D0872048

A HUNDRED DAYS TO RICHMOND

4-12-07

To Johnny,

With thanks for coming to the Round Table.

Best Wishes

Jim Lehrer

A Hundred Days to Richmond

OHIO'S "HUNDRED DAYS" MEN IN THE CIVIL WAR

Edited and with an Introduction by Jim Leeke

INDIANA UNIVERSITY PRESS
Bloomington and Indianapolis

This book is a publication of

Indiana University Press
601 North Morton Street
Bloomington, IN 47404-3797 USA

http://www.indiana.edu/~iupress

Telephone orders 800-842-6796
Fax orders 812-855-7931
Orders by e-mail iuporder@indiana.edu

Letters of Jacob Souder Holtz and Norman D. Egbert excerpted by permission of Mr. Paul Buskirk.

Letters of Wallace W. Chadwick previously published in "Into the Breach: Civil War Letters of Wallace W. Chadwick," edited by Mabel Watkins Mayer, *The Ohio State Archaeological and Historical Quarterly* 52, no. 2 (April-June 1943), pp. 158–80. Reprinted courtesy of the Ohio Historical Society.

The paper used in this publication meets the minimum requirements of American National Standard for Information Sciences—Permanence of Paper for Printed Library Materials, ANSI Z39.48-1984.

Manufactured in the United States of America

Library of Congress Cataloging-in-Publication Data

A hundred days to Richmond : Ohio's "hundred days" men in the Civil
    War / edited and with an introduction by Jim Leeke.
        p.   cm.
    Includes bibliographical references (p.   ) and index.
    ISBN 0-253-33537-X (cloth : alk. paper)
    1. Ohio. Militia—History—Civil War, 1861-1865.   2. Ohio—
History—Civil War, 1861-1865—Regimental histories.   3. United
States—History—Civil War, 1861-1865—Regimental histories.
    4. Ohio—History—Civil War, 1861-1865—Personal narratives.
    5. United States—History—Civil War, 1861-1865—Personal
narratives.   6. United States—History—Civil War, 1861-1865—
Campaigns.   I. Leeke, Jim, date.
E525.4.H86   1999
973.7'471'0922—dc21   99-20005

1 2 3 4 5   04 03 02 01 00 99

For the old 37th Division.

When Gen. Sheridan read the application for our discharge, he paid us the greatest compliment we had in our experience. He said, "I did not know that I had any hundred days men in my army, they are all veterans."

—Private George Perkins, 149th Ohio Volunteer Infantry

Thy purpose firm is equal to the deed;
Who does the best his circumstance allows
Does well, acts nobly; angels could do no more.

—Edward Young, 1683–1765 *Night Thoughts. Night II.*

Contents

Illustrations follow page 8.

List of Maps

Introduction

IN THE SPRING of 1864, after three years of military defeats, bungling, and lost opportunities, a begrudging sort of optimism infused the Northern states. At last, the Union employed generals who knew not only how to train an army but also how to command and risk one. The previous summer had seen the first costly defeat of Robert E. Lee at Gettysburg. Vicksburg had fallen simultaneously, and the victor, Ulysses S. Grant, promoted to general-in-chief of the armies, now had the Army of the Potomac poised at the very doorstep of the Confederacy. Grant's friend, Major-General William Tecumseh Sherman, was preparing to thrust into Georgia from Tennessee. Northern armaments factories hummed. The United States Navy strangled Southern ports. Captured rebels overflowed prisoner-of-war camps.

Perhaps now, finally, three years into horrendous strife that many on both sides had expected to last no more than a season, the end was finally in sight. Into this atmosphere of fragile hope was born the notion of the "hundred-days" regiments.

Short-service regiments were not new. Many of the first units on both sides in 1861 had been sworn into service for three months. Although most short enlistments had long ago given way to one- and three-year terms (many of which were due to expire in the approaching summer), regiments serving for a few months were still not uncommon, particularly during emergencies such as Lee's invasion of Pennsylvania.

Yet in many ways the idea of summoning state militias for a hundred days of Federal service in 1864 was novel, even hopeful. The call was intended as a herald to the last great Union thrust that would topple the Confederacy like a sudden wind against a weakened tree. The new regiments were meant to guard Northern bridges, railroads, and forts, and so release veteran long-service regiments to finish the job at the front.

The impetus for forming these hundred-days regiments came from Ohio. So, too, did the majority of the men who first responded, members of a newly reorganized Ohio militia called the National Guard. Four other states in what was then the West but is today generally considered the Midwest also raised regiments. Indiana, Illinois, Iowa, and Wisconsin, like Ohio, filled their rosters with that uniquely American mixture of farmers, businessmen, veterans, students, and boys that had long constituted both armies.

The prime mover behind this campaign was Ohio Governor John Brough, whose election on a Unionist ticket (a coalition of Republicans and War Democrats) over the fiery exiled Peace Democrat Clement L. Vallandigham the previous fall had greatly heartened President Lincoln.[1] A railroad president and former newspaper publisher and state auditor who had been called home from Indiana to run for office, Brough was a memorable figure even for the rough-and-tumble world of Ohio politics. (He was, for instance, the last of three one-term Ohio war governors.)

Brough (pronounced "Bruff") was a fat, untidy man with a reputation for ability and honesty coupled with frequent poor manners. As governor, he displayed fierce personal regard for the welfare of his state's soldiers, plus a brutal impatience with incompetence. Respected in Washington if sometimes and increasingly despised at home, he was a man whose vision and energy could not be taken lightly. His subordinates moved no less decisively than he did.

Benjamin R. Cowen,[2] appointed Ohio adjutant-general when the Brough administration took office in January 1864, had immediately set about reorganizing the state's somewhat chaotic militia system. Cowen later recalled that "before the first day of May, 1864, Ohio had by far the best organized and most effective militia of any state in the Union, and I felt justified in advising Governor Brough that the National Guard was ready for active service in garrison duty, guarding supply posts, military prisons and lines of transportation, thus relieving the regular, disciplined volunteer forces for the more active duties of the field in the then approaching campaign."[3]

(W. H. H. Terrell, adjutant-general of neighboring Indiana, maintained that the idea for hundred-days regiments had come first from his state's chief executive, although he gave Brough high marks for implementing it. Indiana Governor Oliver P. Morton had been inspired by messages exchanged with Sherman, according to Terrell, and had then discussed the idea with Brough in Indianapolis.)[4]

Encouraged from various quarters, Brough visited Washington and formally offered President Lincoln 30,000 or 40,000 Ohio men for a hundred days. "Mr. Lincoln was greatly pleased with the proposition," Cowen later recalled, "but with that wonderful sagacity which characterized all his public acts, he imagined that the acceptance of militia in such considerable numbers at that time would be construed as an indication of our inability to recruit a sufficient force of regular volunteers and of so desperate a state of things as would encourage the enemy and discourage our own people. He also thought that a call for Ohio troops alone, or the acceptance of a volunteer offer of so large a contingent from a single state, might be misconstrued and lead to jealousies and misunderstandings which would embarrass his administration in other directions."[5]

Lincoln and Brough therefore agreed that the governor ("unbeknownst" to the president, Cowen added dryly[6]) should invite his counterparts from Indiana, Illinois, Iowa, and Wisconsin to meet with him, and that jointly the five governors should offer 100,000 men for 100 days. Brough and Morton, together with Richard Yates of Illinois, William M. Stone of Iowa, and James T. Lewis of Wisconsin, made the offer April 21st. All signed the message except Lewis, who wasn't present.[7]

The five governors offered 85,000 troops. Ohio would send 30,000; Indiana and Illinois each 20,000; Iowa 10,000 and Wisconsin 5,000. The government in Washington, however, clung to the 100,000 figure, perhaps expecting contributions from other states. General Grant wired Secretary of War Edwin Stanton, also of Ohio: "As a rule I would oppose receiving men for a short term, but if 100,000 men can be raised in the time proposed . . . they might come at such a crisis as to be of vast importance."[8]

After what Cowen called "two days of diplomatic hesitation," the president accepted the offer with a single sentence: "The foregoing proposition of the governors is accepted, and the secretary of war is directed to carry it into execution. A. Lincoln."

Cowen later declared that it was "well understood between Mr. Lincoln and Governor Brough that the offer of the other states included in the arrangement would probably be merely perfunctory; but this understanding, of course, extended no further, and the other governors named acted in entire good faith in the premises. They were drawn into the arrangement, rather, to give it a more general appearance than because any assistance was expected of them. . . . There was no time to raise such troops. They were wanted immediately, or not at all, and Ohio was the only state in condition to respond to a 'forthwith' process."[9]

If Cowen's description is somewhat unfair to the other states, all did, in fact, experience trouble raising their regiments, and none met its quota. Adjutant-General Terrell offered an explanation for Indiana that applied equally to the others: "The attempt was made at the busiest time of the spring season, just after the heavy calls of February and March had been filled, which the people, who had been so largely drawn on before, confidently believed would be the last. No fears of a draft were entertained, and most of the arms-bearing laboring men of the state had entered into engagements with farmers for the season.

"The militia, what there was of it, was organized on the volunteer system for the protection of the border, with the express understanding that it was not to be called into service except for home defense. The militia law gave the

Governor no power to compel service, or to send the troops beyond the limits of the state; this force, therefore, as a body was not available, though many volunteers were obtained from it for the call.

"In Ohio the case was different, and her quota was entirely and immediately filled by simply transferring the required number from the National Guard to the United States' service. Indiana's quota could only be filled by volunteers."[10]

Late on the evening of April 23, Brough notified Cowen of Lincoln's acceptance, and ordered: "Set the machinery in motion immediately." Because the following day was a Sunday, Cowen couldn't publicize the call until Monday morning, when "the necessary general orders appeared in all the daily papers of the state, and were sent by telegraph to the commandants of battalions and regiments."

The call was short and pointed:

"The regiments, battalions and independent companies of infantry of the National Guard of Ohio are hereby called into active service for the term of one hundred days, unless sooner discharged. They will be clothed, armed, equipped, transported and paid by the United States Government. These organizations will rendezvous at the most eligible places in their respective counties (the place to be fixed by the commanding officers, and to be on a line of railroad if practicable) on Monday, May 2, 1864, and report by telegraph, at four o'clock P.M. of that day, the number present for duty. The alacrity with which all calls for the military forces for the state have been heretofore met furnishes the surest guaranty that the National Guard will be prompt to assemble at the appointed time. Our armies in the field are marshaling for a decisive blow and the citizen soldiery will share the glories of the crowning victories of the campaign by relieving our veteran regiments from post and garrison duty, to allow them to engage in the more arduous duties of the field."

This summons wasn't entirely unexpected, a newspaper noted, since there had been "intimations for some weeks that a call would be made about the first of May for the militia of the Northern States to take the field for a short time."[11] As hundred-days regiments began forming in the Buckeye state and across the West, Secretary Stanton estimated the cost of equipping and supporting them at $25 million. Congress passed an appropriations bill so promptly that a New York City newspaper editor reportedly exclaimed, "What, $25 million in three minutes!"

Ohio quickly reported 35,982 men ready for duty in more than 40 regiments.[12] Her companion Western states mustered more slowly, four to six weeks later, but ultimately contributed another 24,778 men; this total, however, was less than half of their combined quota.[13]

In the coming months, the hundred-days movement expanded to seven additional states (Delaware, Kansas, Maryland, Massachusetts, New Jersey, New

York, and Pennsylvania), fueled in part by the frantic Northern reaction to Confederate General Jubal Early's audacious raid on Washington in early July. Their contribution totaled nearly 20,000 men,[14] which would have given Washington more than its hoped-for 100,000 had all five Western states reached their self-imposed quotas. Still, the combined figure topped 80,000.

Ohio's hundred-days troops therefore did not answer the call alone. The other four Western states primarily saw their regiments sent south into Kentucky and Tennessee, where many guarded railway lines in support of Sherman's army.[15] Most of the Eastern regiments remained in the East, often within their state borders, generally guarding railways and prison camps.[16] The Ohioans, however, who had marched first and in larger numbers, went to relatively more important positions in the field (and because their duty proved eventful, also left a richer public record).

The Buckeyes knew what might await them. Few answered the call with blind enthusiasm or innocent patriotism, although in later years some might like to remember that they had. The historian of the 149th Ohio, George Perkins of Chillicothe, offered a clear-eyed picture of the time:

"The North had suffered an enormous drain upon her resources, had seen her men sent home from the front, suffering from disease and wounds, pitiful survivors of battles in which thousands had gone to their death. The romance and glamour of war had gone, the horror of it remained. There was scarcely a family in the North who did not suffer sorrow that cannot be described, hardly a fireside that did not mourn for a husband or lover, brother or friend, who went forth with pride, never to return. Under such circumstances the men of the hundred-days service, knowing just what to expect, hastily arranged their affairs, and from the stores, workshops and farms, flocked to the defense of their country in the hour of its direst need."[17]

The 149th's weekly hometown newspaper editorialized the day after muster that the call-up "took our citizens by surprise, and found most of them but poorly prepared to respond to the call. The season has been backward, and owing to the scarcity of help, farmers are behind in their work, so that the call was a severe test of their patriotism, but to their honor we can say they met it in an excellent spirit."[18]

Some regiments, in contrast, demonstrated instead what the Cincinnati *Gazette* termed a "spirit of dissatisfaction." In the Queen City, the colonel of the largely German-speaking 10th O.N.G. regiment held a public meeting to dampen what the newspaper called "several serious misapprehensions in regard to the law." Colonel Leonard A. Harris of the companion 7th O.N.G., who was also the city's mayor, bluntly informed the meeting that anyone not reporting for muster would be considered a deserter.[19]

In a proclamation published around the state, Governor Brough assured his guardsmen that he was "not ignorant of the sacrifices this call imposes upon you, nor the unequal manner in which it imposes the burden of war." Despite reverses in the spring (the battle at Sabine Cross Roads, Louisiana, on April 8th had checked the Red River Campaign, and the Fort Pillow massacre of April 12th was still prominent in Northern headlines), "the general military situation is everywhere hopeful," he said, "and those in command of your armies have never been more confident." But he added pointedly that "we can not permit this war, in its present proportions, to linger through another year. . . . [T]he sacrifice gives promise of materially hastening the close of the contest." As the hundred-days regiments left the state, Brough concluded, "the prayers of the people of your State will follow you; and may your return be as glorious as your going forth is noble and patriotic."

One O.N.G. member quipped that he hoped the entire Ohio National Guard would be sent east, since "all quiet on the Potomac" agreed with his idea of war.[20] Despite the support of pro-administration newspapers and encouraging early signs from the battlefield,[21] however, Brough's grand scheme for ending the war proved ephemeral, as had so many others during the long conflict. Lee was still brilliant and tenacious, and Grant's campaign in Virginia deteriorated into a bloody, protracted affair, inevitably drawing Ohio's hundred-days men into it. Then came Jubal Early's tough, resourceful Army of the Valley and its breathtaking swoop toward Washington, a raid during which several Ohio regiments found themselves facing more hazardous duty than even they had imagined.

"My theory as to the service of the Guard was so far modified in the offer and the call," Cowen later recorded, "that [ultimately] they were to serve 'on fortifications, or wherever their services may be required,' the wisdom of which modification is apparent, and the propriety of which was never questioned."[22]

The question of ordering National Guard regiments to the front (rather than seeing the front suddenly turn and engulf *them*) was complex, and shrouded with misinformation by the government and partisan press on one side and the pro-South Copperhead press on the other. Grumbling continued in many regiments, especially those that unexpectedly found themselves within sound of cannon fire.[23] "There is such feeling throughout the whole of the one hundred days men that I do not think that the Republican party could get five thousand votes today out of the forty thousand . . . ," a private wrote home from the fortifications in Washington.[24] But grumbling was and is the right of all soldiers, and although no regiment volunteered for the front, all that received such orders promptly obeyed them.[25]

More than half of the Buckeye regiments would "see the elephant" in battle before returning home. Facing tough, experienced enemies, a few broke or surrendered. Most, however, stood and fought as best they knew how, and several suffered heavy losses. Ohio hundred-days men fought under General Lew

Wallace at Monocacy. An anxious, determined few helped defend Fort Stevens outside Washington (the only time a sitting president ever came under enemy fire). Others served in the works near Petersburg, or tramped through the Shenandoah, or skirmished with Mosby's fearsome partisans in Virginia. One regiment even went to sea. It was a remarkable performance for men who were essentially "home guards."[26]

If, in the end, Brough's and Lincoln's ambitious plan for ending the war in a hundred days failed, it was through no failure of the hundred-days men themselves. Indeed, they and their regiments had done far more than these leaders had asked or expected of them. In the Ohioans' simple willingness to step forward—or, at the very least, their refusal to shrink from the call—they displayed magnificent dedication and courage.

In the years after the war, Cowen and others staunchly defended the performance of Ohio's hundred-days men from the disparagement of longer-serving veterans,[27] who often viewed them as what he called "a grotesque and superfluous appendage to the armies of the Union. . . . Those who thus regard them can not be possessed of accurate knowledge of the circumstances attending the call nor the character of the service performed by those troops."[28]

With the turn of the century and the gradual passing of the Grand Army of the Republic, the hundred-days regiments were nearly forgotten. Their role became a slim footnote to that bloody, thunderous final summer of the war. Yet theirs was a compelling history, one that illuminated many of the best qualities of the men who served both sides, however briefly.

It deserves to be remembered.

Editor's Note

THESE ACCOUNTS DERIVE from regimental histories, newspaper articles, letters, diaries, and individual reminiscences written during and after the Civil War by Union soldiers. Spelling has been updated and some punctuation slightly modified for modern readers, particularly for those unaccustomed to paragraphs of Faulknerian length.

In a few cases, the editor has inserted an amplifying phrase in brackets. Notations in parentheses are the writers' own. Although many accounts are abridged or edited, in no instance has meaning been altered. Ellipses are reserved for denoting abbreviation of individual quotations or of already brief documents such as letters, orders, and poems.

A HUNDRED DAYS TO RICHMOND

1 | The Boys

A CIVIL WAR REGIMENT *typically represented every profession, trade, and class of the community in which it was raised. This was true of the hundred-days regiments, too, but with some important distinctions.*

Hundred-days men were the family and friends of veterans who had gone before them. A large percentage were mature men of substance and position, who had been spared for various reasons (including legal payment to substitutes) from earlier service in the war. Not a few graybeards marched in regiments or even companies with their own sons.[1] Consequently, many held a clear-eyed, unromantic view of the war, and recognized what hazards might face them.

New army ranks in the hundred-days regiments often bore little relation to social or professional standing at home. Many a high private was as likely as his captain to be addressed as "Mister"—a respect that tightened bonds between soldiers while loosening a stiff army hierarchy.[2] The colonels and regimental officers, in contrast, had often participated in the bitter fighting of earlier seasons. Their experience soon proved invaluable in the field for steadying green, nervous regiments their first time under fire.

Like so many men in both armies, many hundred-days men referred to themselves as "the boys" for the rest of their lives. This was often more than poetic license. With tens of thousands of fighting-age men already in uniform, National Guard rosters often included college students or privates still in their teens. "They have took boys that are only 15 or 16 years old," a 20-year-old private wrote home, "and some as short as I am."[3]

Here are firsthand accounts by "the boys" of all ages, beginning with the Ohio adjutant-general.

Benjamin R. Cowen, adjutant-general of Ohio:

A word as to the personnel of the Ohio National Guard.[4] It was composed of the most substantial men left in the state; men of high social position, of wealth and influence in every department of industry and of every profession; men whose whole history from the commencement of the war had been filled with sacrifices and generous deeds, and many of whom had been in the service and discharged for wounds or other disability or by expiration of service.[5]

Ohio at that time had already sent ten percent of her entire population into the army. We had in the field 130 regiments of infantry, 12 of cavalry, three of artillery and 26 independent companies of all arms; in all, about 150 regiments. A draft was pending, and there were indications of resistance to it in several parts of the state. It was upon a community racked and torn in this manner that the call fell, and at a time when the farmers were in the midst of their preparations for active spring work.

One week elapsed between the call and the rendezvous, and it was a week of tremendous pressure on the office. The correspondence by letter and telegraph, and the personal applications, remonstrances and appeals, were unexampled in numbers and fervency, and were a severe tax on time and patience. It must be said, however, to the credit of the Guard, that very little of the trouble and dissatisfaction came from the members.

A few, and but few, of the officers asked leave to resign. They were men of large business interests, whose absence from home for so long a time entailed heavy pecuniary loss. One officer offered to contribute $5,000 to the sanitary fund, and another offered $10,000 for the same purpose, if I would accept their resignations; but both offers were declined. The latter gentleman, who was at that time mayor of the city of Cleveland and at the head of a large business house, went home, arranged his business, painted across the front of his packing house in large letters "Closed for One Hundred Days," and cheerfully went to the front.[6]

Farmers and other outdoor workers were in the midst of their spring work, but they left their plows, their quarries, their teams and their unfinished buildings; the merchant and the professional man left his store and office, and the mechanic his shop, with that unhesitating promptness which was characteristic of our patriotic people during the entire progress of the war.[7] No consideration of what they would lose by going, or how much they could make by staying at home, weighed a feather with them.

The proposition relative to the stations of regiments contemplated the keeping of eight in the state at the camps and prisons. But so far from desiring that kind of duty, it was impossible to find a single regiment willing to remain in the state, and it was only under orders, and then very reluctantly, that any were kept. The comparative safe and easy duty of guarding military prisoners at Camp Chase and Johnson's Island[8] was too tame to suit them, and all were clamorous for duty at the front, regardless of the implied terms of the call.

The service of the Guard was far more onerous than was contemplated when the offer was made. They were only expected to relieve disciplined soldiers in garrison duty. Many experienced military men believe that a regiment's first fight is its best, but a regiment that is essentially raw stands a poor show in the active operations of a field campaign. They may be brave enough in spirit, but they are physically tender.

The arduous labor of the long march, the exposure, the forced and extra duty, the tremendous strain of frequent engagements find them not yet inured by drill and solid rations and outdoor life—not yet acclimated, so to speak. They are also unacquainted with that magnetic touch of the elbow which speaks silently but eloquently, and imparts such confidence to veteran troops. So they find themselves at a disadvantage in all the hard work of camp and march.

But the Guard never claimed immunity from any service on account of their greenness. One company, and but one, refused to be mustered into the U.S. service.[9] It was summarily disposed of in a special order of dishonorable dismissal. This course was deemed preferable to a court-martial for several reasons, not the least of which was that the refusal, though no doubt an act of cowardice, was but the exercise of their legal right, as there was no power in the state authorities to compel the Guard to muster.[10]

* * *

Of all the Ohio regiments, the 150th displayed a special gift for style, self-promotion, and controversy. It was also wonderfully eclectic, listing on its rosters the movers and shakers of Cleveland, farmers from modest outlying districts, and students from a respected nearby college. Adored by some, reviled by others, members of this regiment would see history made during their service.

William J. Gleason, private, Co. E, 150th Ohio:

Our regiment was mustered into the United States Volunteer Service at Cleveland on May 5th, 1864, to serve 100 days. It was composed of Companies A through H of the 29th Regiment, Ohio National Guard, all from the city; Company I, of the 30th Battalion O.N.G., from Dover, Cuyahoga County; and Company K, 37th Regiment O.N.G, from Lorain County, made up of the students of Oberlin College.[11]

The personnel of the regiment was equal to that of any body of men in the Union Army. It was made up of the flower and pick of Cleveland's citizens, having in its ranks many of the leading and substantial businessmen and mechanics of the city, as well as the sturdy farmers of Dover and the scholarly students of Oberlin.

Every wholesale and retail establishment in the city, the newspaper and job printing offices, the railroad offices, the professions, and the shops were all represented. The firm of Sanford & Hayward supplied our able colonel, William Henry Hayward. Three privates also came from this firm. The George Worthington Co. furnished 15 men; William Bingham Co., 13 men; Morgan

& Root, 12 men; Edwards & Townsend, six men. Similar establishments supplied some of their proprietors, bookkeepers, clerks and working men. The newspapers were well represented—the *Herald* by four volunteers, the *Leader,* five; but the old War Democratic *Plain Dealer* bore off the palm, furnishing nine of its attachés.

Our regimental officers and staff were nearly all of them veterans, having acquired their skill and expertise in other commands. They were men of excellent standing as soldiers and citizens, and took the best care of their command. The several captains and line officers were, as a rule, intelligent, able, popular, painstaking soldiers. They had a watchful care over their men, and each of them possessed the ambition to have the best company in the regiment.

After all these many years,[12] when the beardless youth of 17 or 20 years of age, of which the rank and file of the 150th was mostly composed, have grown along down the western hillside of the half century, a retrospective glance over the intervening years will clearly demonstrate that the men of our regiment have been noted no less in peace than they were in war.

The jolly, auburn-haired, freckle-faced youth that served as first lieutenant of Company C in 1864 is now universally recognized as one of the most eminent men of this nation: Marcus A. Hanna, successful businessman and senator from the great state of Ohio.[13] There is Edward W. Wolcott, formerly private of Company D, who went west and grew up with the country, and became the brilliant United States senator of the Silver State.[14]

Here is the quiet, modest George K. Nash private of Company K—the boys who always said grace before and after tackling their sowbelly and hardtack, "skippers"[15] included, and sang the Doxology every night before retiring—elected to the honorable Supreme Court of our state, and recently nominated for the exalted office of governor.[16] Another one of that intelligent praying band of comrades of the Oberlin company is now doing his own duty as county solicitor, just as earnestly as he did as a private soldier in 1864.

Along the line come a private, Company A, and private, Company H, both honored judges of the Court of Common Pleas; private, Company C, and quartermaster, who served our city as mayors; private, Company H, distinguished Ohio state senator and United States district attorney; private, Company F, county treasurer and enterprising educator and financier. Scores of the members of the 150th have ranked among our leading bankers, manufacturers, professional and business men, and have performed their share in building up the institutions and lovely homes of our beautiful city and its surrounding towns.

* * *

The Cleveland regiment included perhaps the least likely yet memorable organization among the hundred-days men: Company K from Oberlin Col-

lege.[17] *Originally one of just two companies in a small O.N.G. battalion, it was suddenly reassigned during muster to the regiment that eventually became the 150th O.V.I. This shift sparked resentment in Elyria, the hometown of its companion company, where the Oberlin boys were suspected of engineering a separation from working-class colleagues—a charge of elitism they vigorously denied.*

"It would be far from the truth to suppose that Company K was a band like unto the Roundheads, of Cromwell's time," Private James C. Cannon later recorded. "We were young men, full of life, and enjoyed the jokes, pranks and activities natural to youth, yet we could not forget that our duty to country was measured by our duty to God."[18]

R. Dwight Burrell, corporal, Co. K, 150th Ohio:

Colonel Frazee[19] no doubt recalls the appearance of the 150th Regiment upon dress parade. His eye followed down the line, and rested upon one company after another—the company of the elegant sons of Euclid Avenue; the company of West Cleveland boys; the companies of businessmen; clerks, of artisans, of stalwart farmers from Dover; and at last upon Company K, the "Little Benjamin," as it were, the smallest boys of the regiment.

It is true we were not martial in our bearing, and did not give promise that in battle we would be able to put to flight the army of the alien, for we were small, and had the appearance of the student of that day, and not of the athlete of the present. But it was not long before we acquired the reputation of doing the most work, and the best "policing," with the least grumbling, of any company in the regiment, and of being the most given to the prayer-meeting.

Do not infer that grace always abounded in Company K; we grumbled as did others; grumbled over our rations and the conduct of the war, and certainly grumbled that Fourth of July when we were ordered to march and take up quarters at Fort Stevens.[20] It was only a short time, however, before each member of our company looked upon that transfer as a special dispensation of Providence, for it enabled us to see President Lincoln, and many other great men, face to face; to engage in the battle that marked the nearest approach to the capital of actual war; and to acquire a fuller experience than any other company of the regiment.

* * *

After he donned the Union blue, newspaper editor Clifton Nichols reported on his regiment for the Springfield News.[21] *Many of its officers were unknown to his hometown readers, as Nichols's company and one other were unexpectedly reassigned to a regiment from outside Springfield. During his service, Nichols revealed a breezy style reminiscent of an early Ernie*

Pyle. The following is a compilation of various articles, which carried the byline "Nickliffe."

Clifton M. Nichols, corporal, Co. E, 152nd Ohio:

The readers of the *News* would probably be interested in knowing something of the Colonel and the other field officers of the 152d Ohio, and we will undertake to gratify their curiosity in this respect.

Our colonel, David Putman (not Putnam) was, previous to the rebellion, a merchant in Darke County. He was appointed a second lieutenant by Governor Tod, October 16, 1861, and authorized to recruit a company for the 69th Ohio. He was elected captain of Company E. Captain Putman remained with the regiment until June 20, 1863, when he resigned upon a certificate of physical disability. He was in the battle of Stone River,[22] and commanded the regiment on the memorable 31st of December, 1862, the colonel being disabled and the major having been wounded.

Need we undertake to give a history of Lieutenant-Colonel Doty[23] to a Clark County public? Surely he is favorably "known of all men" and a good many women. His untiring energy and devotion to his fellows is as marked in the army as it has ever been at home. He is studying the science of war closely and industriously, and practicing it upon all possible occasions.

Our major is John H. Hunter, a local preacher of the M.E. church, and resides in Arcanum, Darke County.

Edwin B. Putnam (not Putman), a lawyer of Greenville, Darke County, and a man of good attainments, is our adjutant. This is the adjutant's first item of experience in military life, but all the male members of his family have been in the service for nearly two years.

Our quartermaster is Jacob W. Shively, who was, previous to the rebellion, keeper of the Darke County infirmary. He joined the 69th Ohio as a private and was promoted to be second lieutenant, served six months and was then discharged upon a certificate of disability.

Dr. J. C. Williamson, the surgeon, is a resident of Versailles, Darke County, and was in the Ohio Legislature from 1856 to 1859.

Dr. J. A. Jobes, of Palestine, Darke County, a graduate of the Medical College of Ohio, is our assistant surgeon. Dr. E. H. Larsh, of the same place, formerly a practicing physician and now a horticulturist, is our hospital steward.

The chaplain, Rev. J. S. Guthrie, a Universalist clergyman, resides in New Madison, Darke County. He superintends our mailing arrangements, and is assisted by J. H. Wood, of Rensselaer County, Indiana.

In the ranks, serving as privates, are some of the best men of Clark and Darke counties.[24] From the latter is William H. Morningstar, who is a wealthy citizen and a prominent Union man of his section. It is his special duty to take care of the sick, and his kindness of heart prompts him to constant and laborious effort in their behalf.

Corporal J. C. Miller will be as corpulent as his father, the magistrate, by the close of the 100 days, if he continues as he has begun.

* * *

Some National Guard regiments were relatively tightly knit groups that discouraged the common and entirely legal practice of paying substitutes to take one's place in the rank. Others reported a brisk market for "subs" in the days before muster. A former sergeant in a six-months regiment, discharged in February and living in Tiffin, Ohio, recorded the appeal of that market in his diary.[25]

Charles L. Morehouse, veteran of the 86th Ohio:

Monday, April 25:

The militia are ordered out for 100 Days—causing a big commotion among our "Blues." Substitutes are in demand—and "Yours Truly" is on the lookout for a "posish."

Tuesday, April 26:

The going to war question has been the all-absorbing one today. Substitute trade quite brisk—I'm "up" for a go if someone bids high enough.

Thursday, April 28:

All quiet today—although "Going a soldiering" discussions have been quite numerous. I'm "on the fence" as regards the question. Expect to "fall in" though.

Monday, May 2:

Military business has been on the table exclusively today. George[26] is much rejoiced—as I am accepted as "sub" in his place. I am making arrangements accordingly.

Tuesday, May 3:

Getting ready for war has been my principal "biz" today. . . . Was "sworn" for the call of May 2nd this A.M.—signed the roll and now I'm "stuck." The 49th [O.N.G.][27] have rec'd orders to report at Cleveland tomorrow.

* * *

Short-service and militia units were infamous among veterans for what many perceived—often correctly—as a distinct lack of smartness. Some

Guard companies were less military in appearance than even their own officers could bear. In the works outside Petersburg, Virginia, halfway through their hundred days, Company F (McCook Independents) of the 138th Ohio[28] would be singled out by their colonel at dress parade for "general unsoldierly bearing and slovenly appearance." The rebuke didn't go unchallenged.

Gilbert L. Laboytreaux, private, Co. F, 138th Ohio:[29]

Oh, how it showered the ashes of humiliation upon our heads, how it bowed our tolerably clean faces in the dust. To some it was a feast of merriment, and to others abundant food for meditation. The more solid and matter-of-fact members of our company don't swallow it, can't swallow it and never will swallow it.

I shall take the merry side of the picture. I think it is a "big thing" for the company. It is composed of *men,* not a few of them have been men a long time,[30] and will so continue to the end of the chapter. A three months' drill under a very Nero would not make mere machines of them. They are ever ready, willing and prompt to obey all legal orders. None in the regiment have shown better discipline—we have always cherished a feeling of respectability *that* has kept our heads above the mire and filth, and why should we not be considered respectable?

The McCooks count two Doctors. Put that down, if you please. Three preachers—there is a moral for you; two Ohio Legislators—they are "some in a bear fight" everybody knows, and two postmasters that are not to be sneezed at. The balance of the company is made up of mechanics, merchants and farmers honorable the world over. No company in the regiment can make a cleaner record.

Our commanding officer[31] must have known this—hence I think it must have been a "slip of the tongue" that Company F was designated—when Company Q or Z was meant.[32] So I take it, and I advise all the boys to do the same for the balance of the "hundred days," at least.[33]

Benjamin Cowen, Ohio Adjutant-General (ca. 1885). Reproduced from the collections of the Ohio Historical Society. All rights reserved.

John Brough, Ohio Governor. Reproduced from the collections of the
Ohio Historical Society.

Allison L. Brown, Col., 149th Ohio. Reproduced from the collections of the Ohio Historical Society.

George Perkins, Pvt., Co. A, 149th Ohio (ca. 1911). Reproduced from the collections of the Ohio Historical Society.

Clifton M. Nichols, Cpl., Co. E, 152nd Ohio (ca. 1899). Reproduced from the collections of the Ohio Historical Society.

Asa Bushnell, Capt., Co. E, 152nd Ohio (ca. 1893). Reproduced from the collections of the Ohio Historical Society.

John N. Frazee, Lt.-Col., 150th Ohio (ca. 1893). Reproduced from the collections of the Ohio Historical Society.

Marcus Hanna, 2nd Lt., Co. C, 150th Ohio. Reproduced from the collections of the Ohio Historical Society. All rights reserved.

Jacob S. Holtz, Pvt., Co. H, 164th Ohio (in borrowed officer's coat).
Rutherford B. Hayes Presidential Center.

Nathaniel Haynes, Col., 169th Ohio. Rutherford B. Hayes Presidential Center.

Edward H. Hobson, Brig.-Gen., U.S.V. (ca. 1893). Reproduced from the collections of the Ohio Historical Society.

Commander & Staff. Fort No. 1, Baltimore, 149th Ohio. Reproduced from the collections of the Ohio Historical Society.

Robert Stevenson, Col., 154th Ohio. Reproduced from the collections of the
Ohio Historical Society. All rights reserved.

Benjamin Franklin Kelley Brig.-Gen., U.S.V. Reproduced from the
collections of the Ohio Historical Society.

Jubal Early, Lt.-Gen., CSA. Reproduced from the Collections of the
Library of Congress.

Lew Wallace, Maj.-Gen., U.S.V. (1862). From *Lew Wallace: An Autobiography.*

Company K Memorial (150th Ohio), Fort Stevens. 1907. *From left*: Dwight Burrell, Fred McWade, James Laird, John Frazee, James Cannon. Reproduced from the collections of the Ohio Historical Society. All rights reserved.

2 | Muster

THE NATIONAL GUARD mustered the first week of May. More than 35,000 men were soon passing through camps scattered across Ohio,[1] and with remarkable quickness boarding trains for the East. Within two weeks, most regiments had left the state. By the end of the hundred days, none had served entirely within Ohio.[2]

Benjamin R. Cowen, adjutant-general of Ohio:

The day for rendezvous and report came, and it was one of the most disagreeable May days ever experienced in this latitude. Snow and rain fell upon every camp of rendezvous in the state.[3] It was such a day as will make the average man hesitate to leave his home or office even for a pleasant jaunt or a social visit, and when it came to leaving home for so long a time, to encounter the uncertainties and perils of a service to which they were not yet inured, and in the face of the doubts that had been so freely expressed as to the power of the state authorities to make the call, would it have been astonishing had the guard failed to respond?

But neither the unpleasantness of things present, nor the uncertainty of things to come, could dampen their ardor or induce them to disregard the plain demands of duty. Each man had set his house in order and repaired to camp, and at 7:30 P.M. of May 2, I had received telegrams from the commandants of regiments, battalions and companies which enabled me to telegraph the secretary of war: "Thirty-eight thousand National Guards in camp and ready for muster."

Then came the exasperating work of preparing the Guard for muster into the service of the United States. The brigade and division organizations had been eliminated under the new law, and we were thus spared the embarrassing presence of divers and sundry ambitious major and brigadier generals at this most difficult stage of work. Some of the companies were below the minimum in numbers, after the unfit men had been weeded out, and wherever such was the case consolidations were made promptly and remorselessly. Thus were company and regimental organizations broken up in many cases, and worthy officers left out. Such a result was unavoidable.

There was a mysterious delay in completing organizations at Camp Dennison, and I went there one evening on a locomotive, to find a colonel who had been consolidated out haranguing his men and advising them to refuse to muster unless he was restored. The trouble was very promptly settled by locking up the disgruntled officer, mustering in the regiment and starting it to the front before daylight. Another colonel at the same camp a few days later caused considerable delay by trying to get himself made brigadier general. He was settled by sending him off with a single regiment.

Notwithstanding all the hindrance and embarrassments of the work, however, the first regiment left the state on May 5, three days after the rendezvous, and the last one was to move on the 16th. Between those dates, 41 regiments and one battalion of seven companies—in all, 35,982 men—were consolidated, organized, mustered, clothed, armed, equipped and turned over to the United States military authorities for assignment and transportation.

On the 10th of May, I advised the governor that we should have six or eight regiments more than our quota, and that none of them were willing to be sent home. This fact was communicated to Secretary Stanton, who at once responded, "I will accept all the troops you can raise. The other states will be deficient and behind time. We want every man now. They may decide the war."

* * *

On receiving Cowen's muster order, Colonel Gustavus Swan Innis ordered his Third Regiment, O.N.G., to assemble in Columbus, the state capital. Companies from outlying towns in Franklin County marched into town to join the regiment at 7 A.M. on May 2nd. More than 30 years later, Sylvester Sherman still vividly recalled the scene at "the hall of Company B, (Meade Rifles), in the Carpenter block on Town Street between Third and Fourth." Within days, like so many others, the 3rd Regiment would be consolidated.

Sylvester M. Sherman, first sergeant, Co. G, 133rd Ohio:

Promptly at the hour the men began to pour in. The companies from outside the city came in wagons with their fifes screaming, drums beating vigorously, and flags flying, giving spectators the impression that they were full of martial spirit and ready to meet the enemy at once. The feeling seemed to be that we were called for a special purpose and that the emergency was something beyond any which had yet presented itself, and all seemed to feel the importance of it.

Soon the whole regiment was gathered at headquarters and speculation was rife as to where we were to be sent. Of course we could only guess, and this we did to the best of our ability all day, starting anew at every rumor that came to our ears. During the day quite a number of members of the regiment who thought they could not go, or who disliked the idea of going, secured substitutes at some price or other, many agreeing to give their representatives a dollar a day while in the service, besides their pay from the government.

Thus the day passed, and at 6 P.M. companies A. and B., being composed entirely of men who lived in the city, were dismissed for the night, but with strict orders to report at 7 o'clock in the morning or be considered deserters. The balance of the regiment was marched to Tod Barracks.[4]

Here all was hurry and bustle; drums were beating, provost squads coming and going, and soldiers in their blue uniforms moving about the enclosure which seemed to fairly swarm with them. All this was new to our unprepared minds, but it was the beginning of our soldier education. Once inside the gate the boys were under more restraint than they had ever been used to, and although many of them desired to step outside for a little while to secure additional articles of baggage or make final arrangement of their business, the guard was an obstacle which could not be surmounted. They all yielded gracefully after doing a little grumbling, which they considered a soldier's privilege.

As night came on we realized that we must find someplace to sleep, though the very thought of passing the night in such quarters seemed repugnant. We thought of the great numbers of soldiers, some of them not very cleanly, who had been quartered here, and we were suspicious that the bunks were already occupied by those very interesting little insects that accompany the soldier through his service unless he takes extra precautions to keep rid of them. The thought was anything but pleasurable.

The old soldiers were friendly in giving us advice as to how "to git rid of 'em." "Soak your clothes in strong salt water," or "Boil your clothes, that'll knock 'em," all of which advice we treasured up for future use.

The different companies selected their bunks, which were in tiers at the sides of the large frame buildings, each bunk being about four feet wide and the length of a man. The bedding was nowhere to be found, so each man had to spread his coat or whatever he happened to have with him on the bare boards and use his spare pair of socks for a pillow. After they were comfortably settled it was announced that we had taken some other regiment's quarters, and so we had to get out at 10 P.M. and go to another building no better furnished.

At 5 A.M., the reveille sounded, when all were supposed to rise and prepare for breakfast. If anyone was slow about rising, he was sure of plenty of assistance from his bunkmates. The facilities for morning ablutions consisted of wetting the hands at the pump, a swipe or two at the face, and then drying them on whatever was handy, from a blouse sleeve or handkerchief to a newspaper or the tail of a shirt. Breakfast was the same as last night's supper, though it seemed a little better owing to the growing appetites.

Being unorganized we had no duty to perform, so we spent the day lying in our bunks, or reading, singing or lounging around the barracks. In the meantime, a few absentees were sent for and brought in.

A physical examination [May 4th] of the members of the regiment who claimed to be unfitted for service was conducted by the surgeons in a hurried way, and did not exclude many from service.

It was not known what would be done with us, so the boys again put in their time guessing where we were to go. In the morning (May 5th) the guessing continued and the probability that we were to be sent to the Kanawha Valley seemed to increase. During the forenoon orders came for us to march to Camp Chase.

At 2 P.M., we took up our line of march and after a hot, dusty tramp of five miles reached our destination. Here we found the ground had been cleared by a detail which had been sent ahead for the purpose. Pitching tents was a trick which the boys had to learn, but fortunately some few of them had had a taste of service, and under their direction we were under cover and got supper by nine o'clock.

Sleeping on the ground was a new experience with most of us, but the boys took hold with a determination to do their part cheerfully, and although next morning there were many aching bones, nobody complained.

Our orders were to perfect the organization of the regiment as quickly as possible, that we were needed immediately. Two telegrams were sent to Governor Brough by the Secretary of War. The first read, "Has Ohio a regiment that can be sent at once to West Virginia? It is needed badly." This was followed by a second, which read, "For God's sake hurry up and send a regiment. The rebels are threatening our stores at New Creek."[5]

The regiment was filled up by adding two companies of the 76th Battalion O. N. G. from Franklin County, and two companies of the 58th Battalion O. N. G. from Hancock County to the 3rd Regiment O. N. G. from Franklin County. This work of consolidation was done by the regimental officers without assistance, and was the only hundred-days regiment whose officers performed that duty.

Numerous changes were necessary before everything was satisfactorily adjusted. There was an excess of officers after the organization of the new regiment. This was arranged for the most part among the officers themselves, but in a few instances choice was made by the men.

The captains of the absorbed battalions accepted first lieutenants' commissions. Some of the first lieutenants became second lieutenants, and those who did not get places remained at home except two lieutenants who enlisted and served as privates. These changes made it rather unpleasant for the men, for being transferred in small numbers to other companies it separated them from companions with whom they had enlisted, and with whom they expected to mess and bunk. But they were men of intelligence and did not need to have the necessity explained to them. They accepted the situation and were soon hail fellows with all.[6]

The mustering in was done in the night of May 6th, and was not completed until 4 o'clock on the morning of the 7th, the field officers being mustered last, though all was dated May 6th. When mustered into the service of the United States, the regiment was designated the 133d Ohio Volunteer Infantry.

The uniforming of the regiment was done at night, or rather in the morning of the 7th. Before this was finished, urgent orders were received by the Colonel to march at once, that the regiment was badly needed to protect the Baltimore & Ohio R.R., which the rebels were threatening in West Virginia.

Everything was hurly-burly. Snatching up their knapsacks and canteens the men fell in, some only partly dressed, and the march was begun at 5 o'clock A.M. to the State Arsenal on West Friend (now Main) Street.

Here we were each handed a Springfield rifle and the necessary accouterments, and the noncommissioned officers in addition a straight sword, a piece which they called "toad stickers" and "cheese toasters," which they afterward learned were of no earthly use, unless it was to get between their legs when on the double quick.

Friends and relatives had collected, and lined the streets as we marched to the depot. Many "good byes" were said, and many of the boys looked sadly at the stores and shops along High street where they had been employed and wondered if they would ever take their places in them again.

Just after we arrived at the depot, the Colonel was approached by a prominent citizen who requested that one of the men be granted a leave of absence, as his mother was very sick. But the Colonel, being under imperative orders to march at once, could not grant the request and was roundly abused by the citizen.

We were not permitted to lose any time but were loaded into boxcars, and were at 11 o'clock A.M. on the way south over the Little Miami R.R. This was pretty quick work, the regiment being mustered, uniformed, armed and equipped for the field and on the way to the front in less than 12 hours. It was the first Hundred-Days regiment to leave the state.[7]

* * *

The 27th O.N.G. mustered in Chillicothe under Colonel Allison L. Brown, "Colonel Ally" to his regiment. None could have known that they would be perhaps the most battle-hardened of the hundred-days men when they marched back home—if they were fortunate enough to return at all.

George Perkins, private, Co. A, 149th Ohio:

On Wednesday, May 4th, the 27th Regiment O. N. G. of Ross County reported at Camp Dennison.[8] It was a cold, disagreeable day. Snow fell that afternoon, a day on which men would rather have remained by their own firesides, but a firm determination to duty urged them on.

The 27th Regiment reported 596 men. It was found necessary now to have a reconstruction of the regiments and battalions. The eight companies of the 27th were by consolidation reduced to seven. The companies of the 55th Battalion from Clinton County were added, making ten companies. By orders, the lieutenant-colonel and adjutant were relieved, and returned to their homes. The regiment entered the United States service as the 149th Ohio Volunteer Infantry.

From May 4th until the 11th the regiment remained at Camp Dennison, during which time they were uniformed, armed and equipped. On the night of May 11th orders came for the regiment to report to Gen. Lew Wallace[9] at Baltimore, Md., going by way of Columbus and Pittsburg.[10] We started at midnight, being crowded into boxcars, without a seat or bed except the floor. We rode in this manner for three days and four nights.

Thursday noon found us still south of Xenia,[11] and we did not reach Pittsburg until Friday evening. There the regiment was handsomely received. We marched to a hall where a bountiful supper was provided for us by the loyal ladies of that city. That supper to the tired, hungry soldiers was an event long to be remembered. The good people of Pittsburg fed every regiment that passed through, going or returning.

Early the next morning we passed Altoona, Pa., and the great "Horse Shoe Bend." At this point one of the brakes on our car dropped to the track as we were descending the steep mountain grade; we could hear it "bump, bump" on the track, but luckily it held or the history of the 149th would have ended then and there. Nothing could have prevented the train rolling over the mountainside.

However, the longest ride must have an end. Our train pulled into Baltimore at 3 o'clock Sunday morning. As soon as possible Col. Brown reported to General Wallace, and the regiment was assigned to duty at several points in the city, relieving the 8th N.Y. Heavy Artillery. The command, two thousand strong, immediately left for the front, and after six weeks but seven hundred remained, the colonel and all of his staff being killed.[12]

* * *

Colonel Robert Stevenson's regiment gathered on Monday morning, May 2, at Xenia, Greene County.

Joseph A. Stipp, private, Co. B, 154th Ohio:

The 60th Regiment, Ohio National Guard, was composed of eight companies and mustered about 700 men. In obedience to orders, the several companies scattered throughout the county assembled at the appointed time and place.

The streets of quiet Xenia presented an animated and decidedly warlike appearance.

On Tuesday morning, May 3rd, the regiment was drawn up in front of the courthouse, and made the recipient of an elegant and beautiful silk flag, the gift of the patriotic and spirited ladies of Clark Run district, No. 3, of Xenia Township. This was the signal for our departure, and father, mother, sister and brother, sweetheart and friend were present to bid us an affectionate good bye and God speed in the work before us.

We were soon on our way to the depot, drums beating and banners flying, and in due time we were located in barracks at Camp Dennison. *The Xenia Torchlight* of May 4th says: "Our Greene County Regiment departed for Camp Dennison yesterday. The boys left in good spirits and are anxious to do their duty in the coming crisis. God grant that they may be preserved, and in due time returned to their families and friends."

Upon our arrival at Camp Dennison we were mustered into the service of the United States Army, and our regiment was invested with a new title and designated as the 154th Ohio Volunteer Infantry.

At this time and place our strength was augmented to a full regiment of ten companies by the addition of the 23rd Battalion, Ohio National Guard, comprising two full companies from Madison County. They were most cordially received by us, and by their soldierly bearing and sturdy qualities of manhood they merited and received our confidence, goodwill and esteem.

Our stay at Camp Dennison—just nine days—was spent in further perfecting the organization of the regiment, in company and battalion drill and in routine camp duty. Here we were supplied with new arms—Enfield rifles—and accouterments, blankets, knapsacks and camp equipment.

Camp Dennison having been selected at an early period of the war as a place of general rendezvous for Ohio troops, and 17,000 or 18,000 men having assembled at this place under the call, afforded the opportunity for a grand review. To that end Governor John Brough and his staff paid us a visit, and after reviewing the new soldiery, complimented them upon their military bearing and precision.

We left Camp Dennison May 12th, our destination being New Creek, West Virginia, where we arrived Saturday evening, May 14th. We remained aboard the cars until the next morning, Sunday. What a dreary, desolate and deserted appearance that camp presented. The boys, however, smiled at fate, cheerfully accepted the situation and conducted themselves in a manner becoming true soldiers.

* * *

Henry Vail, a diminutive Vermonter who taught school in Ohio, joined a militia company during antidraft riots in Dayton in 1863, and served as a "Squirrel Hunter" during Morgan's raid.[13] His National Guard duty consisted of drills and a week of summer camp, where he concluded that "our colonels and generals were not well acquainted with the handling of large bodies of soldiers." Vail was surprised but pleased by Governor Brough's call.

Henry H. Vail, sergeant, Co. C, 131st Ohio:

When we marched to the station in Dayton,[14] everybody turned out to see us off. We went to Columbus in freight cars; only regimental officers went in cars having seats. On reaching Columbus, we marched some two miles out of the city to Camp Chase. This was on a large meadow and it was enclosed by a high fence, for it was a prison for Confederates, and there were thousands of them.

We were held there several days, awaiting the mustering officer of the United States, and we became very weary of our confinement. Men in the ranks never know what their next order will be, or where they will go. Some of our hot-headed men talked of making a petition that we be sent directly to the front. But in due time an officer came to muster us into the service of the United States, and at the same time our company was made a part of the 131st Ohio Volunteer Infantry. This regiment was formed on May 14th, and on the same day our colonel received his order to take the regiment to Baltimore.

Several days later, the privates learned where we were going, but even then we could not know whether we would be kept in Baltimore or be sent elsewhere.

Before we left Camp Chase,[15] we were ordered to take three days' rations in our haversacks, and barrels of hardtack, pork, coffee, and sugar were opened for us to help ourselves. It was our first acquaintance with the army ration, and we did not know how to handle it. We felt pretty sure that we could do no cooking in the freight cars, so we took nothing but a dozen or two of the big round crackers that were always called "hardtack." By carrying, these soon crumbled into small fragments; but they were our only food for more than three days.

Before leaving Columbus, we marched to the state arsenal there and gave up our good Springfield muskets and took Belgian guns instead. These were wretched pieces, fit only for show. They were often out of order and were really dangerous to the soldier who discharged one.

From the arsenal we marched to the station, and we then knew that we were going east. It was nearly dark when we broke ranks beside a train of freight cars. We scrambled in and the train started. In a few minutes we discovered that we should need more air; so with the butts of our muskets we dashed off half of the boards that covered the sides of the cars. We spread our blankets and lay down. There were so many of us that when one turned over, all must turn. We then turned over only on the order of the Captain, who happened to sleep next to me.

We were on the Baltimore & Ohio railway, and this road was then often broken by the attacks of small bodies of Confederates. Rumors of a late attack reached our colonel, and he remembered that we had not a single round of ammunition. So he obtained leave to stop at Cumberland[16] for a supply. It was really our first stop, and we were all hungry. There was a line of soldiers drawn up on each side of the train, and we soon saw that the officers passed through without any trouble, but the common soldiers were stopped.

As I was studying the situation, a private in our company, a handsome soldier, touched my arm and said, "Hold on, sergeant, I will show you how to get through."

We jumped down and went up to the nearest guard and my friend entered into conversation with him, asking him what regiment he belonged to, and I remember that he was a soldier of the First Loyal Virginians. While they were talking, I slipped across the guard line, and while the guard was trying to get me back, my friend stepped across the line. We then made a straight course to the village.

There was a hotel; but my friend was too old a soldier to crowd in where the officers were struggling for food. It was about the usual time for supper, and we turned in at a very nice looking house and went down to the basement kitchen door. There my friend rapped and a neat maid opened the door.

We were as hungry as wolves, and before us was an ample supply of food. My friend was too wise to ask for food, but he played the agreeable so sweetly to the two maids that we were invited to share their supper—and it was a good one. We offered them money, but they declined it. They did not refuse my friend's farewell kiss.

When we returned to the train, well filled, we listened with pleasure to our officers' description of the wretched meal served them at the hotel at a high price. We knew enough to keep very still about our good luck.

* * *

Mustering could be confusing even to the guards—a newly consolidated regiment might include troops from four O.N.G. units, all with a different number. (One Columbus newspaper reported the plight of an unfortunate substitute who couldn't recall his new regiment and so spent weeks under arrest.)[17] *Here journalist Nichols explains how he, like so many others, left home with one regiment only to serve in another.*

Clifton M. Nichols, corporal, Co. E, 152nd Ohio:

Camp Dennison, May 3.

It is the purpose of the writer to give a plain, unvarnished history of the movements and doings of the 35th regiment of the Ohio National Guard, from the time of leaving Springfield until its return.

We formed in Market Square on the morning of this day, bidding adieu to thousands of our friends, and passing through Yellow Springs, Xenia and other towns on the Little Miami road, arriving at Camp Dennison without incident at four o'clock and going into the rough wooden sheds to which we were assigned.

May 4.

Three companies from Madison County have just arrived and been assigned to the 35th, so that the regiment is now full, and will therefore, we hope, preserve its regimental organization, with Israel Stough as its colonel. This would give a great deal of satisfaction to the line officers and men. Surface indications are to the effect that Colonel Stough would put us in good fighting trim. Last evening we had our first dress parade.

May 5.

Neither clothing nor blankets have yet been issued to us. The 35th is in good condition and good spirits, ready for any sort of work that may be demanded. On Wednesday night and this (Thursday) morning, much time was spent in the work of consolidating the Madison County battalion with the 35th, and in perfecting the process of making and getting requisitions. We are already in one respect like the great Army of the Potomac: namely, we are reported to be just about to do great things!

Here is a record of camp occurrences:

Surgeon, to raw but enthusiastic "One Hundred Days" recruit: "You won't do. Your front teeth are gone, and you can't bite a cartridge."

Recruit, mistaking a cartridge for hardtack, "Well, if I can't bite it, I can swallow it whole."

The 8th cavalry boys were rather out of humor because they were ordered out of their barracks to make room for Hundred Days' men, and by way of revenging themselves took a good-sized comrade, spotted his face artistically with red ink, wrapped him in blankets, affixed a "small-pox" label, and put him near the entrance to the barracks. The new men came up, saw the point, and immediately applied for different quarters.

Governor Brough reviewed six to eight thousand of the National Guard here this afternoon. He made a good speech, which was greeted with a hearty demonstration of approval.[18]

May 6.

It seems that the members of a regiment just going into active service know but very little about their destination until—they find out. That is now the fact as to the 35th. We have rumors and echoes of rumors, and Nashville, Knoxville, West Virginia, et cetera, are knowingly mentioned by parties who are blissfully ignorant as a babe unborn of all the future of the regiment. When marching orders come, however—whatever they may prove to be—they will find a hearty, active response. Colonel Stough is at this hour drilling the commissioned officers of the regiment, and they form by no means an awkward squad.

We are today advised that we shall be known as the 146th (?) O.V.I. Since the addition of the Madison County battalion, we number 700 men, and we are told that an addition of a battalion from Lawrence County tonight will give us 1,000.

May 9th.

Today we are *not* to be known as the 146th, and Colonel Israel Stough is *not* to be our colonel. All former assignments have fallen through, and on Friday the organization of a brigade, of which we are a part, was announced.

Colonel Stough made all possible effort to have the 35th preserved intact, but finally we had to submit to a new deal. The Colonel had the boys of the old organization called together, and he and Lieutenant-Colonel Doty addressed the men with directness and force, explaining the circumstances, and impressing on them the great necessity of submitting cheerfully to the demands of the situation, so that the men could be got into the active service as soon as possible.

The organization of the brigade is:

Colonel H. Crampton, commanding.

146th O. N. G., Crampton, colonel; composed of the 31st and two companies of the 35th.

152d, David Putman, colonel; composed of the 28th and two companies of the 35th.

153d, Israel Stough, colonel; composed of the 41st and two companies of the 35th.

154th, R. Stevenson; composed of the 60th and 23rd battalions from Greene and Madison counties.

The companies of Captains Asa S. Bushnell[19] and Charles A. Welsh go with Lieutenant-Colonel Doty in the 152d.

This disposition of the 35th Battalion was quite unsatisfactory to the men, as those belonging to the Clark County regiment wished to be together. But, really, this is a small matter, and not at all to be considered in connection with what is endured by every soldier in the three-years' service. As fresh "soldiers," new to camp experience, we are apt to make a great deal of matters of slight consequence. We came out to try to render what little service we could for a hundred days, and to do that which will be most helpful to the Union cause. Our regiment, as the smallest one in the camp, naturally fared the worst in the transformations and combinings.

May 10.

Last night we had a two-hours' rain, and this morning the hills which encircle the camp are clothed in that beautiful verdure yearly brought out by the ethereal mildness of spring. May today appears in modest but charming colors and tints, and her sweet breath comes to us, but unhappily, not unmingled with the unfragrant smell of an aged military camp, which smell it would be base flattery to call a stink.

The work of mustering in, clothing and equipping the Clark County men is being pushed forward today.

This afternoon we had several hours of rain, which, mingled with Camp Dennison clay, makes expansive areas of mud that adheres in large quantities with an affectionate tenacity.

May 16th.

The companies of Captains Bushnell and Welch left Camp Dennison with the 152d Ohio on Thursday, May 12, at 12 o'clock.

Coming from Camp Dennison, on our way to the front, we were met with crowds of people—at South Charleston, Xenia, and other places—and pleasantly greeted. It was night before we arrived at Columbus, and we were at once crowded into boxcars and began to suffer, in a mild way, for our country.

* * *

An officer in the 157th Ohio, a veteran of hard service in Tennessee, was startled by the public's emotion during the long eastward journey from Columbus.

William M. Eames, surgeon, 157th Ohio:

All along the route we were saluted with cheers and smiles and waving of handkerchiefs and flags from early dawn to long after sunset. Never in all my campaigning have I seen anything to compare with those manifestations of rejoicing for the promptness of the 100 days men of Ohio. From the costly mansion and the Irish hovel—from the school houses and farm houses and manufactories—from laborers on the R.R. track and from the cottage far up on the hillside or among the distant trees were handkerchiefs and aprons and hands and hats and newspapers and flags waved till the train was out of sight.

I noticed one man who had nothing else to wave pull off one boot and swing that vigorously and shout "bully for the Buckeyes," and another one seized a small child and swung it high above his head in his zeal to demonstrate his joy. At one place in Maryland the students of a young ladies seminary had formed themselves in line by the road, and such a snapping of linen handkerchiefs as they got up would be hard to beat.[20]

3 | New Creek

*L*ITTLE REMEMBERED TODAY, *the rail and river town of New Creek,[1] West Virginia, was well known to Ohio's hundred-days men. Nearly every regiment passed through on its way east; a few remained either here or nearby for their entire service. "This is quite a small place but presents something of a warlike appearance," one corporal recorded.[2]*

Although situated just across the Ohio River from home, West Virginia often seemed like enemy territory. This was a new, breakaway state, after all, admitted to the Union just the previous year. Confederate sentiment often ran high,[3] and the hundred-days men had several scraps here (and later in the Shenandoah) with the feared rebel partisans they called "bushwhackers." Theirs was a dangerous, unsettling, and sometimes comic sort of war.

"Nickliffe" offered his readers several vivid portraits of New Creek, beginning with his arrival by train.

Clifton M. Nichols, corporal, Co. E, 152nd Ohio:

May 16.

We reached Piedmont [West Virginia], a fine town located in a deep valley, noted for coal and iron products. We found two of the three engine houses in ruins, having been destroyed a few days since by a party of about 40 rebels. They also destroyed three locomotives. They remained in the town about three hours, and ruined property worth not less than $100,000. The sight of these ruins aided us to appreciate the fact that we were in an enemy's country.

The trip from Piedmont to New Creek was a short one. We arrived at about five o'clock Saturday evening, having been about 52 hours on the route, during which period few of the men enjoyed much sleep. Saturday night was spent on the cars. A few of the men slept in government sheds, and more room was left in the cars for the remainder.

Yesterday (Sabbath) morning, notwithstanding the rough trip, our men all seemed to feel well. Many of them seemed to be generally improving. A little after eight o'clock, the regiment was called out, and a camping ground and shelter tents furnished. Just as the stakes were driven and we were preparing to pitch our canvas tabernacles (in which two only can be "taken in and done

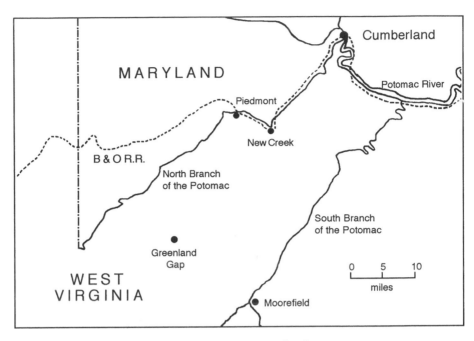

Maryland–West Virginia border

for"), it began to rain vigorously, and continued to do so all day long, with perhaps an occasional interval of ten minutes. We arranged our habitations, however, in spite of the torrents of water that fell upon us; dug ditches around them to carry off the floods; and then got inside and took, patiently, the drops that strained through upon us.

Our present location, New Creek, is the headquarters of Major-General Sigel,[4] who is away at present, aiding General Grant in the vicinity of Richmond. Our colonel reported to him on Saturday evening [May 14], by telegraph, for orders.

This camp somewhat resembles Camp Dennison, only it is on a much larger scale every way. It is encircled by mountains, whose tops are frequently covered with clouds. Upon the summits of these hills and mountains our men do picket duty, remaining out 24 hours.

This place was once the headquarters of General Fremont,[5] and the old residents have a variety of large stories prepared with which to "chaff" the new arrivals. One is that General Fremont shelled Stonewall Jackson from a high bluff on the eastern side of the camp, and drove him up the New Creek valley.

We are well fortified here, and have men enough for any emergency. The rebels have a force of 15,000 or so within from 30 to 100 miles of us, who have been cut off from Richmond by Sigel.

New Creek is 190 miles this side of the Ohio River and 20 miles west of Cumberland.[6] It is located on the north branch of the Potomac. Just east, across the Potomac, on the Maryland side, rises a rocky hill to the height of 200 or more feet, from the summit of which projects a bold cliff which has the appearance of having been cut into columns by a skillful sculptor. From this summit, in every direction, can be seen Alleghenian peaks of various heights and at various distances, from one mile to ten or 20.

The camp itself is in a vast plain, ample enough for 50,000 men. In the center is a fort well provided with heavy guns, and there are other means of defense adequate to the protection of the vast quantity of army supplies which have been gathered here.

There is not much to be said about the village of New Creek. It is composed of a railroad station and other buildings, an express office, a post office, one or two "stores" and offices, and a small city of sutlers' shanties. Three-fourths of the old inhabitants are secessionists, whose able-bodied connections are in the rebel army. Occasionally, a scoundrel remains to give information of our movements to the enemy.

Ohio troops are passing through here by thousands. Just how many thousands we are not permitted to say (if we knew), but it is certain that our state is covering herself with glory by her promptness in taking the field to assist in winding up the affairs of the Southern Confederacy.[7] Is not John Brough a little ahead of Governor Morton (whose praises are in the mouths of all loyal men) this time?

The Springfield companies in the 152d are in excellent condition. The food we eat is of a good quality. Cyrus Albin cooks for Captain Bushnell's company, and our "cooked rations" are well prepared. This is a matter of some importance, as the health and lives of the men are involved in it.

The 154th Ohio is encamped close to us.[8]

The camp of the 152d is being fitted up in good style, and our quarters are increasingly in comfort. We may remain here during the hundred days, but matters of this are always uncertain.

May 18.

To the natural and proper inquiry, "How do you do in camp?" we reply, "Pretty well, we thank you; how do you do yourself?"

We dwell in tents like the Arabs, but no Arabs, we take it, would consent to live in a shelter, or "dog" tent, such as is furnished to the United States soldier.[9] They are, in the center, about four feet high, and the "gables" are quite open, exposing the two occupants to whatever wind may prevail at the time. On the sand, with which the plain is covered, we spread two "gums" and one government blanket. On these we lie, and over us we throw another government blanket, which, in turn, is covered by another gum blanket. On this may fall dew or rain without seriously wetting us.

We can hear the roar of the north branch of the Potomac, its haste to join its mates and rush on to "report at Washington," furnishing a fair parallel to the multitudes of hundred-day Ohio troops who pass through here daily on the same errand.

We have guard and picket duty to perform, the former at the government warehouses, and the latter in the mountains surrounding the camp. The commander of the brigade, Colonel Wilkinson[10] of the 6th [West] Virginia, undertook to test the faithfulness of one of the "hundred day" guards yesterday. The guard had been instructed not to allow any smoking on the platform. Soon the Colonel came along, smoking a cigar, and the guard saluted and halted him, informing him that he must remove his cigar or leave the platform.

Apparently very much enraged, the Colonel swore at him and declared he was a "d———d pretty fellow to halt a colonel." The guard replied that he was "that same," put his bayonet under the Colonel's breast and ordered him to throw away his cigar. The lightning glance of his eye showed that he meant business, and the Colonel complied. After he had passed him, he turned and commended him for his faithfulness.

We have a line of pickets on all but the Maryland side of the camp, a mile and a half out, a line a mile beyond, and another still farther out, with cavalry pickets (or videttes) still beyond. Mr. Segrove[11] was out yesterday and the officer who made the "grand rounds" in the night tested him also, but he stood the test. The officer asked him for his gun so he could examine it as to its condition, but Segrove replied that he could "see it tomorrow, but not to-night."

May 24.

The 152d is doing some heavy drilling—some six hours per day. This is necessary not only to give military efficiency to our men, but to give them that exercise which is the only preventative of disease in such a climate as this—with hot days and cold, damp nights. Lieutenant-Colonel Hoy[12] assists in the drilling and is doing good work. If we come back to Springfield at all, and we hope we do, we shall be well-drilled men and shall hope to have the appearance, at least, of veterans.

Colonel Hoy said yesterday, "The Ohio National Guards have saved the whole of West Virginia from being overrun by the rebels, the Baltimore & Ohio road (an all-important government route) from destruction, and sent 20,000 veterans to Grant."

This is undoubtedly true, and does anyone in our ranks, or at home, regret that we have come? And are we not entitled to a better name than "Home Guards?"

May 28.

We have marching orders, and leave for Martinsburg, [West] Virginia, 100 miles east of here, on the Baltimore & Ohio road tonight. It is the old residence of Captain C. A. Welch of the Lagonda company.[13] The whole regiment goes. Direct letters to New Creek, to follow regiment, until we write you again, as all letters must be forwarded to us from this point. The 154th goes 25 miles west, up the New Creek Valley, to Greenland Gap tomorrow.[14]

* * *

Little more than a month after muster, the departing 154th would be the first Ohio hundred-days regiment to have a significant skirmish with a rebel force.

Joseph A. Stipp, private, Company B, 154th Ohio:

The 154th remained at New Creek until it received orders to march to Greenland Gap, a very important pass in the Allegheny Mountain range, 27 miles distant and south of New Creek.

A junction of the Moorefield, Petersburg, Altamont, Oakland and New Creek roads was formed at this gap. It was held by the forces of Brigadier-General B. F. Kelley as a key to a wide and important area of country to the south, as well as for the protection of the Baltimore & Ohio Railroad.

Our march from New Creek to Greenland Gap was without incident and made in about ten hours, a pretty good test of our soldierly qualities so far as marching was concerned. Upon our arrival at Greenland Gap, our force was slightly augmented by the addition of a small detachment of the 2nd Maryland Mounted Infantry, or Potomac Home Brigade, about 20 in number, and one section of Battery L, 1st Illinois Light Artillery. Our camp was established at the brow of a hill that commanded the gap, as well as a wide scope of country on our right and left.

The mountain range was grand and majestic, clothed with a heavy growth of pine, fir, hemlock and various other kinds of wood. The air was healthful and invigorating, and an abundance of pure water from never-failing springs flowed from almost every crevice in the rocks. The scene was beautiful to behold and unsurpassed in loveliness.

But we were now in the enemy's country, which was for miles around thoroughly infested with bands of guerrillas under command of McNeill, Harness, Mosby, Imboden, Jones, Rosser[15] and others too numerous to mention. The enemy's forces in this section were always mounted, and had perfect knowledge of the country, the roads and numerous mountain paths and by-ways which facilitated escape. Our forces were "strangers in a strange land," compelled to grope their way in the darkness, occasionally aided by a scout upon whose head a ransom was placed.

We were pretty thoroughly schooled in drill, picket and outpost duty. The roads leading from Greenland Gap diverged in every direction, and every avenue of approach was guarded with the utmost vigilance.

During the afternoon of Sunday, June 5th, two mounted couriers presented themselves to our regimental headquarters and handed Col. Stevenson a little document, which was hastily opened and read. The appearance of the cavalrymen attracted no little attention. They looked like *old soldiers,* and with their warlike trappings, each armed with a brace of navy revolvers, they plainly indicated that they were prepared for business. One by one our boys would quietly draw near, eager to catch every word spoken, hoping thereby to solve the mystery attending our presence.

Some of us did not have to wait very long. The orderly sergeants of the several companies were seen to leave their captains' quarters. Then going down the company streets, they ordered this man and that man to provide himself with four days' rations of hardtack, coffee, sugar, salt and pepper and report to regimental headquarters at once. About five o'clock on that quiet Sunday afternoon, 126 men reported as ordered.

Under the command of Captain Joseph F. Bouck,[16] we left camp, taking the Petersburg road, and continued in that direction for a distance of about five miles, when we filed to the left and passed around a spur of one of the large mountains that entered into the formation of the gap. After marching about ten miles, at least four of them over and through the foothills, traversing paths and byways heretofore unknown to us, imagine our surprise when we arrived at the white house owned by Mrs. Babb, and only about four miles from our camp. Darkness was coming on, and some mutterings were heard concerning the lateness of our supper hour.

Finally we came to a large spring near the roadside. Here we halted, kindled fires, made our coffee and indulged in our evening meal. After a short rest, we were drawn up in line and made acquainted with the object of our scout. Captain Bouck, a kind-hearted Christian gentleman, told us in a manner that betrayed his deep concern and solicitous feelings for our safe return, that we were going to meet the enemy, in what numbers he did not know. With a spirit of earnestness, he invoked the Divine blessing upon our little command. This scene awakened within us sober thought and serious reflections.

We trudged along in the darkness and stillness of the night, our music being the cadence of our marching feet. Soon the clatter of horses' hoofs, accompanied by the rumbling sounds of a wagon, came stealing upon our ears. What could it be? Was it the enemy with a piece of artillery? Our anxiety in this direction, however, was soon relieved when we learned that it was a wagon with supplies, accompanied by an ambulance in the charge of our assistant surgeon.

About midnight we came upon a picket post of cavalrymen, which proved to be a detachment of the 22nd Pennsylvania, or "Ringgold Cavalry," under Captain James P. Hart. We ascended a pretty good-sized hill called Walnut Knob. Here we went into camp for the remainder of the night. About four o'clock in the morning we were roused from a sound sleep, ordered to fall in and proceed on our journey, our detachment of infantry being in the advance. About six o'clock we came to a mountain stream, where we halted, kindled fires, made and partook of our breakfast, consisting of coffee and hardtack.

Resuming our march, we began the ascent of a mountain, and upon reaching its summit we halted. The detachment of cavalry, just 104 in number, passed us and led the advance. Here our ammunition was inspected, each man having been provided with the usual 40 rounds. We were instructed not to allow ourselves to become separated in the event of an attack. We marched on until about nine o'clock, when we were startled by the rattle of carbine fire in our front.

The command *double quick* was given, and the promptness with which that command was complied with would have done the old soldiers credit. The firing became more rapid and terrific as we drew nearer the immediate scene of conflict. Imagine our surprise when we were met with one-half of the cavalry force coming back. On we went, down that narrow, winding mountain road with bayonets fixed, and in a very short time we were right upon the enemy's forces.

The rebels were in full possession of the road, and were formed in sections or platoons as thick as they could stand, occupying the ground as far as we could see. We immediately opened fire, and continued the fight until we discovered that an attempt was being made to flank our right. We fell back a reasonable distance and extended our right up the mountainside, and advanced in line of skirmishers, keeping up a stead fire upon the enemy.

About one-half of the cavalry had charged through the lines of the enemy, and had crossed the South Branch of the Potomac that glides through the Moorefield Valley. The half that had fallen back returned in due time and assisted in putting the enemy to flight.

We pressed forward, only to find the enemy beating a hasty retreat. We soon reached an open space where we were able to obtain a good view of the entire force of the enemy. At this point, we were reinforced by the detachment sent out by Colonel Higgins,[17] having with it a genuine jackass battery. This little piece was soon placed in position, and the retreating enemy was given a parting salute of several rounds.

We now returned to the ground where the fight opened, to find four men killed and nine severely wounded. The dead were placed in our wagon; after the ambulance was filled with the wounded, the remaining wounded were placed in the wagon with the dead.

Our situation now became embarrassing. The cavalry were determined to return to Green Spring, and they turned their faces in that direction. So long as we remained together we were comparatively safe; but, if separated, no one could tell what might befall us. We were told that we must reach Mechanicsburg Gap as early as possible to effect our escape, as the forces we had engaged with would join the forces that were to cut off Captain Hart's return. So we set out with a very quick step and kept pace with the mounted men, reached the gap and passed through it safely, remaining together until we reached the junction of the Romney and New Creek road.

Here the infantry and cavalry separated, the infantry returning to Greenland Gap, reaching that place on Tuesday evening, June 7th, at about eight o'clock. We had marched 83 miles, had experienced a genuine fight, and were tired, hungry, and footsore.[18]

* * *

The 154th soon sent another scouting expedition from Greenland Gap after McNeill's elusive band. Although Private Stipp pronounced it "a disappointment to many of us in the light of our former experience of June 6th," a 39-year-old farmer turned second lieutenant sent a vivid account of the march to his wife.

Isaac Hambleton, second lieutenant, Co. C, 154th Ohio:

Greenland Gap, June 23

Dear Wife,

Well, we had considerable of a march. We went to Moorefield twenty miles from here. It's the county seat of this county, a perfect Secesh hole with the exception of two or three families.

We arrived there about 5 o'clock, encamped, ordered the citizens to furnish supper for us, which they done. It is a very nice town about as large as London.[19] It's on the south branch of the Potomac, a very nice country, rich bottom land. There's but few men in the town but lots of women & children. The women looked very sour at us. They all have a very sad look. We expected to find McNeill there, but did not. Some of the women threatened us that we would be run out of there before two days.

We stayed two days and nary an armed Reb came in sight. So we started back, come six miles, encamped, sent out the cavalry scouting on different roads. Some of them went back in sight of Moorefield (we had about 80 cavalry with us). They heard that McNeill was over between Moorefield and

Petersburg, distance twelve miles. So the next morning all but sixty of the men and the wagons, one captain and myself started to hunt them up. We stayed to protect the provisions.

When they got in sight of Petersburg, the cavalry were in the advance. The infantry concluded they [would] rest a while and let the cavalry [pass] through the town and see if there was any Rebels there or not. Some of the boys thought they would take a swim while they were gone. They had just got in when they heard guns firing and the cavalry coming back as hard as they could run. They were in a narrow gap in the mountains, in a hard position. So they fell back a mile or more and formed a line, but the Rebs didn't come any farther.

The Swamp Dragoons[20] and the Rebels had a skirmish the day before near there. Several wounded and a few killed on each side. So they came back where [they] left us and we stayed a couple of days, and concluded to go back to Moorefield and see if we could find them. We started at 12 o'clock at night, got there about 5 in the morning. Found some of them digging a grave to bury Lieutenant Doland, one of McNeill's men that the Dragons had killed. They broke and run when they saw us, but we captured one of them.

There was a Union man told us there was two hundred back in the mountains a couple of miles, but our Colonel concluded not to follow them. He is a very cautious man. So we returned to our old camp. Fetched a family of slaves back with us, a man & his wife & seven children, two girls, young man. They done some washing for Ted & me yesterday. Done it well. So you see, our tramp didn't amount to much. I hardly think we will take another soon.[21]

4 | Washington

As OHIO'S HUNDRED-DAYS *regiments rolled east on the Baltimore & Ohio railroad, the long-awaited Union push toward Richmond was fast becoming a shambles. During five murderous weeks, from early May to mid-June, first at the Wilderness then Spotsylvania,[1] North Anna River, and Cold Harbor, Grant's army lost 50,000 men. The Confederate forces under Lee lost 32,000. The North's advantage was its ability to supply more men and material, while the exhausted Confederacy could not. The South's hope now lay in Lincoln's defeat in the November presidential election, followed by a negotiated peace.[2]*

The green hundred-days men weren't yet engulfed in the carnage, however, and initially deployed in the rear as planned. Thirteen regiments reported to Washington, where some glimpsed the president.[3] To one Ohio soldier, the capital seemed "the center of creation, the Head Quarters of the world, and Mr. Lincoln the Chief Bugler."[4] Here a private from near Cincinnati began writing to his wife.

Wallace W. Chadwick, private, Co. F, 138th Ohio:

May 23rd.

We are now situated at Fort Tillinghast.[5] How long we may be here I know not. We may move in two or three days, or we may be here a month. It is about six or eight miles from Washington, on the south side of the Potomac. We are in nice barracks at present. I can sit in my bunk and look over part of Washington City.

I have been shaved and had my hair cut and feel all the better for it. I suppose our duties will be arduous here, but not severe. I feel pretty well, except a little soreness of throat from fast marching and then cooling off too quickly. I wonder that some of the boys are not sick, for it was warm, and our march was too long for raw troops.

We left North Mountain[6] last Saturday evening, being brought direct to Washington and from there to this place. We came through Harper's Ferry about nine or ten o'clock in the evening. The moon shone brightly and we had

a very nice view of it. It was a grand sight to see a train of over 30 cars crossing the river on a bridge. They had to wind around so that the train was in
about three curves at one time, and it passed through a tunnel cut out of solid
rock.

We traveled through Maryland. One little town was the most loyal place
I have seen since I left home. The women and children were out with flags and
handkerchiefs, as though it were some big political meeting. About 20 miles
from Washington the country began to look like living, but the soil was very
thin and in quality inferior to the best parts of Hamilton County.

Washington did not meet my expectations by any means. There are a few
nice buildings, but the majority cannot come anywhere near Cincinnati. I was
through the Capitol yard, a nice grove of several acres, all laid off with nice
walks. It is a very beautiful place. The Capitol is a splendid affair, but I think
rather too low for the amount of ground it covers. There is one main building
with two wings with large pillars cut from solid rock. Many pieces of sculp-
ture are located in different parts of the building, some of them very nice, but
it will be some time before it will be completed, perhaps years.

We marched through the city and crossed on the Long Bridge to this side.[7]
We camped in front of the residence and on the lawn of the rebel General Lee.
It is the most handsome situation I ever saw, commanding a full view of the
Potomac for miles up and down the river, in a natural grove, on Arlington
Heights.[8] I send you a couple of flowers we pulled from the flower garden as
trophies of the home of the rebel general.

If we stay here any length of time, we will be luckier than some of the
boys, for as we passed Martinsburg, [West] Virginia, they told us that five regiments of the Guards had gone to Sigel and there were lots of them stationed
on the railways in the heart of the enemy's country.

I feel that we are doing good here, as I read in yesterday's paper that in
the late fight,[9] where the rebels tried to turn our right flank, two regiments of
heavy artillery from these defenses charged the enemy, scattered them, and
frustrated a well-conceived plan to break our right flank. While we had no
hand in it, if it had not been for the Guards taking their places, they could
not have been spared from these forts. So we may have been the means of
saving our army from serious losses, though the credit is due those men and
not us.[10]

* * *

*The 150th Ohio also reached Washington by rail. Despite the drudgery
of garrison duty ("Washington soldiering is a humbug," a bored veteran
huffed in his diary)[11] and the city's often tawdry reputation ("I pity the poor
soldier who has to make his abode in that place of red tape and prostitu-*

tion," another Ohioan wrote home),[12] *duty in the capital suited the regiment, especially Company K of Oberlin College.*

William J. Gleason, private, Co. E, 150th Ohio:

We arrived in Pittsburg in the evening [of May 12]. Our coming had preceded us, and the ever patriotic women of that hospitable city treated us to a substantial, elaborate feast, also filling our brand-new haversacks with palatable food.

The next stop was at Baltimore, where we disembarked and marched through some of its principal streets to the Baltimore & Ohio depot. We received an ovation from thousands of colored people. This was the first introduction that a majority of our boys had to the genuine southern negroes. The white people seemed to be mighty scarce in Baltimore when the union soldiers marched through their city, while the loyal colored element turned out in full force, with shouts of welcome.[13]

A brief ride from Baltimore took us into Washington, where we arrived on the evening of the 13th. Here we were marched to the Soldiers' Rest, where we were furnished with our first army meal—sowbelly, hardtack and so-called coffee. We had not yet felt the pangs of hunger, our haversacks still containing a goodly part of the substantials provided for us by the patriotic ladies of Pittsburg; so instead of indulging in the government fare, we plastered the walls and floors with the sowbelly.

Soon we got tired of firing hardtack, and orders were received to unroll blankets and retire. What a delightful night's rest and sleep we enjoyed in the memorable and never-to-be-forgotten Soldiers' Rest! Although we were somewhat shy on sleep, we carried away with us a scratching collection, some lively reminiscences that multiplied and continued to entertain some of the boys during the campaign. Blue ointment applications along the seams of our shirts and trousers and frequent bathing were essential to destroy the neighborly attachments we formed within the walls and on the grounds of the lively Soldiers' Rest.

We were soon at the Capitol. The conundrum went around: Where do we go next? It was answered on the morning of the 14th. The command was given to "Fall in by companies." This being done, the roll being called, and "all present and accounted for," we set off, in heavy marching order, for our respective soldier homes on the northeast of Washington. The entire regiment was assigned to garrison duty in Forts Lincoln, Thayer, Saratoga, Slocum, Bunker Hill, Slemmer, Totten and Stevens.[14]

* * *

James C. Cannon, private, Co. K, 150th Ohio:

Companies H and K were the two companies assigned to Fort Slocum, to which we marched that Sunday afternoon, and found very good barracks that had been occupied by the 11th Vermont for nearly two years. Company L, 5th U.S. Artillery, was also stationed there, and the strictness of the regular army discipline made a deep and valuable impression on our minds.

Bible classes were instituted on the first Sunday, and continue regularly throughout our period of service.

Guard duty became something important, and some of us took it very seriously and solemnly. One newly fledged United States Army sentinel, having received orders to halt anyone attempting to cross his lines, tried to halt the whole company one morning when their drill exercise threatened to bring them over his beat.

So much is said about the soldier's fare that only one brief reference will be made to it here, and that is the actual account written home by one of the [Oberlin] seniors. He said: "On my plate I found a piece of pork one inch square surface, half an inch thick, and a piece of boiled turnip containing about two cubic inches. But there was plenty of bread, and what in my inexperience I called coffee."

Some variation of the routine gave new interest to barrack life almost every day. On May 18, the regular drill was livened up by a change to the practice of Zouave[15] Drill. Another day we were ordered out to march under sealed orders and were led to the river, where the orders proved to be for a bath. In a week or ten days, the change of living began to have its bad effect, and names of the sick began to be dropped from roll-call.

After supper, May 22, we moved over to Fort Thayer, about a mile and a half from the East Potomac. During the hot weather we made good use of the yellow waters of that stream, for they were a few degrees cooler than the air, and seemed quite refreshing. At Fort Thayer, we bunked on the floor at first with Company E, as the barracks were occupied by the 16th Massachusetts Battery. But they left the next day, and the quarters were at once thoroughly cleaned and fixed up.

Our nearness to Washington was, of course, a source of great pleasure to our student soldiery. It mattered little whether the day was clear or rainy, if we could get passes for outside trips. On May 24, with the mercury at 95 in the shade, a bunkmate and the writer visited the Senate while the internal revenue bill was under consideration, and from the gallery of the House looked with intense interest upon the able men guiding the ship of state, and especially noted the massive frame of James A. Garfield.[16]

One amusing experience was that of Sergt. Robbins[17] on a trip to the city. For some trivial and perfectly innocent reason, the sergeant wanted to buy a pair of overalls, but none of our blandishments could induct the store men to sell—they evidently suspected him of a scheme for desertion.

The first week of June passed with some hard experience of hot weather, and the drills were sometimes omitted. Usually 10 or 12 men were daily on the sick list.

The company went to Fort Slocum on the 8th [of June], but the provisions did not arrive until afternoon, and rations for dinner were reduced to a small private stock of ginger cookies. The variations of our barrack life had a very wide range from grave to gay; writing of daily journals, jotting down scientific notes from the last excursion, jolly times of singing, games, reading class lessons, the seniors diving now and then into Plato, the juniors into some other fountain of knowledge, all these and many more issues filled the days and sometimes a large part of the nights.

We had taken to the artillery drill with great interest, and in that as well as the usual infantry tactics had now greatly improved. Corporal Barnard[18] was detailed to give instructions in projectiles, and made us familiar with the qualities and uses of shells, case, canister, spherical, grenades, etc.

A favorite visiting place was the Soldiers' Home, where veterans of the Mexican War were happily spending their declining years. It was President Lincoln's summer home, and sometimes we would meet him coming from the city after the anxious work of the day. Once we saw the old hero, Gen. Casey,[19] white-haired and worn by long service, sitting in his carriage at the gate.

Under order, we went to Fort Bunker Hill on June 15.

On June 17, Mrs. Stephen Douglas visited the fort, which afforded an agreeable topic for camp talk. The next day was a red-letter day, on account of the arrival of a box of cake from home to Corporal Ells,[20] one of the five seniors. Sergt. K[21] remarked: "How strange it tastes!"

This was a very trying week for heat, and at 4 A.M., just when we wanted to sleep, it seemed as though all the flies in Maryland wanted to visit with us. During the hot spell, brief windstorms swept over the hills, covering us in clouds of dust. Now and then some outside items of news came to us of special interest, as when we heard that Congress had made some increase in our pay. Sergt. Keyes was sent to Washington with three prisoners, one of whom ran away. But the sergeant put a bullet hole in the fellow's hat as a souvenir of freedom.

Then, on July 4, "Special Order No. 77," the sixth item of which was: "Col. Hayward will order one company of his regiment from Fort Bunker Hill to Fort Stevens."

Under this order Company K was moved to Fort Stevens, which was soon to prove the special post of honor of the whole service.

* * *

Jake Holtz, a 21-year-old farmer's son, had been turned down by the army in 1862 because of heart problems. He joined a National Guard company in April, only to see the unit scattered during consolidation. He was nonetheless thrilled to be sent to Washington.

Jacob Souder Holtz, private, Co. H, 164th Ohio:

Fort Woodbury, Va.

Dear Folks,

I thought I would write you a few lines to let you know that I am well and feel first rate. Yesterday we came from Washington and arrived here last night. We are on Arlington Heights and guard Fort Woodbury. It is a beautiful place. We can see down on the City of Washington. If I only keep well I would not have missed this for a good Deal.

I was at General Lee's (rebel) house yesterday. It is a beautiful place. I wish you could be here to see us. We have as good Quarters as any. Kitchen and good bunks to sleep in. They are better than my bed that I had at home. Two sleep in one bunk. Courtney and me sleeps together. There is a good stream of soft water here and nice grove of trees about like them at Mr. Dunage's.

Our regiment is divided in divisions of two companies each and placed in the fort. The forts are about 1/2 mile apart. We can run around and go down to the river. Some of the boys are fishing today. I will tell you more next time. I will send a Dollar home, it will not go here. I got it in York[22] and I want you to send me some stamps. It is so much trouble to get them here. I can get everything else here. . . .

Arlington Heights, Va., May 26th / 64

Dear Father, Mother, Brothers and Sisters. . . .

I was on guard yesterday. Standing guard here is nothing to what it was in Cleveland. We just stand around in the fort and watch the guns. And the picket guard is easy, all they have to do is to examine the passes of the folks passing the road. We have a first rate Company. . . .

Fort Woodbury, Va.
June the 17 / 64

Friend Isaac. . . .

We are situated in a beautiful place in Arlington Heights Va. near the Potomac River and have a grand view of the City of Washington. We have first rate barracks to live in. Have to do guard duty and throw up entrenchments, build magazines and a little bit of everything. I have been drilling on the Artillery. I like it a great deal better than infantry. This thing of carrying a gun I do not like. If you enlist go in the artillery. I like soldiering very well as long as I keep well. I feel first rate so far. I hope I may continue to feel so. . . .

Fort Woodbury, June the 18th

Dear Father. . . .

We do not drill much Infantry. I do not drill any more in it. I belong to the artillery. There is two sections in our Company. I like it very well, a good deal better than infantry. . . .

* * *

Duty in the Washington forts involved more than garrison duty and artillery drill. Pickets also stood constant guard beyond the walls, in a line of sentinel posts extending from fort to fort around the capital. One young picket got a scare one night outside Fort Ethan Allen, Virginia.

M. B. Lemmon, private, Co. B, 169th Ohio:

The men for interior guard came for duty at guard mount, dressed in blouse, with gloves, gun and sidearms. Then, to the left of the line thus formed, were the men for picket duty. They also have 24 hours to serve. But what a difference! They have their guns and sidearms also, but they have besides these their blankets, overcoats, haversacks, with one day's rations and a canteen of water. When the guard was formed, this picket guard was taken charge of by its commanding officer, and without fuss or delay marched at once to the relief of the men on picket.

Leaving the fort, the detail marched down the right side of the Potomac River, fully a mile. Here was Post No. 1, whose men, on arrival of the new detail, fell into line and saluted. Here our sergeant, corporal and several men were left. The march then continued, going at right angles from the Potomac, along a sort of cow path made by the sentinels and squads marching up and down the line. The posts were stationed not so far apart but that they could easily communicate with each other, both day and night. These posts were placed at intervals, in a sort of semicircle, about the same distance from the fort.

Our first squad was located on the river road. Only one other post was on a road. That was about the center of the line, and here was a great deal of travel to and from camp, and here was stationed a lieutenant and half a company of men. Then on to the last post. Our tramp of some three miles ended abruptly at the foot of a mountain rising very steep and high. So steep was it that one could scarcely go up it without pulling himself up by the branches of trees and brush. Here it was that we met the picket guard sent out from Port Marcy, making the line continuous.

All the time at each post there was at least one man kept on duty, two hours on and four hours off, but he marched no stated beat, to and fro. He wore no white gloves. But one thing he did, and that was his full duty; he was the watch-guard for his comrades. When first we did duty there were those in our company, and I suspect in others also, who, when detailed for picket duty, would swap with one detailed for interior guard, and 25 cents each. After a time, and nobody being killed on picket, the 25 cents premium went the other way. When night came, telling stories far into the night kept the sentinel company. Then the men would, one by one, drop into sleep, and all would become quiet, save the crick of the bugs, the call of the night-birds, the sigh of the wind in the forest trees.

A little incident occurred on this last post one night. It was about one o'clock in the morning. There was no moon, but the stars shone bright and the air was clear and quiet. To my left as I faced away from the fort was the squad of men, good comrades, about six rods behind me quiet in restful slumber. To my right was the mountain. I was surrounded with trees and brush, save where a military road and our own little station had been cut. There silence and foreboding of still night was all around and about.

My birthday of sixteen was August 7th of that year. In youthful trust I stood there, not afraid, but with a sort of solemn awe hovering about me. My dead mother was in my thoughts. My father at home also. My three brothers were all in the service. The occasion was both grand and, to a boy like me at the time, dismal. I knew my duty and was doing it.

When so standing, wholly engrossed with my thoughts of home and loved ones, there came with a leap, a bound, a large tiger-cat from the mountainside directly in front of me, some ten paces. With a scream, growl or yell, such I never heard before or since, the animal stood a few seconds looking at me, and I looked at it. Then with a growl and bound, it disappeared in the darkness. Strange to say, during this ordeal I stood perfectly still, carrying my gun at right-shoulder shift. The roar of the brute awoke the boys, who inquired what was the matter.

To which I replied, "Oh, only a panther-cat!"[23]

5 | Maryland

MARYLAND, AN OHIOAN *wrote home, "is composed of Negroes, dogs &* *fools & Rebs."*[1] *The 149th Ohio, from rural Chillicothe, arrived in beautiful* *and cosmopolitan Baltimore, where many of its citizens were indeed South-* *ern sympathizers.*

George Perkins, private, Co. A, 149th Ohio:

Companies A and F were assigned to Fort No. 1 on the outskirts of Baltimore, Capt. Wm. W. Peabody of Co. A being appointed garrison commander. Companies A and F settled down to routine garrison duty. Cooks were detailed and the men assigned to barracks, Co. A occupying the first floor and Co. F the second. The duties of the day after roll call consisted of dress parade and guard mounting. Guard duty was by detail, two hours on and four hours off, each being held for duty twenty-four hours.

Time was given the men for many trips into the city, and this part of our service was very pleasant and safe. Many of our friends from Ohio came to visit us while we were there and brought money and good things to eat for the boys. Four Companies of the regiment were assigned to Fort Federal Hill, and Cos. D, K and I at headquarters in Baltimore. On May 25th several companies were sent to the eastern shore of Maryland, with headquarters at Salisbury. They had orders to quell the rebellion sympathizers, do provost guard duty at that point, guard the telegraph lines and patrol the Bay for smugglers.

A chain of forts encircled Baltimore, from Fort No. 1 on Baltimore Street to Fort No. 12 in Druid Hill Park. Details were made from the men at our fort for guard duty at these outposts. One guard at each fort was to remain all day, his duty being to keep a strict watch.

One day at Fort 11, a squad of 12 cavalrymen came on a full gallop down the road past the fort. Just as they came opposite to where I was standing guard, the officer in command shouted, "There they are, fire." A volley from their carbines followed and two men who were in a field running through the high wheat threw up their hands and tumbled over dead. I heard afterward that they were deserters trying to escape from Lafayette Barracks.

The discipline was severe—some may think too much so—but it was necessary to control the great variety of characters that made up the army. When our company first came to Fort No. 1, we found the guardhouse full of rough men of the New York Artillery. We were detailed to guard them. Of all low, rough New York toughs, these were surely the worst. They took great pleasure in guying the boys fresh from home, and their actions were disgusting. Luckily, they went away in a short time.

One night, two of them attempted to break guard and escape. Our boys who were on guard fired at them and alarmed the garrison. A search squad was at once formed and the two men were found lying on their faces in the ditch surrounding the fort, nearly frightened to death. They were taken back to the guardhouse, saying they "did not think the 'century plants' would shoot." These fellows had a better opinion of us after that episode.

The hundred days service was hard, but it had a humorous side. Many were the pranks played by the boys. Many pleasant hours we spent together. At Fort No. 1, we had our own string band, and every evening we had dancing or singing. Some played cards, others went down into the city taking in the markets, theaters, etc.

At one time downtown a gentleman asked some of us, "Boys, what regiment do you belong to?" We answered, "The 149th Ohio." He mused awhile and said, "One hundred and forty nine, that means a 149,000. My goodness, boys, do men grow on trees in Ohio?"

* * *

Schoolteacher Henry Vail of Dayton also served in Baltimore, where he found time for cosmopolitan activities such as attending his first opera. During duty hours, he patrolled the often angry border city to enforce martial law.

Henry H. Vail, sergeant, Co. C, 131st Ohio:

At Baltimore our regiment was divided, going to the different forts around that city. Some companies went to Fort McHenry, one company to Fort Marshall, and three companies to Fort Federal Hill.[2] This latter fort was our post for the summer. It was also the headquarters of the regiment.

Colonel Lowe[3] and the other regimental officers occupied a two-story wooden building just west of the parade ground. The barracks for the common soldiers lined two sides of the parade. This fort was built under the order of Gen. Benjamin Butler[4] and its purpose was to overawe the people of that city, for most of them were Confederate in sentiment. Our cannon could reach every part of the city, and more than once the guns were loaded and the city was told that we were ready for any outbreak. We relieved a regiment of regulars who had been there for more than a year. This regiment was sent to the front and was in the battle of the Wilderness, where it lost very heavily.

Our duty at Fort Federal Hill was to guard the fort and hold hundreds of drafted men who were on their way to their regiments, and to patrol the streets of the city at night and arrest soldiers who were absent from their place of duty. For most of the time that we were in Baltimore it was my own duty to command a squad of a dozen men, and with them to march through certain streets, halting all soldiers and examining their papers. These streets were lined with saloons and dance houses.

As the city was under martial law, I was authorized to enter any house and make arrests, sending the person arrested to the provost marshal. Nearly every evening we picked up drunken soldiers who had stayed in town beyond their leave. If possible we sent them back to their duty without making an arrest; but if they were offensive, they were arrested.

One night I found a cavalry lieutenant in a saloon and I demanded his pass. He was indignant that a noncommissioned officer should demand his papers; but I showed him my written authority to halt any officer, and again ordered him to show his pass or suffer arrest. He then very reluctantly brought out his paper. It was short—so short that I can remember every word of it except the name of the man.

It read, "Lieutenant——is hereby dismissed from the service of the United States for cowardly conduct in the face of the enemy. Gen. Philip Sheridan."

I was myself ashamed for the man and said, "Why do you linger here with such a paper as that for your only protection?" The man broke down and said that he had no money to get home. I advised him to walk. I doubted whether he would be welcome in any home with that record.

At this time few men volunteered for service. Men were drafted. If the drafted man could not or would not serve, he hired a substitute who went in his place. Such men often received several hundred dollars for their services. Great numbers of these substitutes were sent to our fort on their way South. We had to see that they did not escape and go back North. Such men as did escape were called "bounty jumpers."[5]

As these substitutes usually had their bounty money in their pockets, pickpockets and gamblers came along with them to rob them of their money. All day long and late into the night gambling went on in the barrack filled with substitutes. Most of them were stripped of their money before they reached their regiment. If these substitutes reached the front they were seldom good soldiers. They were always looking for a chance to run away and get out of danger.

When we marched into Fort Federal Hill, we found cannons on the walls. These were the old-fashioned, cast-iron guns with smooth bores, mounted on two wheels, and resting on a platform of wood. It was very evident that if these cannons were to be used for any purpose, some of our number would have to handle the guns. So three of us went down into the city and bought little books which gave the drill for handling artillery. We then went into one of the redoubts and studied the guns and the books until we were familiar with them. We enlisted as infantry and even our officers had no skill in artillery.

It was not long before at guard-mounting the call was made for men to drill the soldiers in handling the big, unwieldy guns. That was just what we three had prepared for, and we volunteered at once. The squads were called out to drill several times in the hot sun; but we three fellows never had to put our hand to a gun; we had only to instruct others. Our commissioned officers never learned the drill. The artillery was handled only by the sergeants in our company.

We never fired balls from these guns. We were called upon to fire salutes with blank cartridges several times, and on the night when the Confederate cavalry was near the city,[6] we loaded the guns that bore on the city with ball cartridges and notified the city that if there was any outbreak, we should fire on the city. The leading citizens of Baltimore were Confederate in their sentiments; but our fort dominated the city. In the morning after this alarm the charges were withdrawn.[7]

I believe that only one man of our regiment was at any time under the fire of hostile guns. It happened that a private was sent to Harper's Ferry, and was there just at a time when the Confederates made an attack on the place. [He] had to do some service; but he was not harmed.

I greatly enjoyed my service. I kept well during the whole time, and performed my duty every day. To me it was like a vacation. My regiment was not engaged in any battle. I did not hear a hostile gun. No decision of my own kept me in the rear of the line of actual conflict. The government placed us in the forts in and around Baltimore because other troops had more drill and were more useful in the line of battle. Some regiments had to perform duty in these forts, and some general placed us there. We were very fortunate; but I have no tale of bloodshed to tell my children and grand-children.

* * *

Many hundred-days regiments served with African-American regiments. The performance of these "U.S. Colored Troops" was often as much of a revelation as the East itself to men who shared the common prejudices and slang of the day. From coastal Maryland, an officer wrote home to his brother about duty at a prisoner-of-war camp.[8]

Jeremiah Kiersted, second lieutenant, Co. A, 139th Ohio:

Point Lookout, June 5, 1864.

Tomorrow will be one week since we landed at this point. We are here doing guard duty. There is here 11,900 troops, in one large enclosure, of every shade and color. It is quite a sight to see Mr. Nig, marching with fixed bayonets guarding a squad of the "Southern chivalry."

At first it seemed strange, but the short experience we have had has learned us a lesson so far as nigger soldiers go. I witnessed guard mount on Friday last of about 160 of them, and their evolutions were as good as any I ever saw; they are well disciplined and well drilled. There is no making fun of nig here; the men find that won't do, and there is but little disposition to do so. Perhaps a little time may teach us all that some things can be done as well as others.[9]

We are encamped in the nicest place in this section of the country. Our location is at the mouth of the Potomac where it empties into Chesapeake Bay, 95 miles from Washington and 40 from Baltimore. There is the nicest salt-water bathing imaginable, and I assure you we have made the most of it. Donevant and Wilson[10] have been fishing two or three times, and brought us a fine lot of soft-shell crabs. Oysters are also said to be plentiful yet, but few have been brought into our quarters. I imagine this is a very healthy place, for the reason that our shanty (we had to build them all ourselves and buy the lumber to build as far as we went) has been open at one end ever since we built it, until last night, and then we stopped it up to keep out the rain, and from all this exposure neither Nat[11] or myself have experienced the least cold or bad effect.

Bartley Fanning[12] was on guard at the Pen the other day and found his cousin Charley, but was not, of course, permitted to speak to him; he will try to do so when he goes on again.

One hundred and sixty of our men are on duty today, which is the second time we have been on since we camped. I was officer of the day in our regiment yesterday.

One of our men died this morning; we buried him this afternoon—Old Mose Phillips[13]—he went in swimming last night and cooled off too quick in the cold air, which produced congestion of the brain and lungs. He lived only about twelve hours, perfectly unconscious until the last.

* * *

William Miller, a farmer near Lake Erie, in a quirk of consolidation also served in the 139th, one of the regiments from Cincinnati on the Ohio River.[14] *Altogether, three Miller brothers wore a uniform. George, a sharp-*

shooter, had died in January of wounds suffered at Missionary Ridge, Tennessee; Wilson was still a captain in the 41st O.V.I. Here William tells him how he landed in probably the most plum assignment enjoyed by any hundred-days company during the war.

William Miller, corporal, Co. K, 139th Ohio:

Piney Point, Md. June 15th 1864

We left Pt. Look[out] last Saturday the 11th on board a steamer and came up the Potomac to this point. Only our company and a squad of twenty-five from other companies came up. The rest of the regt. is still at Lookout. Our company is guarding a lighthouse. We have nothing to do in the daytime, but have to stay at the lighthouse during the night with loaded guns by our sides, ready to go in at the first alarm. The rebs have occasionally made a raid across the river and destroyed the lighthouses and other government property. A light ten miles above here was destroyed only two weeks ago.

We are quartered in an old oyster house during the day. It is a very nice comfortable place, on the banks of a creek about twenty rods from the Potomac. We have plenty of small boats, canoes, skiffs, etc. which furnish fun for the camp; not a day passes but someone gets a wetting. We catch eel, sea crabs, fish, oysters etc. The country around here is a pretty fine one, for the south. We "draw" plenty of milk, cherries, onions and many other things to tickle the palate of a hungry soldier. The people are nearly all secesh, and the commanding officer tells us to take anything we want, but [we] must not be caught doing it.[15]

There is no buildings here except a lighthouse, and a large hotel, which was used as a summer resort before the war. The squad which came with us are scattered up and down the shore doing picket duty. They are there to prevent goods being smuggled across to the rebs, and to arrest deserters. Their captures are brought to us for safekeeping. Not a day passes but what some deserters are brought in either from the rebel or union armies. Most of them profess to have been in the rebel army, but it is plain to see that many of them are not southerners. Tis said that the woods back of here are swarming with just such fellows.

I hope we will be permitted to stay here all summer. The only objection I have to the place is poor mail facilities. I have seen and learned enough already to amply repay me for the time and expense of the hundred days. If I only keep well until "these hundred days are over" I shall ever look back upon them as one of the brightest periods in my life's history.[16]

* * *

The 157th Ohio also went to Baltimore, but soon left for less congenial duty in nearby Delaware. There it guarded rebel prisoners at formidable Fort Delaware.

J. Fletcher Daton,[17] first lieutenant, Co. C, 157th Ohio:

Baltimore, Md., June 18th, 1864

On last Sabbath morning, when there was a comparative lull in camp, and everything was quiet and still, an order came from the Commanding General announcing that we should prepare to march immediately. The camp of quiet and tranquillity soon became one of confusion and anxiety, and all in a short time were ready to move to the point of destination. The majority of the regiment, having become attached to the camp and its associations, preferred remaining, and General Tyler[18] did all in his power to have the order countermanded, but "the powers that be" had decreed otherwise, and like good soldiers, we cheerfully obeyed.

Shortly before departure, General Tyler, accompanied by Colonel McCook,[19] appeared on the camp ground and addressed us in highly flattering terms. The General complimented the regiment for its marked improvement in military evolutions, and its commendable state of discipline, and declared that the regiment was an honor to "old Jefferson,"[20] and an honor to the state from which he was proud to hail.

Soon we were on board the cars and off to Baltimore. It was highly gratifying to us to arrive in the city at the same time with those bronzed and gallant veterans, the Pennsylvania Reserves[21] — who had just returned from the thickest of the fight. At the beginning of this terrible contest they had left the endearments of home 15,000 strong, and now they were returning, about 1,700, to the scenes of their homes and their childhood. Forward they marched with their battle-torn and bullet-rent banners, through the principal streets of the city of Baltimore, and the 157th felt itself highly complimented with a place in the rear of the column of such brave and valiant heroes. As we passed along, those two distinguished sons of Ohio, Governors Dennison and Tod,[22] were introduced to us, and enthusiastically cheered, who also accompanied us to the depot, and passed around familiarly and socially among the members of the regiment.

At Fort Delaware the principal part of our duty is to guard the many prisoners who are stationed there, who, however, will be sent in a few days to Elmira, N.Y., to be guarded by New York State troops.[23] In the meantime, the Commissary General of Prisoners, at Washington, has directed that all officers and men now confined in the Old Capitol Prison be immediately sent to Fort Delaware.

Several members of the regiment, having been detailed to remain behind on General Court Martial, had the pleasure of attending the National Convention.[24] It was enthusiastic in the extreme, and the popular feeling for "Old Abe" was beyond description. It was truly gratifying for every son of Ohio to see the prominent part she took in the Convention. Ohio led the van in everything.

* * *

Alexander S. Sharon, private, Co. B, 157th Ohio:

Fort Delaware, June 17, 1864

We are located on an island[25] in the Delaware River, about 10 miles above the bay, which contains 92 acres, in the center of which is built the Fort, built of granite.[26] The fort mounts 180 guns, which is manned by three artillery companies of 150 men each. Gen. Schoepf has a very nice residence here, and lives in style.[27] There is one hotel, a sutler store, an ice cream saloon and some private residences, our little town.

We occupy very nice quarters, white frame houses built close by the Fort, and have everything we could expect or wish. The water we use is brought every morning from the Brandywine river, about 12 miles off, which is good and fresh. In addition to this we have as much ice issued to us every day as we can use. Our rations consists of fresh beef, pork, bread, coffee, sugar, molasses, rice, potatoes, beans, etc. So you can see there is no danger of us starving.

We are on light duty, one day in three, which is occupied in guarding the rebs, who number 10,600 including officers.[28] There was also 486 more brought here this morning. Their barracks are on the upper portion of the island, and a poor, wretched, depraved looking set of men they are. There was a mutiny among them this morning, but by the prompt appearance of the 157th they were soon dispersed, with the loss of one reb, who got killed in the affray.[29]

Among the rebel prisoners here is Lieut. Col. James Urquahart, formerly of Steubenville, Ohio, but belonging to a Louisiana regiment. He was taken at the battle of Chickamauga, Sept. 20th, 1863, and has been here ever since. His brother William was up and had a long talk with him concerning the war, etc. He is large, and rather good looking for an Ohio reb. There is also a Capt. Miller here, whose father lives some twelve miles below Steubenville; so you see we have some Jefferson county boys here among the rebs. There is also 246 convicts, or Company Q men here. There were ninety-three sent to the Dry Tortugas from here on last Sunday, there to remain for from one to seven years at hard labor. Their offenses are murder, desertion and bounty jumping—mostly the latter.

The regiment enjoys very good health, better than at Camp Relay.[30] The sea breeze makes it cool and pleasant here of evenings, and we all sleep sound till the tap of the drum: some to guard, some to reading and writing, and others to fishing. We can sit on the bank and view Delaware City, one and a half miles from here, the nearest point of land, to us; and also see steam and sail vessels, ironclads, etc., and be fishing, catching catfish, perch, eels, etc., at the same time.[31] All the boys are well and in good cheer, except an occasional one who is homesick, or would not be satisfied in any place or situation in life, and therefore should have no account taken of him.

Some of our regiment have gone to Philadelphia and some to Fortress Monroe,[32] and there is talk of taking some 2,000 rebs to Johnson's Island,[33] and if so, we will have a chance, some of us, to pass through Ohio again.

* * *

Rebel prisoners at Fort Delaware, General Schoepf reported, were "accustomed to insult and trifle with the sentinels because they are militia." The mortal wounding of Lieutenant-Colonel E. P. Jones of the 109th Virginia, on the night July 7, was "one of the results of it."[34] The guard soon testified before a review board.

William G. Douglass, private, Co. C, 157th Ohio:

On yesterday [I] was acting as sentinel at post No. 20; went on guard between 7 and 9 P.M. Some time between those hours a rebel came out of the sink—the officers' sink—and stopped about ten minutes. I told him to "leave"; think he was about twenty or thirty feet from me; went back and turned the light; came back and said, "Now, you must leave." Then I said the third time, "If you don't leave, I'll shoot you." The man still stood there. I said again, "Leave." He muttered something, and then I shot him.

Regimental surgeon Eames wryly noted,[35] "The boy who shot the reb Col. Jones was tried and acquitted, and I presume he will try to kill another one."[36]

6 | The Shenandoah

SEVERAL HUNDRED-DAYS regiments went no farther east than the Shenandoah Valley, which had been a contested area of operations throughout the war. Duty here quickly proved far more burdensome—and hazardous—than manning the forts in Baltimore and Washington. An Ohio clergyman serving as a company commander in the 160th Ohio arrived with his regiment at Harper's Ferry, West Virginia, at the mouth of the fabled valley, on May 14th.

Rev. Simeon Siegfried, captain, Co. E, 160th Ohio:

We went into camp on Bolivar Heights, a bold promontory which rises above the Potomac and Shenandoah rivers, facing Loudoun Heights on the south and Maryland Heights on the east. An introduction here to soldier's life and fare was pleasant and agreeable; but soon we were ordered to Martinsburg,[1] to do guard duty along the Shenandoah Valley, as guards to government provisions and forage trains.

We were ordered to Sigel's army, with a large wagon train. This march was one that tried our powers of endurance to the utmost, but we accomplished it,[2] and found ourselves at the *front* at Cedar Creek,[3] where Sigel was superseded in command of the army, by Hunter.[4] Our battalion of nine companies up to this time was commanded by Lieut.-Col. W. D. Marsh, but Col. [Cyrus] Reasoner, having been assigned the company, from Gallipolis, Ohio, came on, met us here and assumed the command.

We advanced with Hunter as far as Woodstock, when a large return train was turned over to our guardianship, and we returned to Martinsburg. When we reached Strasburg, we had strong intimations of the presence of the enemy's prowling guerrillas. Passing on to Middletown, our cavalry, guarding a laden train to the front, came dashing up to us with intelligence that at Newtown, four miles on, the guerrillas had attacked and driven them, and were then burning the train they had been guarding. Col. Reasoner no sooner received the word than he threw his column forward at double-quick, reaching Newton in time to see 15 to 18 wagons burning, some of them in the street, but not in time to see the rebels who, though they had run the cavalry, skedaddled for life at our approach.

We formed line of battle, scouted awhile and bivouacked for the night. Newtown has the name of being a *"secesh hole"* and has among its population many who are sanctimonious Union men in the daytime, when the Yankees are around, and at night are guerrillas of the meanest type. There are hundreds such in this valley. Col. R. assured them that night that he would hold them responsible for their conduct while he tarried with them; and that if they did not behave well he would burn their town. They were quiescent, for they knew that he did not wear the *spread eagle* for nothing.

In the morning, our Col. went out with five companies to secure anything valuable he might find in the wreck of the train, over night within our picket line. His advance was strongly assailed by the rebels, who charged upon it from the woods; but the right wing in line, and the left in supporting distance, met the onset like veterans, and pouring in their well directed volleys into the guerrilla band, sent them reeling back in disorder. Nor could the rebels rally. Our rifles cracked too fiercely—our line was too steady—our aim too deadly, and seeking the shelter of the woods they *hid* themselves from us, nor could we find them again after feeling for them with our elongated balls, and bantering them to return as we stood in line of battle to meet them. But they were gone—they had enough.

A captain of cavalry was killed; our regimental bugler Jackson, wounded; [these] were all the casualties on our side necessary to report in this engagement.[5] To the coolness and soldierly bearing of the 160th, when thus beset by guerrillas, flushed with the success of having driven our cavalry the evening before, is due the credit of saving a large train in their charge, and much of that in charge of the cavalry guards, on its way to the front.[6]

* * *

The hundred-days men often escorted wagon trains through the valley. The course of one epic journey by the 152nd Ohio was shaped by the movements of rebel General Jubal Early before his Maryland raid. The regiment hosted an abundance of newspaper correspondents, including its lieutenant-colonel; this report appeared in the Springfield Republic *under the pen name "Valedo."*

A. P. L. Cochran, Esq., corporal, Co. E, 152nd Ohio:

The trip was commenced from Martinsburg on the 4th day of June. Our regiment, together with five companies of the 161st [Ohio],[7] some artillery and cavalry, to which was added afterwards the 2nd Maryland, were detailed to guard a train of 200 wagons, containing provisions and clothing, to General Hunter's army. Hunter was then supposed to be at New Market,[8] a place distant 65 miles from Martinsburg.

Having only this distance in view, we all left camp this bright June morning [the fourth] with full haversacks, flowing spirits and pleasing anticipations, supposing that we were only embarking on a brief and jolly tramp, which would be a happy release from the tedious routine of camp life. But our eyes were very soon opened to the true nature of the duty we were called upon to perform.

To a soldier loaded down with a gun and accouterments, 40 rounds of ammunition, haversack, canteen, and blanket, a long march must necessarily be fatiguing. But when you add to this the necessity of accommodating his speed to that of a long train of wagons, halting (not, however, sufficiently long for rest) with every chain that loosens or trace that breaks or strap that unties, and then running until the gap in the line caused by this detention has been closed, the labor of the soldier is increased one-half, and the distance traveled each day materially lessened.[9]

Owing to this fact we only reached Bunker Hill the first day, a point about ten miles distant from Martinsburg.

The day following, the train getting into a little working order, we marched a little over 20 miles, camping at Newtown, ten miles beyond Winchester. After this we seldom made less than 17 miles a day, generally going farther.

On the evening of the third day, quite an amusing incident occurred. The 2nd Maryland was in the advance and had gone into camp. The rear guard (the train being several miles in length) was still some distance behind, dragging their weary limbs through the mud occasioned by the heavy shower which had fallen during the afternoon. All at once, a brisk firing was heard in the advance.

In the rear, it was supposed to be an attack. The rear guard, consisting of companies H, A and L, was formed into line of battle, skirmishers were thrown out, and the excitement was intense. In a few moments, some cavalry orderly who had been sent to the front returned with the information that the firing had been occasioned by a squad of the 2nd Maryland advancing on a drove of hogs which they wished to secure for supper. It is needless to say that a calm immediately prevailed.

Just before entering Harrisonburg, our cavalry took one of McNeill's[10] men prisoner, named Charley Clare. Charley was quite a good looking young man, and had formerly resided in Harrisonburg. On entering the place, our prisoner was the cause of much display of feeling by the fair sex, who were at all the windows to see us pass by. One threw him a blanket, another a haversack, another provisions, and soon through all the vocabulary of a soldier's wants, until the poor fellow was loaded down to his utmost capacity—when, with the hot rays of a summer's sun beating upon him, he could truly realize the truth of the old adage, "Save me from my friends."

His other admirers, with more regard to his comfort, displayed their devotion by showering kisses from their hands and shedding tears most profusely, carrying this to such an extent that many of us almost envied Charley in his position. A little below Harrisonburg we captured another prisoner, a major in a Virginia cavalry regiment.

On reaching New Market, we fondly hoped to find Hunter's army, unload our wagons and return; but our hopes were doomed to disappointment. Hunter had advanced to Staunton. So Staunton was our next object of attention. We reached Staunton on the 10th of June, only to find that Hunter had passed through it in his rapid advance toward Lynchburg. It was now resolved into a foot race between Hunter and ourselves. The advantage was in Hunter's favor, he being in the advance.

To overcome the distance between us was a somewhat difficult task, Hunter traveling every day as fast as we did. But it was absolutely necessary to do this, in order to perform the duty upon which we had been detailed. We therefore passed through Staunton on the evening of the 10th, at a rate of speed nearly approaching a double quick, and traveled all night. During the morning of the 11th, our eyes were greeted with the welcome sight of the rear guard of Hunter's army.

We naturally supposed when we reached these forces that our wagons would be unloaded, and we would be dismissed hence with them; but lo! such was not the case. We were put into Colonel Wells's brigade of General Sullivan's[11] division of Hunter's army, reaching Lexington at 9 o'clock on the evening of the 11th, the advance having on the forenoon of the same day attacked and taken the place.

We rested on Sunday on a hill overlooking the camp, having a fine view of the burning of the Military Institute[12] and adjoining residences occupied by the professors in the institution. The institute was built of brick, the front being plastered and lined so as to resemble stone. It was of large and elegant proportions, and built in the Gothic style of architecture.

It was a sad sight to witness the destruction of such a beautiful specimen of American talent and handicraft; and nothing could reconcile the mind to the loss but the fact that out of those burning portals the rebels had been wont to lead their youths, with minds and hearts educated to combat, to destroy those glorious institutions through whose fostering care American talent had been so developed as to enable it to plan and rear such tasteful structures.

Whilst at Lexington, we visited the grave of that great but erring chieftain, Stonewall Jackson. A simple flag pole marks the spot where he lies. A rebel flag had floated from its head previous to Hunter's arrival. When he entered the town, the retreating rebels lowered the flag and took it with them.[13]

From Lexington, we advanced with Hunter to within 18 miles of Lynchburg, where we were halted and our heads turned homeward—that is, toward Martinsburg, our Soldier Home. The question now was, What road should we take? Breckinridge had got into the rear, so as to cut off our return by the way we had come, and another had to be looked for. And further, our strength had been greatly weakened. Our cavalry, artillery, and the 2nd Maryland were left with Hunter. The 152nd regiment and five companies of the 161st regiment were alone, left to bring the wagons through, and 150 rebel prisoners.

After some deliberation, a course homeward was determined upon; a course, not a road. We traveled over turnpikes, mud roads, mountainsides, ravines, creek beds, meadows, through bushes, over logs, through rivers, over creeks, and through and over every other imaginable shape and phase of the earth's surface, so nearly in a state of nature that the most liberal construction could not bring them under the head of a common highway.

In the former part of the journey, a large number of horses had died from exertion, and the wagons to which they were attached were in consequence burned. But now this became more frequent than ever. Not only fatigue from the intolerable roads, but also want of food contributed to marking our line of march with those dead animals and burning wagons. Still we pushed ahead, for starvation likewise held out her gaunt arms to us, threatening to envelop us in her dread embrace.

We started out with ten days' rations in our haversacks, and these were now nearly exhausted. Whilst in the valley, our forage train could gather enough cattle, sheep, etc., for our daily wants, but could get very little ahead even of these. As to bread, flour and meal, not enough could be obtained to supply us fully through the valley. Gloomy apprehensions were entertained as to our means of sustenance whilst in the mountains, through which the greater part of our course lay. Yet relying on Providence and our Yankee instinct, we pressed on in good spirits.

On reaching Fincastle, the mayor of the town moved out under the flag of truce to surrender the place. What the conditions were we do not know, nor do we think any in the command stopped to ascertain; matters of more importance were occupying our minds at that time.[14]

Our course led us by the Sweet Springs of Virginia. The building accommodations here are the finest I have ever seen, and kept in perfect order. The grounds in themselves have no particular attractions. The water has a peculiar taste, slightly sweet, and warm and unpleasant. We lay here one night.

The morning we left these Springs, and about two miles from them, we were fired into by bushwhackers, perhaps 40 in number, who were concealed in the mountains. Two wagoners were wounded. One or two volleys from our men dispersed the crew, and as the nature of the ground prevented our pursuing them, we soon went on our way.

The next night, we encamped in the grounds of the famous White Sulphur Springs of Virginia.[15] The grounds here are very attractive. Indeed, nature has been more lavish than art. With the exception of one central brick building, which is truly a fine structure, and some few cottages surrounding it, there are no accommodations at all desirable. We found on the grounds limestone, red and white sulphur water.

Near these springs two roads unite, one leading to Beverly, the other to Charleston.[16] We took the Charleston road, but had advanced only a few miles when we found the road strongly defended by a heavy line of breastworks. These works were more than half a mile in length, and had been thrown up a year or two ago. They ran along the brow of an immense hill, up which we would have had to advance through two high mountains.

Strange to say, our regiment was ordered forward, not in line of battle, but in columns of four; nor did the mistake seem to be discovered until the enemy's bullets were being hurled upon us like hail. The ground we occupied and the manner in which we were being pushed forward prevented us from returning the fire of our assailants. This position is of all others the most trying to new troops, but not a man fell back until the order was given. One man was killed in Company H, and several wagoners taken prisoner.

The regiment fell back a short distance, was halted, and formed in line of battle. Some companies were sent up the mountain to endeavor to flank the enemy, and that was almost accomplished when another order for the flanking parties to fall back was received, our commandant deeming it impracticable for us to scale the mountain in sufficient numbers to make any impression on the occupants of the fortifications—in which opinion his command by no means concurred. He further considered that he had not come through this unconquered country to subdue it with his small force, but that his duty was simply to guard the wagon train safely to our lines.

Had a general engagement ensued, a stampede would most probably have occurred among the wagoners and negroes who had flocked to us for protection to the North, which might have proved more disastrous to the train than any injury the enemy could inflict. Further, the best information that could be obtained led to the belief that if all the defenses before us were demolished, similar ones would be encountered all along the route. The shortness of our supply of provisions rendered it impracticable for us to encounter all these delays.

These reasons, much to the chagrin of the men, led to a change of front. The course we now pursued was rough, rugged and mountainous to a degree almost beyond belief. Our provisions grew daily perceptibly less.

Our stock of negroes rapidly increased, and these had to be fed out of our scanty supplies. The rear of our train at this time presented a really ludicrous appearance. Cattle, sheep, negroes (men, women and children in indefinite numbers, with their beds, banjoes and bundles of every description hanging around them, and rags to cover their persons) and soldiers who had given out (mounted on mules broken down like themselves, thrown from the wagons as worthless) followed the train in all its meanderings through the mountains of Virginia, constituting such a gathering as Falstaff would have gloated over with delight.[17]

But all had to be fed, and the wherewithal to feed us gradually disappeared. Nothing could be done in the foraging line amongst these mountains. Scarcely a house was to be seen, and when found the inmates were destitute. We still had some fresh beef, but often had to dispense with using it, for want of time to kill and cook it. All salt meat had disappeared. Hard bread, flour and meal were among the things that were. At last we were reduced to coffee and corn, and even the supply of corn came to be less than half an ear a day to a man.

As soon as we were sufficiently near our lines to admit of a carrier being safely sent forward for provisions, it was done. A supply accordingly reached us Sunday noon, June 26th, within 18 or 20 miles of Beverly. This supply was greeted by the men with more hearty applause than any former occurrence ever drew from them, and was lustily enjoyed.

On the following day, at noon, we arrived at Beverly.[18] We rested until the 29th, at noon of which we started for Webster, arriving there on the 1st instant. We there found orders to go to Cumberland. Transportation being furnished us on the morning of our arrival, we at once embarked on the cars, reaching Cumberland on the following morning.

In 26 days we traveled on foot some 460 miles, resting altogether about three days. However, we marched several entire nights, and more or less of almost every night, in this way fully compensating Uncle Sam for the days of grace allowed us. But few marches were made by any body of men during the war under more trying circumstances than that we accomplished.[19]

7 | Cynthiana

*B*OTH OHIO AND WASHINGTON *had learned to keep a wary eye on Kentucky, Ohio's supposedly neutral neighbor across the river. If anyone doubted it, General Braxton Bragg's invasion of Kentucky in 1862 clearly revealed the significant rebel sentiment in the state. This Southern thrust also threatened Cincinnati and resulted in a bitter Federal defeat at Perryville.*

No Confederate officer, however, bedeviled Ohio more than John Hunt Morgan. His daring raid into Indiana and Ohio in 1863 terrorized both states. Although captured by Union troops under Brigadier-General Edward Henry Hobson, Morgan escaped from the Ohio State Penitentiary in Columbus and made his way home. In early June, 1864, his cavalry again struck northward through Kentucky.

The Union again sent Hobson, himself a Kentuckian. He caught a riverboat to Cincinnati and crossed to Covington, where his immediate challenge was finding enough troops. Later in the summer hundred-days regiments from Illinois would help control Kentucky,[1] but they weren't here yet and most of Ohio's hundred-days men had already gone east. Hobson received just two of the few remaining Ohio regiments, along with a handful of Kentucky troops.

One of these regiments was the 171st Ohio, which on June 9th had hurriedly left Johnson's Island, the prisoner-of-war camp in Lake Erie. A 19-year-old private in the 171st found time before departure to scrawl a quick note to his father. Just three days earlier, he had invited both parents to visit the island for the 4th of July.[2]

Mortimer C. Thompson, private, Co. B, 171st Ohio:

Father, I am well at [present] and feel well. We are ordered to march to Covington Ky. We will move this afternoon I expect. We have a lot of secesh to tend to, but I don't think we will go any farther. Our time is about now half out and I don't want you to be any ways alarmed about the news. I will write all the particulars about us. Our order may be countermanded yet. We will be in Cleveland today. I hope you will come if you can find out if we are there.

Our orders came so soon for us this time. I believe that's all at present—will write when I can.

Mort

* * *

As he set aside his pen, Thompson had two days to live. The following accounts of the fight at Cynthiana, Kentucky, between green Ohioans and Morgan's hardened cavalry are drawn from official reports. They reveal both the weaknesses and strengths of hundred-days regiments.

Edward H. Hobson, brigadier-general, U.S. Volunteers:

I heard of the capture of Mount Sterling by Morgan and the destruction of two bridges on [the] Kentucky Central Railroad; and knowing there was but a small force to oppose Morgan, and that nearly all my mounted force was with General Burbridge[3] in the hills of Eastern Kentucky, I immediately gathered up the men at Covington, intending to advance toward Lexington. To my chagrin, I found only 230 men could be raised, including the militia which I had ordered to be called out. There were nine miles of fortifications around Covington to protect, and this force was much too small to do it.

I represented the scarcity of troops in Kentucky and the situation to Governor Morton, of Indiana, and Major-General Heintzelman,[4] commanding [the] Northern Department. I directed the movement of the small force at Lexington and Louisville by telegraph, and also sent the news of [the] capture of Mount Sterling and the whereabouts of Morgan to Col. S. B. Brown, at Louisa, to be forwarded to Brigadier-General Burbridge, who was supposed to be at or near Pound Gap, with the cavalry force of my division. I continued my efforts to raise more men in the meantime, and at length concluded to leave the fortifications with a small guard and send all the men I could raise to meet Morgan and prevent the destruction of the railroad and bridges.

I raised 130 men, consisting of [the] 50th Veteran Reserve Corps, 50 of [the] 47th Kentucky, and 30 militia, and put Capt. George H. Laird, of my staff, in command, and sent them to Falmouth, where they were joined by 30 more militia. This was done on the 8th of June. Captain Laird deserves great credit for his management of these men and his promptness in furnishing information by telegraph of the enemy's movements.

In the meantime, Governor Morton sent one regiment from Indiana to Louisville to protect the city, or to be sent to Frankfort for the protection of that place. Major-General Heintzelman was furnishing me all the assistance possible by shipping troops from Ohio. I soon had the First and Second Kentucky Regiments, whose terms of service had nearly expired. They were placed in the fortifications and barracks as a garrison for Covington.

On the arrival of 168th Ohio National Guard (100-days' men), they were ordered at once to go by rail to Cynthiana, and guard the railroad bridges on the road. The regiment came to me with no ammunition and very poor guns. I am obliged to report that a few of the officers and a great many men of this regiment refused to march, and Company K actually stacked their arms.[5] Under these embarrassing circumstances, I had but little hope of repulsing Morgan before he had accomplished all the destruction of the road.

At 4 P.M., 10th of June, Col. J. F. Asper, 171st Ohio National Guard, reported to me with his regiment in Covington. I at once ordered a train of cars to convey the troops to Cynthiana, knowing that the 168th Ohio would probably be attacked in a day or so. Two hundred and fifty horses were also ordered to be drawn from Captain Webster, assistant quartermaster, Covington, and loaded on the train. These horses were drawn for the 30th Kentucky Infantry, and were to have been taken to Lexington for their use.

At 11 P.M., 10th of June, I got on the train with my staff and proceeded with [the] 171st Ohio National Guard to Keller's Bridge, about one mile north of Cynthiana, arriving there at 4 A.M., June 11. Colonel Asper had got his men off the cars, and was distributing rations and extra ammunition to them, when firing was heard in direction of Cynthiana. A man from the town reported that a detachment of [the] 168th Ohio were needing assistance.

Colonel Asper immediately sent two companies to reconnoiter from a small hill, and to ascertain how far the enemy were from us. Soon after they had reached the top of the hill, a squad of rebel cavalry came toward the train. I suppose they had heard the noise of the train, and had been sent out to reconnoiter. Our two companies fired into them and they ran in the direction they had come. A few seconds after this we observed a force of cavalry moving to our right, as if to intercept the train, which had been ordered back with the horses, and a line of skirmishers was seen advancing through a field upon our position.

Capt. J. S. Butler, assistant adjutant-general of my staff, immediately mounted one of the few horses which had been taken from the train, and taking one company of [the] 171st Ohio National Guard and some convalescent men of [the] 52nd Kentucky who had accompanied us, threw out a line of skirmishers, and attacked the rebels in the field, and drove them until they were reinforced and had sheltered themselves in the woods.

Our line was reinforced and skirmishing kept up for an hour more, when the town was seen to be on fire and the firing ceased in Cynthiana. The shouts of the rebels led us to believe that the detachment of the 168th Ohio in town had surrendered.[6]

Immediately afterward, the rebel cavalry were seen moving to the right of us, and a heavy force of dismounted men advanced upon our front. Our line of skirmishers was slowly pressed back on the main force, and the detachment of [the] 47th Kentucky, about 30 strong, under Captain Wilson, who was ordered to hold a small eminence under the protection of a fence, was driven from its grounds after a few rounds and with very slight resistance. Captain Wilson was slightly wounded on the side of the neck, and left the field.

The 171st Ohio National Guard had never been under fire as a regiment, and, with the exception of two companies, the regiment was moved to the rear and formed on a small hill in the woods, for the purpose of better protection and to prevent being flanked by a force still moving on our right.[7] This last position we stubbornly defended for five hours, until we were completely surrounded by a largely superior force, and General Morgan sent in two flags of truce and demanded our surrender. Colonel Asper met the flags and reported to me that the terms were that we should surrender as prisoners of war.

I called my staff and the field officers of [the] 171st Ohio together, and after learning the number of men left, and knowing of no chance of being reinforced, and the troops in town having surrendered, and the train having been captured, and knowing of no good to be accomplished by a further loss of life, being completely surrounded by about 2,500 rebels, while my small force left was but from 275 to 300 effective, I thought it useless to attempt to repulse the enemy, as my men were entirely exhausted, and a great many not even able to reach the river to procure water to quench their thirst.

When General Morgan came up to our position, he modified the terms, and allowed officers to retain their sidearms and private property and the men to keep their haversacks, private property, and blankets in consideration of our stubborn fighting.

I am happy to report that the conduct of Col. J. F. Asper, Lieut. Col. H. R. Harmon, Maj. M. A. Fowler, Captain Hatch, and all the officers of the 171st Ohio National Guard, with a few exceptions, deserve the highest praise; and had the men ever been under fire before they would have been equal to veterans.

General Morgan soon after the surrender moved all the prisoners, except myself and staff and field officers of the 171st Ohio, about two miles from the field, and it appeared from the preparation that the officers kept were to be sent off at once with a strong guard to prevent our escape or recapture. General Morgan then suggested to me that I should select such officers as I thought proper and proceed to the nearest point of communication and attempt an exchange for the men captured by him in Kentucky for some of his men who were in the hands of Federal authorities. He proposed that we should sign such an agreement to return to him in case I could not effect an exchange.

I refused to sign such an agreement for three reasons: First, I thought that if General Burbridge was informed of Morgan's movements he would be pursuing him, and by negotiation I could delay Morgan's march. Second, I thought he would be compelled to informally parole and release the prisoners, as he had done on previous raids. Third, I was a prisoner and, of course, had nothing to do but submit to any mode of imprisonment my captors should think proper, and was entirely at their disposal.

At the request of Colonel Asper of the 171st Ohio National Guard (100-days' men), I afterward consented to sign the agreement, in order that we should do what was in our power for the benefit of the captured 100-days' men. The agreement was then drawn up by General Morgan's assistant inspector-general, Captain Allen. When I read it, I found it contained an obligation not to take up arms or give information, and contained the requirements of a parole. Every officer present emphatically refused signing the paper, and told Captain Allen we would not accept a parole, and preferred going to Richmond.

After a negotiation, in which the enemy had been delayed for four hours after the fight, the annexed agreement was signed,[8] and we returned under flag of truce to Falmouth,[9] arriving there at dusk on the 12th of June.

The night of the 12th, the three rebel officers and one private were placed under guard by the provost-marshal of the town, under the charge of violating the privilege of flag of truce by associating with rebel sympathizers and receiving visitors and walking around the town. It is proper to mention here that the Federal officers were the prisoners of the rebel officers, and that they passed into our lines without being met by a flag of truce, and took us with them.

As the situation of myself and other officers is a peculiar one, I would respectfully ask the decision of the proper authority in regard to the latter part of this report.

* * *

Joel F. Asper, colonel, 171st Ohio:

I have the honor to report to headquarters, Northern Department, a full account of the march of my regiment from Johnson's Island[10] into Kentucky (General Burbridge's district), with an account of the disaster which occurred to it there, together with the condition and situation of the field officers, as well as the situation and condition of the line officers and men since their capture by General Morgan.

About 8 A.M., June 9, I received an order for the march of my regiment to Covington, Ky., to report to Brig. Gen. E. H. Hobson, eight companies being on Johnson's Island on duty. My orders [were] issued at once, and preparations were commenced by cooking rations, etc. At 10:30 o'clock, I received a copy of a dispatch from General Heintzelman, and was ordered to march at once.

The cooking of the rations ceased, and in one hour and a half the regiment was on the march.

It was taken across the bay, loaded, and at 4 P.M. the train started for Cincinnati. At Springfield, it was delayed two hours waiting for our baggage and horses, which had been stopped at Urbana with the train containing [the] 24th Ohio Battery. I arrived at Cincinnati at 1 P.M. on the 10th. Here I was ordered to report at Colonel Marker's headquarters, which I did. I made requisition for two days' rations and 30,000 rounds of ammunition, crossed the Ohio River, and reported to General Hobson about 4 o'clock of the 10th.

In pursuance of orders, I placed my command in light marching order; loaded it on the train; also assisted to load over 300 horses. When ready to move, I reported in person to General Hobson, and was ordered to move my train at once, proceed to Cynthiana, and await orders. The train moved about 10 P.M. Having heard that a small body of rebels or guerrillas had been seen near the railroad about 25 miles up the track, I gave the strictest orders to guard against any surprise, ordering sentinels posted in each car, the men to be ready with guns and accouterments, and all line officers to remain with their commands.

We proceeded without interruption to Keller's Bridge, over the Licking River, which is about one mile over the railroad track and two miles by the dirt road from Cynthiana. The bridge had been burned by Morgan's men two or three days before. On Thursday, the 168th Regiment Ohio National Guard, Colonel Garis, had been sent up this railroad, dropped in detachments along its line, with five companies under Colonel Garis in Cynthiana. This I had been advised of.

The train arrived at Keller's Bridge at 4 o'clock in the morning. I immediately ordered my men out of the cars, had them stack arms on the left of the track, the ground offering a good position for defense. I had details made, and the rations and ammunition unloaded and distributed, and our private horses taken from the train. On getting out, I placed a picket, consisting of one company, on duty on the top of the hill which overlooked the valley and much of the country about. Having taken off our regimental stores, and while the men were putting rations and ammunition into haversacks and cartridge-boxes, I then went to inquire about getting off the government horses, four car-loads of which were on my train.

I went back to the second train, which had followed us closely, and in a short time found Captain Butler, assistant adjutant-general on General Hobson's staff, who directed me to make a detail of 230 men and 10 officers to mount a portion of the horses, and this detail was to get the horses out of the train. I ordered the detail made, and the adjutant set about it. About this time picket-firing had been commenced at the town in our advance. I was also notified by a man from my advance company that a large cavalry force was moving on our right. I saddled my horse, rode to the point of observation, saw a considerable force which I knew was rebel cavalry.

At this time, the sergeant-major of Colonel Garis' regiment came to me and reported that Colonel Garis had been attacked by 1,500 of Morgan's cavalry; that he would hold the town as long as he could, and wished me to come to his assistance as speedily as possible. I ordered the lieutenant-colonel to form the line, and rode back and reported to Captain Butler. He directed me to wait until General Hobson should come forward. He soon came forward.

My line was forming in good style, faced toward the rebel approach. By the time General Hobson came up, a large column of cavalry was coming down the road toward us, either for the purpose of getting between us and Colonel Garis or to get to Colonel Garis' rear; and by direction of General Hobson, I placed two companies, under command of Major Fowler, on a point of the hill across the railroad. These companies opened fire upon the column immediately and drove it back, several saddles being emptied at the first fire.

I had in my command 690 officers and men. This included musicians, hospital attendants, and all supernumeraries. There were about 100 men of different detachments on General Hobson's train, mostly from Kentucky regiments. These men and one company from my regiment were thrown forward as skirmishers, General Hobson assuming command of the whole force, and Captain Butler, of the staff, having charge of the skirmish line.

The battle opened about 5 o'clock in the morning. It was hotly contested on both sides. The force directly opposing us from the start was Colonel Giltner's[11] brigade, of Morgan's command, 1,500 strong, armed with the Enfield rifle. This brigade dismounted and advanced as infantry. We held them in check and drove them back twice, and had there been no other force, we should have been the victors on the field. Between 11 and 12 o'clock, another brigade came into our rear and took position in a wheat field; besides, another had flanked around and took position on our right flank and rear. This was commanded by Colonel Martin,[12] and the other by General Morgan in person.

I made disposition of my exhausted and scattered command to meet it. I placed all I could spare from my front line against a high fence to our rear, where they would be partially protected by the two fences of a lane. By the time the dispositions could be made, a flag of truce was seen approaching our lines. I was directed by General Hobson to receive it. I went out and met Captain Morgan, of General Morgan's staff. He carried a demand from General Morgan for our surrender as prisoners of war. I started to report to General Hobson, and on my way was summoned to meet another flag carried by the rebel Colonel Martin. I replied to him that I was considering then a demand from General Morgan.

I reported to General Hobson. He asked my opinion about it. I told him that I could hold out an hour longer, but that the end was plainly to be seen unless relief was at hand, and we knew of none. General Hobson thought I could not hold out more than 20 minutes, or 30 at most. We were unanimous in the conclusion that from the exhausted condition of the men, having been fighting six hours without rest or water, that we could not hold out much longer if attacked vigorously from front, rear, and flanks, and to save the slaughter that must ensue from such an attack policy and duty alike required a surrender.

Colonel Garis had surrendered as we believed more than four hours before.[13] No firing had been heard from that quarter since early in the morning, and a scout we had sent to ascertain the result had been driven back by rebel pickets. I was then deputed to arrange the terms of surrender, which I did with Captain Morgan.

The terms were: General Hobson's forces to surrender unconditionally as prisoners of war; the officers to retain their sidearms; all private property to be respected except horses; public property to belong to the captors. After General Morgan rode up, he said we had made so gallant a fight that we should all have our horses. Lieutenant-Colonel Harmon had a valuable horse which Colonel Martin insisted upon keeping, and he was permitted by General Morgan to do so, but with this exception the terms as modified by General Morgan were strictly observed.

I was ordered to form my command, stack arms, and march them off; and then make a list of names, companies, and regiments. Before this could be done they were ordered away under a guard, the field officers being detained with General Hobson and staff.

Our loss was 14 killed[14] and 45 wounded. My surgeon stated to me on his way down to Covington that he thought our loss in killed and wounded would reach 75 or 80. I have no means of stating accurately, having been separated from the command since the surrender. Our loss in prisoners is about 500, some men having escaped.

I fought my command as well as I could and to the best possible advantage, General Hobson giving no general directions during the battle besides his personal assistance to keep the men up to the work. General Hobson surrendered only when to have held out longer would have been mere idle bravado, and would have induced reckless and wholesale slaughter.

I cannot speak too highly of the conduct of most of my officers and men. Two or three officers failed to do their duty, and some men skulked away; but no more than is usual in most regiments. Most of these men had never been under fire, but they fought splendidly, coolly, and behaved like veterans.

General Hobson was cool, brave, and judicious; was exposed all the time to the rebel fire, and deserves well of the government.

My own horse was shot under me and disabled, and I had several other evidences of the close firing of rebel sharpshooters, but escaped unhurt.

General Hobson refused at first to go into the [surrender] arrangement. After consultation, I advised that it be done for the benefit of our officers and soldiers, who are only hundred-days' men, as it would be peculiarly hard to take these men south to languish in Southern prisons for several months, and I believed the government would not permit it. It was then agreed to accept the proposition of General Morgan.

The paper being signed, horses obtained (General Morgan had ordered a horse given me to replace my disabled one), with an ambulance for those who had no horses, General Hobson's and staff's horses being on the train, which had been run back, thrown from the track, and destroyed, we started for some point where communication could be had with the military authorities by telegraph. We expected to find such communication at Boyd's Station, on the Kentucky Central Railroad, but the operator had abandoned the station, and we proceeded to Falmouth, where we arrived Sunday evening.

Our escort was Capt. C. C. Morgan, aide de-camp, and Surgeon Goode, of General Morgan's staff, Major Chenoweth of the line, a Mr. Voorhies, said to be a soldier, lately joined them at Lexington, and an ambulance driver, who was also a soldier. These men were all armed. Voorhies carried a flag of truce in advance. We were received into our lines at Falmouth; the rebel officers were assigned quarters and kept close. General Hobson immediately placed himself in communication with General Burbridge, his superior officer, commanding the District of Kentucky, and the result is, two telegrams, copies of which are annexed.[15]

On Friday morning, General Hobson and staff in pursuance of said telegrams, started overland for Lexington (having first obtained permission to go that way), to report to General Burbridge, taking with them the rebel officers and men, and myself and the other field officers of my regiment came to Cincinnati, as directed by General Burbridge, and from thence I came on here[16] to report, leaving the lieutenant-colonel and major at Cincinnati. The regiment, with the line officers, was paroled on Sunday after the battle between General Morgan and General Burbridge.

There may be some doubt upon the subject, but whatever the strict legal rights may be under the cartel, still I believe it would be policy on the part of the government to accept this parole and exchange them at once, in order that they be again put into the field. It will place them in a condition to go to duty more willingly and heartily, and not with the fear that if again captured they would be murdered. They have yet about two months and a half to serve. (General Hobson and staff and the field officers are under a different obligation. Their parole binds them to return if a special exchange cannot be effected.) They were treated with kindness and courtesy and do not desire or wish to violate their pledge.

Although the proposition came from General Morgan, yet it was for our benefit, for if not accepted we would have been mounted on fresh horses and run into General Branch's [Vance's?][17] lines as soon as possible. This they told us after it had been arranged. If the principle of the cartel that we were not reduced to possession within the permanent lines of the army liberates us, we desire that the Government assume the responsibility of so deciding and then to protect us.

We have fought hard and bravely, and to some purpose, too, as a short statement will show.

General Morgan had planned to sweep down the Licking River Valley, plunder as he went, ride into Covington, plunder and burn it, then turn the guns of the fortifications upon the city of Cincinnati, shell it until he was satisfied, then turn up the Ohio and ride out of the state via Maysville and Pound Gap. He had burned the bridges at Paris and Cynthiana to prevent troops following him on the railroad; he had made a feint upon Frankfort, to draw off General Burbridge, which he partially succeeded in doing. He had fresh horses, was 24 hours the start, with no force at Covington, and none on the line of march except ours.

Our fight was so obstinate and protracted that the fighting, taking care of his killed and wounded and the prisoners, detained him until General Burbridge could come up. The rebel officers admitted that this was General Morgan's plan, and that they had been checked in the execution by our fight. General Burbridge was able in a short and decisive fight to completely rout General Morgan's forces so that they were compelled to fly the state in a scattered condition.[18] We beg to be allowed to believe that we have, by our sacrifice, rendered the government and our own state some service, and ask to have these questions considered fairly, and to be liberally and fairly dealt with by our government.[19]

* * *

Richard O. Swindler, captain, Co. B, 171st Ohio:

After the surrender, many of the arms were burned on the field by order of Morgan as worthless, and the others put into the hands of his unarmed recruits. The line officers and men were marched to town, where the afternoon was spent in preparations for paroling the prisoners, name, and descriptive lists being prepared, etc. In the evening, we were marched out of town, together with those of other commands previously taken,[20] and turned into an open field without food and but few blankets.

The night was very chilly, and on Sunday morning we were marched out on the Augusta road, taking our line of march by 4 o'clock. We were made to double-quick, miles in succession, fording [the] Licking River, at Claysville, waist deep, and smaller streams many times. Blankets, shoes, and all impediments were thrown away, and with bleeding feet many of the prisoners continued to march only because threatened with death if they fell out.

Having reached a distance of perhaps 20-odd miles, by the route taken, and still without a morsel of food, the officers were told by Morgan if they would accept a parole for themselves and men he would grant it; if not, he would parole the men and take the officers with [him] to Richmond or other point in the Confederacy—mounted, if they would give the parole of honor not to escape; on foot, and at double-quick, if they would not give such parole.

The line officers present, consisting of all who had been in the fight, except Lieutenant Earl,[21] of Company I, accepted the parole for themselves and men. The men were also sworn not to bear arms against the Southern Confederacy, or do other military service till exchanged or released from parole, under the penalty of death. They did not sign any paper.[22] The whole number of paroled men and officers belonging to the 171st Regiment is about 400, but the undersigned can not state accurately now for want of reports. A descriptive list was not furnished General Morgan, but the names of the men were given him.

After being paroled, the men were some 22 miles from Augusta on the pike, on which for a considerable part of the way stone had been newly broken and was so sharp as to cut shoes. The country had been entirely stripped of food, the men had eaten little, many nothing since Friday evening, their clothing insufficient, and the undersigned being senior captain, put in command by Colonel Asper immediately after surrender, thought best to reach Augusta by the night of the 12th. This was done by dark, the men having marched on that day over 40 miles, though unused to marching, being composed of farmers, merchants, clerks, lawyers, etc. A few horses were procured on which were carried those unable to walk.

The citizens of Augusta had no notice of our coming, but supplied our wants to their utmost ability, and on the morning of the 13th instant, by my order, [the] captain of the steam-boat —— with two barges brought us to this place, where we arrived in the afternoon, the men exhausted and fainting.

The loss of the regiment in the fight at Keller's Bridge was 13 men killed and 50 wounded, many of them very seriously, some of whom have since died. Not over 400 were in the battle, and if portions of other commands were engaged with us it escaped the notice of the undersigned.

It would not become me perhaps to say much as to the conduct of the troops or the manner in which they were handled, but I saw no reason to complain of either. The regiment was armed badly, many of the pieces failing to reach the enemy at all; very many became useless early; while they had many very fine guns—short Enfield rifles, Spencer rifles, etc.

The number actually engaged with us was not less than 1,200 to 1,500, supported by as many more. Morgan acknowledged a loss of 74 killed and wounded at Keller's Bridge, but from the number of wounded carried from the field, seen by me and many of our men after the battle, I do not hesitate to say his loss exceeded the number given.[23]

8 | Petersburg

OHIO'S HUNDRED-DAYS *men went east expecting garrison or guard duty. In June, however, to general surprise plus some anger (both at home and within the ranks), ten regiments were ordered up to the front to join Major-General Benjamin Butler's newly formed Army of the James.*

Butler was situated among the sinuous rivers outside Petersburg, Virginia, a key railroad and river town 20 miles below Richmond. His army was to pressure the rebel forces from the south, while Grant pressed Lee's Army of Northern Virginia and the rebel capital from the north. President Lincoln caught this strategy in an earthy country phrase: "Those not skinning can hold a leg."

The Army of the James landed between the James and Appomattox rivers on May 5th and 6th, and was soon entrenched at Bermuda Hundred,[1] eight miles northeast of Petersburg. After a defeat at Drewry's Bluff on May 16th, there it largely remained, bottled up, while Grant continued his brutal slog southward. Butler ordered an infantry and cavalry expedition against Petersburg on June 9th, when the town was defended by a handful of batteries and militia. The prize was Butler's for the taking, but his officers overestimated the opposition and bungled the attack. The fiasco prompted the removal of the X Corps commander, and Butler and Grant would never again see such an opportunity.

Grant skillfully withdrew the Army of the Potomac from Cold Harbor on June 12–13, and the next day began crossing the James to link with Butler in Lee's rear. The hundred-days regiments were already headed toward this new front. In time, they would constitute two brigades[2] in the fortifications and trenches around Petersburg, some nearly within sight of rooftops in Richmond. These Ohioans performed more as laborers than soldiers, wielding picks and shovels beneath broiling skies; occasionally they took up muskets for a skirmish or to repel a rebel attack. Although spared heavy fighting, these regiments served far from the relative ease and safety of Baltimore or Washington.[3]

Sylvester M. Sherman, first sergeant, Co. G, 133rd Ohio:

The 133d so far has been quite actively engaged in Uncle Sam's work, not fighting to be sure, but in guarding stores, picketing the approaches to this important military depot [New Creek], carrying supplies to the garrisons of different posts near here, and like work. The men have done their duty in a soldierly manner, and will be ready for any work they may be called upon to perform.

We got our traps[4] ready, rations cooked, and at five o'clock P.M. June 7th took the cars for Washington city. On arriving at Washington, our colonel reported to General Augur. He was ordered immediately to put his command in light marching order, so that no man should have more than 14 pounds to carry. Then we were to proceed to the Potomac River at the foot of Sixth Street, there take shipping and proceed to the White House[5] on the Pamunkey River in Virginia, and report to General Abercrombie[6] to be sent to the Army of the Potomac. This order caused some fluttering of hearts. The boys who had originally expected to do home guard duty only wondered how they could be taken right into the thick of the fray, for the Army of the Potomac had been for weeks fighting the battles of the Wilderness etc., and were still at it.

This feeling of trepidation was soon gone, and when the order to fall in was given every man took his place willingly and most of them cheerfully, although they had every reason to believe that the majority of them would leave their bones on the sacred soil of Old Virginia.

While in Washington, the boys took advantage of their spare time to look about the Capitol and other buildings and enjoyed it very much, for few of them had ever seen the seat of the national government. The people of Washington were amazed at the numbers of soldiers coming from Ohio. One exclaimed: "Great God, man! What kind of a damned machine have you got out there to make soldiers with?"

The regiment marched without delay to the landing. Here we received another reminder of what might be our fate; boats we expected to take had just arrived loaded with wounded soldiers from the Army of the Potomac, where we were going. Their wounds were of every conceivable description. We were directed to assist in placing them in ambulances which were to take them to the hospitals, and did this service before we could embark.

We boarded the *Wenonah* at three o'clock P.M. on June 10th, steamed down the river to Alexandria, coaled up and anchored for the night. The steamer was a good sized boat, but our regiment and the necessary baggage and supplies crowded it a good deal. As we came down the river we had a very good view of the forts and batteries with their cannon pointing toward us, and

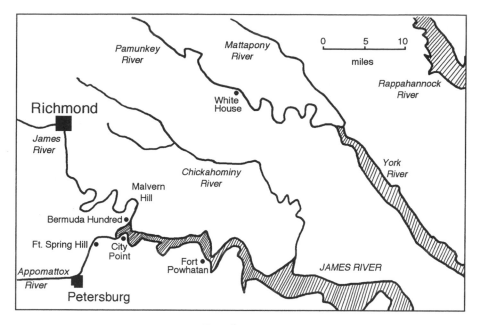

Petersburg area

we realized how quickly our steamboat could be sunk by them had we not worn the blue.

The decks were very dirty, but tired soldiers can sleep anywhere, so the night was passed quite comfortably. It was much better than being jolted in cattle cars. The weather was quite warm, but a good rain in the night cooled the air off nicely. In the morning it got quite cold and drizzly, with a strong wind blowing from the southwest. A little after noon, we got out into the Chesapeake Bay. Here the wind caused the waves to roll up pretty well, forming whitecaps as far as we could see. The result was that the rocking of the boat made many of the men seasick.

Just before we started from Washington, the Colonel had a large envelope handed him by an aide from General Augur's staff, endorsed "Not to be opened till in the Chesapeake Bay." It proved to be an order changing our destination from White House to Bermuda Hundred, where Butler had lately established himself with the Army of the James.

Sunday morning, June 12th, we started on up the James, which is very wide, with low banks and level land beyond them until we got some distance up. Old Jamestown, the first settlement in Virginia, seemed ruined and deserted, as did most of the towns we saw. This river is the main thoroughfare to the seat of war, and consequently we were continually meeting ships and boats of all descriptions coming and going with their freight of soldiers or provisions and munitions of war.[7]

About two o'clock P.M., we landed at Bermuda Hundred without any mishap, and on reporting to General Butler were ordered to Point of Rocks about four miles up the Appomattox. We arrived there about five o'clock, and while waiting to be assigned our place in the works, took notice of what was passing around us.[8]

Our men had built a lookout near where we stopped, and the rebels had fired at it so much that it had to be abandoned; they were still firing an occasional shot at it. Captain Steely[9] went up to take a look at the structure, which was built of pine poles after the fashion of a windmill frame. There was the report of a cannon from the rebel works, and a conical shell struck the ground some distance in front of the captain and came tumbling end-over-end in his direction, throwing a shower of sand over him. He did not wait for it to come up with him, but turned and made tracks away from it at a 2:40 gait, calling forth cheers from the boys commending his agility. We pitched our tents in a woods close by and ate supper.

Our regiment was assigned to the First Brigade, First Division, Tenth Army Corps. Our brigade commander was General A. H. Terry, who just then was promoted to division and then to Corps commander. Colonel Joshua B. Howell of the 85th Pennsylvania Volunteers took command of the brigade, and General R. S. Foster of the division. In our brigade was the 67th O.V.I. To the officers and men of this veteran regiment, the 133d was placed under obligations by many acts of kindness.[10]

Monday, June 13th, after breakfast, we marched about a mile and a half from our camp to a point along the works about half way between the James and Appomattox. Here we pitched our tents back some distance from the breastworks and cleared the ground of brush and fallen trees by piling it up and burning it. Every little while, there would come a report from one of the burning brush heaps and there would be a scattering of the brands. This was caused by the unexploded bombshells which the rebels had thrown over at our men. The fires heated them enough to cause them to explode, but luckily no one was hurt by the flying pieces though several had narrow escapes.

As soon as we were settled here, we were directed to build bomb proofs. This was done by building up poles four feet high, and then placing a roof of poles sloping up from them for ten or twelve feet. Then inside of this, the ground was dug out a couple of feet deep also from around the shed, and the earth thrown back of and on top of the poles, thus making a sort of earth-covered shed with the open side away from the enemy. Being covered with three feet or more of earth, they were tolerably secure for us when firing took place from the rebel batteries.

The bomb proof of each company was about 50 feet long and 10 feet or so wide, with a six-foot space between companies. We were so diligent in getting them done that the old veterans laughed at us, saying that the old soldiers would have been three times as long about it.

One reason for the work being done so soon was that the shells and cannon balls were alighting all about, which was quite a stimulant to exertion. Another was that most of our men were farmers, inured to hard work and accustomed to driving their own business, and they took hold of this in the same way. Two of our companies were city men, not used to the shovel and spade, so when they fell behind the others turned in and helped them.

Our fortifications here extend from the James to the Appomattox, across the neck of a peninsula made by the junction of the two rivers. It comprises about 30 square miles of high-and-dry, land which seems to be almost clear sand, and yet the cleared places are covered with corn which looks well. Our troops have only been here about four weeks and the crops were planted before we came. It is a mystery to us northern men who have been used to rich land how anything grows on this sand.

Our line of fortifications here is very strong. At the banks of both rivers, there are bluffs about 120 feet high. A deep and impassable ravine runs for half a mile from the James, and one of the same kind for nearly a mile from the Appomattox across the neck of the peninsula toward each other, so that only a mile or so of strong works remained to be built. This rendered the line almost impregnable. The rivers were both deep up to the line of works, so that our gunboats could protect the peninsula. It was thus a splendid place to gather an army and to operate from, as troops and supplies could be brought by water very cheaply and quickly; and being close to both Richmond and Petersburg, it was a valuable point to hold.[11]

The rebel works are full of men in plain view about half a mile or less in front of us, and their pickets and ours are close together. We got our bomb proofs completed, but only occupied them about three hours when we were ordered to the breastworks to help repel an expected attack by Beauregard[12] on Butler's center.

Their attack was a little slow, and a couple of brigades from our side sallied out and took a rebel redoubt with small loss. We laid in the trenches all night. On the morning of the 14th, all the men able for duty, about eight hundred, were detailed to work on the fortifications. After marching to several places, they were finally put to work, and made a road for Gen. A. J. Smith's[13] corps of General Grant's army to pass over.

We again laid all night in the trenches. The nights are uncomfortably cold, while the days are very hot. On the 15th, we could hear heavy firing all day in the direction of Petersburg. Troops are pouring in by the thousands and our position is constantly becoming stronger.[14]

On the morning of the 16th, after another night in the trenches, we got our breakfast and were notified that all men able for work were detailed for fatigue duty in repairing, strengthening and extending breastworks around Bermuda Hundred. The detail was made, the men placed in line, and had shouldered muskets, picks and shovels when another order came directing the commandant to march to the front[15] with every available man in his command—with not less than 40 rounds of ammunition and two days rations per man—prepared to support a battery of artillery.

We were ready at once, and marching outside of our works and on through those of the rebs we formed a line of battle and advanced for a mile or more. The advance portion of our line reached the Richmond & Petersburg railroad, tore it up for some distance, burned the ties and bent the rails.

[The party then met rebel opposition. At 2 P.M., Terry reported,] "Prisoners taken say that the force in our front is Pickett's division, that it with other troops crossed the river this morning. They say they saw Lee in person at the crossing. They also report that other troops, Lee's whole army are following Pickett."

[At 3:15, Butler replied,] "Dispatch received. You must withdraw as quickly and speedily as possible. I have sent word to Turner[16] to withdraw also. You had better send an aide to him, so to do, also. See that your working parties are drawn in with their tools."

In withdrawing, our brigade was assigned to the place of rear guard. The rebels advanced rapidly three lines deep and crowded us. Colonel Howell, commanding the brigade, ordered us to about face and give them the warmest reception we could.

He sent for Colonel Innis, and handing him his field glass, said, "Look at those devils over there. They are going to charge on us." On looking through the glass, Colonel Innis could distinctly see the Johnnies forming line of battle. Colonel Howell said, "Now, Colonel Innis, do not let them catch you without fixed bayonets."

"When shall I fix bayonets?" Colonel Innis asked.

"Take your own time, only do not be caught with them unfixed."

On came the rebs, and about 25 rounds were exchanged with them about as rapidly as they could be fired. The effect of our fire on the enemy could not of course be told, but our brigade lost several men in killed and wounded, two of the latter being members of our regiment. In withdrawing, our regiment was ordered to march by the right flank to close the line, which fortunately brought it back of the rebel works and thus prevented our sustaining greater loss.

We arrived inside our works at 11 o'clock at night, having been under fire for about 15 hours. Three companies on the left of the regiment (B, G and K) were detached from the others when we went out and placed on the extreme left of the line, and did not participate in the engagement.[17] But the skirmishers in front of them were continually engaged; the bullets and cannon balls flew over their heads thickly, and kept them anxiously waiting for the order to go in, for which they were quite ready.

During the hottest part of the engagement, the Second Maine Infantry on the left of our brigade, finding their ammunition exhausted, made a movement to the rear for the purpose of filling up again. Seeing this, a good part of the 133d supposed an order had been given to retreat, and they became excited and went back in a hurry.

They soon discovered their mistake, however, and reformed their line on the double-quick, when the whole brigade cheered lustily and opened up a furious fire along the whole line. They exchanged some 25 rounds of musketry, when the enemy fell back leaving about 90 prisoners in our hands. During the balance of the engagement, the 133d behaved like old veterans.

About a company and a half of the men did not run, and while General Howell was rallying the rest he ordered Colonel Innis to remain in front in charge of the line, which he did to the entire satisfaction of the brigade commander.

Colonel Howell says in his report of the fight: "The 133rd, being new to fire broke and ran, with the exception of two or three companies. I respectfully beg leave here to state that the conduct of Colonel Innis was irreproachable. I rode up and down the line and saw him cool and composed, and trying to rally his men. My horse was shot under me at this time. I wish to say to the general that these men are unused to fire, they have to be educated to it. My belief is that they will never break again. I believe they are brave men, they came back with a cheer, those that I saw."[18]

The rebels kept up their cannonading at intervals all night, as also did our artillery, while we maintained our position at the breastworks until one o'clock the next day. A staff officer rode up and inquired for Colonel Innis. Finding him, he said, "Colonel, you are the hardest man to find there is in Bermuda Hundred."

The Colonel explained how we had been ordered about on various duties and that we had been busy.

The officer then said, "General Butler sends his compliments to the 133d for the handsome manner in which they behaved after rallying from their break. He understands that they are new to fire and was pleased that they did so well."[19]

* * *

Repeated Federal assaults beginning June 15th gained ground but failed to break stubborn rebel defenses. Robert E. Lee reached Petersburg on June 18, after which the Federal push became a siege punctuated by frequent sharp actions. The 138th Ohio, suddenly ordered from Washington, arrived about the same time as the Confederate commander.

Wallace W. Chadwick, private, Co. F, 138th Ohio:

Fort Spring Hill [Virginia], June 19th.

Little did I think I would so soon be a part of the Army of the Potomac, but so it is. We are only four miles from Petersburg on the road between Petersburg and Bermuda Hundred, on the south bank of the Appomattox River, eight miles from the mouth and opposite Point of Rocks. We came here yesterday and have been in hearing distance of the battle the whole time.[20] It was terrific at times. Though we were eight miles from the battlefield Friday night, we could distinctly hear the roll of musketry.

We marched here yesterday, making three days we have put in in successive marching. I tell you, my shoulders feel pretty sore. Hale, hearty men have given under, while some of the weaker ones are looking almost as well as ever. But another day or two of marching would have been as much as we could stand.

We came to the Petersburg road, within six miles of that place; then marched to City Point;[21] then crossed to Bermuda Hundred; then next morning back to City Point; then marched down here yesterday. We could hear cannon at Petersburg, and cannon west and northwest of us all at the same time. Still we were safe, as there were old troops between us and the enemy in every direction. However, the rebel lines are only two miles west of us, and it wouldn't be very safe to go blackberrying out there.

This morning the ball has begun again in the direction of Petersburg, although some say it surrendered yesterday evening. They say that in the rear of the town is a lot of high ground that the rebels are occupying. This is going to be harder to take than Petersburg. Still, the troops seem very confident, but the losses are very great on both sides.

June 22nd.

I write this letter from my post on picket duty, where I can see six or eight rebels on picket. I am but 2,700 yards from Port Clifton, which has torn up the ground in my rear between me and our own fort. That was before we came here. They have exchanged no shots since. Towards Petersburg, there has been continual firing of artillery all day. I fear the war will not be over in the next hundred days.

June 23rd.

The firing was very heavy last night on our right and left. That on the left was at Petersburg, that on the right was up the James River, perhaps mortars at Fort Darling.[22]

Old Abe Lincoln was out here yesterday, but he did not visit us, however. There is a rumor in camp that we are going to be sent back to Point Lookout.

I hear it is reported that the 138th refused to go to the front when ordered. Now all such stories are base slanders on the regiment.[23] There were one or two companies, supposing that Colonel F———[24] was to blame, that wanted to get up a remonstrance; but they were hooted down by the other companies. If there was a single man laid down his gun it is news to me, the Copperheads[25] notwithstanding.

We believe it to be our duty to obey orders when they come. Some say they haven't enough to eat. Well, it is not always regular nor fancy. It is frequently under or over, but no one has starved. Grumblers are always found in large bodies of men; to deprive a soldier of his privilege of growling would be depriving him of one of his most undoubted rights. If it were not one thing, it would be another.

June 30th.

We know little about the situation of our armies. We are within range of a rebel fort, rather an ugly customer, but its attention is kept in another direction. We can stand here and see shells that fall short burst over Petersburg. Grant is fetching up siege guns. Both Generals Grant and Butler were taking observations between our fort and the river on the west yesterday.

Some think the object is to throw another pontoon across and seize Fort Clifton, and thus get part of our army in the enemies' rear. I have seen whole divisions completely covered with dust, feet sore, faces worn and haggard, marching at the rate of four miles an hour to throw themselves between the enemy and some important position. They are not as lighthearted as they were at the beginning of the war, for they face stern realities. Some are discouraged, but most of them think Grant will finally take Petersburg. There must be suffering there and at Richmond both, for we harass their railroads, and the number they have to feed must use up their supplies rapidly.[26] I hope we may be able to crush them this season, or we will be financially used up ere long.

* * *

The 134th Ohio was also ordered to move from Washington to the front, where it arrived on a ship named Dictator. *The regiment's lieutenant-colonel provides a brief history of the first strenuous weeks near Petersburg.*

D. W. Todd, lieutenant-colonel, 134th Ohio:

Reaching Bermuda Hundred on the James River at 9:30 A.M., June 11th, the regiment disembarked and marched to Gen. Butler's headquarters near City Point. The regiment had scarcely pitched their tents before the rebels commenced shelling their camp.

On June 12th at 3:30 A.M. the long roll beat and the regiment was hurriedly moved to the fort and laid on their arms until late in the morning.

On the evening of June 13th, Lt.-Col. Todd with a detail of 150 men was ordered to move by boat to the north side of the James River and report to Gen. Weitzel.[27] Our work to remove the rubbish and growing timber along the north bank of the river was marked out to us the next morning by Gen. Weitzel, with strict orders to have it done by 12 m., as the left wing of Grant's army coming out of the wilderness would reach the river by 1 P.M.

The head of Grant's army reached the river at 2 P.M. and at once commenced to cross on the pontoon bridge at that point.

During the night of June 14th, the detail moved back to camp. On June 14th, Grant ordered Gen. Butler to move against the rebels in Petersburg, and on the 15th and 16th the 134th regiment was placed on picket and along the breastworks.

On the morning of June 17th, the rebels drove in our picket near Port Walthal and made an assault upon our line. The engagement last until 12 m. The rebels were driven back and our picket line reestablished. The Union forces lay upon their arms in the advance line until 5 P.M., when they were relieved by other troops. In this engagement the 134th was on the extreme left of the line, with the 62nd O.V.I. on their immediate right, and had one killed, one mortally and three severely wounded. Had the rebels aimed lower, our loss must have been much greater.

On the 21st day of June at 5 A.M., the regiment started for the north side of the James River, crossing the same day on a pontoon bridge about one mile above Turkey Bend. Here the regiment was engaged in digging rifle pits, and picket and skirmish duty until June 22nd when the regiment was ordered back to the pontoon bridge and took rowboats for the north side of the river at Turkey Bend.

Here on a high bluff extending from the river, the regiment with a large force of the enemy in their immediate front and with no support but one gunboat, the *Hunchback*,[28] commanded by Captain Joe Fyffe, laying in the bend of the river, was engaged in building fortifications until the evening of the 23rd, when it was ordered to recross the river to the south side at a point near the pontoon bridge. Having but two boats, the last of the regiment did not cross until after midnight.

About 10 o'clock, just as part of Company F was pulling away from the shore, the rebels under cover of night and a narrow strip of timber, stole down near where they were crossing and fired a volley at them. Captain Fyffe instantaneously opened fire upon them with his gatling guns and we had no further trouble except deep anxiety for our safety. To the writer this was the most fearful day and night of his army life. Nothing but Captain Fyffe's gunboat saved us from being captured. On June 24th the regiment was ordered back, reaching their camp the same day with most of the men exhausted.

On June 26th the 134th was brigaded with the 130th, 132nd, 138th and 142nd Ohio regiments. The brigade was denominated the 2nd brigade, 3rd division, 10th army corps. Colonel J. B. Armstrong was placed in command of the brigade.

* * *

The hundred-days regiments of the Second Brigade endured such arduous, unhealthy duty outside Petersburg that the colonel commanding it—James B. Armstrong, a veteran of the 95th Ohio and a banker in civilian life—took the extraordinary step of appealing for relief directly to President Lincoln.[29]

"This is the only Brigade of this class of troops so near the front," Armstrong wrote. "The unusual nature of our fatigue duties has borne so heavily upon our unseasoned men—together with the climate, that, unless we are relieved, I have reason to fear our numbers will be so reduced by disease and death as not even to leave skeleton Regiments to take home the middle of August."[30]

This admittedly "unmilitary" appeal failed. Each of the colonel's four regiments remained at the front for nearly another month, by which time the 100 days were expiring. In aggregate, his Second Brigade suffered three deaths in combat and 141 to disease.[31] *Armstrong's men may never have learned of his appeal on their behalf; indeed, some suspected him of wanting to stay at the front.*[32]

Sergeant John Harrod of the 132nd Ohio hid the brigade's condition from his worried wife,[33] *if only by describing the raggedness of his enemies. He wrote that he was glad to leave the "God deserted hell deserving" capital, and from outside Petersburg continued his awkwardly reassuring letters home, excerpted here.*

John Harrod, sergeant, Co. C, 132nd Ohio:

White House Landing, June 3rd 1864

Sue—Here the prisoners are sent. There was 900 brought in last night, amongst them a woman. She is dressed in [an] officer's uniform, a lieutenant, I think, and had command of a battery. She does not disguise her sex. She has been in the service 2 years and over. She has been a good looking girl, under 25 years and very intelligent looking. There is another but did not see her.[34]

White House Landing, June the 10th

Susan—There are more prisoners than wounded. This lot of rebs that came in last night were the hardest looking set that has come in since we have been here. They are a rough dirty black ragged mean savage heathenish looking set as was ever seen in any country since the world began.

Bermuda Hundred, Sunday July 9th [sic]

Susan—We have never been put in an engagement yet nor do I think we will. We are kept very close to those that do fight but we have never been asked to fire a gun yet. We have been several times close enough to fight, but as soon as it was discovered we were moved back out of danger and the old soldiers done the fighting and let us go to our quarters. There has never been a time that I considered we were in much danger.

There was two men wounded two weeks ago today in Co. H, the next company to us. I was standing right next to one of them when he was struck. The Johnnies had been trying to keep us uneasy all night Saturday night and kept us pretty close to the works all day. The order was not to leave the ditch but the boys could not see enough there and they were out more than in, but it was at their own risk. The one that I was by was struck in the leg above the knee. He did not know what was the matter. He commenced scratching his leg and wanted to know what in hell was the matter with his leg. Pretty soon the blood commenced running down his leg. He pulled up his pants and there was a hole through his leg by one of these big Miniés. He did not mind it much. The other is shot through the head. But Sue we have not been in range for several days and our pickets in front of us are quiet and if there ever was danger it is gone.

* * *

The companion First Brigade was more fortunate than the Second. Its regiments received orders shifting them to the numerous Federal forts along the rivers. Sergeant Sherman here resumes his narrative of the 133rd.

Sylvester M. Sherman, first sergeant, Co. G, 133rd Ohio:

We now [June 17th] left the front for Fort Powhatan, about 12 miles down the river. During the forenoon, while we were lying at the breastworks, before receiving the order, there was quite a skirmish in the woods in front of us. Our gunboats had been throwing shells occasionally all day. Just as we were about to leave, the Johnnies began to shell our camp but did not harm us.

At the landing where we were to take the boat we met several of the 5th U.S.C.T.,[35] some of whom are from Columbus. Boarding the steamboat we were not long coming in sight of the fort, but instead of landing us the boat anchored for the night.

We had been in the trenches several nights and on fatigue duty in the daytime, then came the days marching and fighting, so that the men were very tired. The boat's decks afforded a good place to lie down, and there was no guard duty to perform. So as soon as we cast anchor and dusk came, everyone laid down and put in a full night sleeping. This was the best night's rest we had had since we left home.

On June 18th, as soon as it was light, our boat moved up to the wharf and we landed and marched up hill into the fort.

An army on the move! Just ahead of our boat is a pontoon bridge, on which a portion of Grant's forces, Meade's[36] Army of the Potomac, is crossing the river. Above and below, they are crossing by ferry boats. They have been crossing without ceasing for three days and nights, which gives one some idea of the immense number of men there are. The immense lot of stores, ammunition, provisions, tents, etc., and droves of cattle, numbering thousands, all go to make up the army.

Our regiment was quite well satisfied to change from active duty in the field to garrison duty in the fort. They thought it more in accordance with the orders under which they were called out. They did not think they had been sufficiently prepared for duty at the front, though the active drilling they had at New Creek made them better than many old regiments in the field.

In speaking of Fort Powhatan, General Butler says:

"Although it was some twelve miles below City Point on the James, yet if it were once in possession of the enemy, it would be impossible to get any troops or supplies up the river, as the channel ran close under it. . . . It may be asked why, if it was of so much importance, I entrusted its defenses to a garrison of negro troops? I knew that they would fight more desperately than any white troops in order to prevent capture, because they knew that if captured they would be returned into slavery under Davis' proclamation, and the officers commanding them might be murdered."

The colored troops held the fort, and Grant's army was crossing when we got there. We relieved these colored troops who were expected to do such desperate fighting. It can be seen by the foregoing account how important a duty we had to perform.

On arriving here Colonel Innis, being the ranking officer, assumed command of the post. In the forces serving here, every arm of the service was represented: two naval officers in command of gunboats, one placed above, the other below the fort, a detachment of the Third Pennsylvania Heavy Artillery, a squadron of cavalry, a detachment of the First New York Engineers, also a signal corps and telegraph station.

After marching up the hill, we pitched our tents both inside and outside the fort, those outside being within the line of fortifications and of easy access to the fort in case of an attack. Some of the men built up poles or boards a foot or two high and put their tents on top of that, thus making quite a roomy place. We then cleaned up the ground, dug trenches around the tents and along the streets in front of them for drainage, and had quite a respectable camp.

In fact, the 133d was always noted for the neat manner in which they did everything. When we established our camp at Bermuda Hundred, the boys did it so nicely that it attracted the attention of General Foster. He came galloping by with his staff and when in front of our camp suddenly reined in his horse, almost bringing him on his haunches.

"By George!" he exclaimed, "whose camp is this?"

"The 133d Ohio," answered someone.

"Send your commander to me."

Colonel Innis appeared and saluted.

The general said, "Colonel, I want to compliment you on the neatness of your camp. You have the nicest camp in Bermuda Hundred."

The Colonel thanked General Foster for the compliment, and added, "I ought to be able to lay out a camp, for I am a civil engineer when at home."

The 133d was now brigaded [at Fort Powhatan] with the 138th, 143d and 163d regiments of Ohio Volunteers, and formed the 1st Brigade, 3d Division of the 10th Army Corps. While we were here, our duties were various. For fatigue duty, we completed the fort and fortifications around it in the most substantial manner. Part of our work was to keep up 20 miles of telegraph line through a rebel country and connecting General Grant's headquarters with the government at Washington City.

Our most important duty was to guard the James, to allow the passage of vessels back and forth with troops and supplies and wounded and prisoners. The river being the main thoroughfare to the seat of war, it was very necessary to keep it open. There was hardly any time that boats could not be seen going and coming. Sometimes as many as 30 were in sight at once. When the rebels were firing on our transports, the passing boats hove to under the guns of the fort until there was quite a fleet of them, passing on as soon as the danger was over.[37]

Some of the vessels conveying prisoners were fairly swarming with Johnnies in their butternut suits. They seemed to take their captivity very cheerfully, and when we would cheer at their passing they would yell lustily in return. One thing that bore evidence of the destruction that war causes was the number of dead mules that floated down the river.

It was a common occurrence for the enemy to attack our shipping loaded with supplies for the army investing Petersburg and Richmond. The guns of Fort Powhatan were turned upon these raiders, and in no instance was the foe successful in capturing a boat or the least article on its way for the convenience or subsistence of our comrades at the front.

Frequently while at this fort, the commandant would receive a note of warning from General Grant's headquarters, informing him of the importance of being vigilant and being at all times fully prepared to repel an attack from the enemy. These notes wound up generally by saying, "The safety of this whole army depends largely on your vigilance at Fort Powhatan."

Our men worked on a lookout and signal station, 96 feet high, which they completed late in July. By means of this tower, the country for miles around could be continuously watched through the day, signals conveyed from the station at Fort Pocahontas, eight miles below on the river, and repeated here to the one at City Point, ten miles up the river. By means of telescopes, these signals—communicated by flags by day and torches by night—could be seen and read, thus conveying information as quickly and as accurately as by telegraph.

The [first] engineer officer in charge was afraid he would be sent to the front and therefore delayed the finishing of Fort Powhatan all he dared. He made considerable complaint about not being furnished with men for the work. He also was a pretty hard drinker, which interfered with his usefulness. The new engineer officer was a gentlemanly and energetic man, and the works were soon finished. On making a tour of observation with the Colonel, he commended the works all round, and when he came in, said, "Colonel, the devil himself couldn't get in here now, even with his wife to help him."

* * *

While operating from Fort Powhatan, the 133rd Ohio was also troubled by bushwhackers. Two of its privates later recalled turning the tables on them.

John C. Ender, private, Company I, 133rd Ohio:

One of my never-to-be-forgotten adventures while serving with the telegraph corps happened shortly before we left Fort Powhatan.

The rebels got bolder every day, as they found our force was quite small. The old saying, "What is one man's loss is another man's gain" came true on the trip out in question. On the day previous, the 1st Lieutenant of Company D., 1st U.S. Colored Cavalry, was thrown from his horse—which was a very vicious animal—and got badly hurt. That evening I got him to consent to let me ride the animal out the next day.

We started about daybreak, got beyond Brandon Mills and found the wire cut. In testing between us and Swan Point, we found the circuit also broken. We spliced the wire and started to find the next break, which we did at a place called Spring Grove, about 11 miles out. There the wire ran across lots to the next crossroad. The old man upon whose plantation the wire was cut told us that some 300 southern cavalry had just gone by and cut the wire. We tested and found all right, but a break between us and Fort Powhatan, which had been made since we left a few hours before.

The Lieutenant said, "This means trouble."

We were only about 50 men. One officer (second lieutenant of Company D., 1st U.S. Colored Cavalry), the man who repaired the wire and myself with testing battery [were white]. The balance were all colored troops. We repaired the wire in the field and notified the man of the place.

General Butler had given strict orders to arrest any person upon whose place the wire was found cut. With the explanation he gave us, we concluded to report our finding and arrest him later if the authorities thought proper. Making our way back to find the new break, we met a colored woman who told us her boy had just come from near Brandon Mills and had met a large body of southern cavalry. They had taken down a large stretch of wire where the line runs through the woods, had placed tripwires across the road, and a fence of rails back of it.

The Lieutenant said, "They have laid a trap. The party who cut the wire through the field is not the same which is between us and Powhatan. Their game is to start us toward the trap and massacre the whole outfit, as they are bitter against white officers of colored troops and never give the colored troops any quarter.

"We have no time for planning. To go to the river means to get caught. If we go farther into the country we are liable to meet larger forces, as scouts from Petersburg are always out there. We have only one remedy—to cut our way through.

"I will take four men for advance guard, go to the trap, take up the wire and take down the fence. They will not be likely to fire on so small a force. At the first fire, you must all come forward on a charge."

As the Lieutenant afterwards explained, there was no firing until they had several rails off the fence. His horse cleared the obstruction, when from the woods nearby voices hallooed. By this time, the advance had the wire loose and quite a gap in the fence; a continuous firing commenced. The vicious horse I had did me good service, clearing the gap without a break.

The whole command scattered along by ones and twos. There were two killed[38] and several wounded. Some had their horses shot, and did not get to the fort for several days. As we left there shortly afterwards, I never heard a full report of the engagement.

* * *

Howard B. Westervelt, private, Company F, 133rd Ohio:

The special service required of us was to keep the James River open and to protect the telegraph line.

This was the great problem. A telegraph line runs out into the country, across streams, over bogs, through forests, along miles and miles of lonely roadway. An army might not get there, but a few men could work through and, covered by the dense underbrush which filled those pine forests, could go where they wished and be completely concealed at almost any point. As would be expected, the wires were cut frequently.

The linemen were kept busy. Scouting parties were frequently sent out. A few prisoners were brought in, but the nuisance was unabated. Often, before the scouts or repairers got in, the wires would be broken again. This state of affairs gave rise to the incident I relate.[39]

On Monday, August 1st, I came off picket duty and was allowed to rest during most of the day. In the evening, about the time we were spreading our blankets, someone called my name. I went out and was taken a little ways from the tent and the case was laid before me.

The interruption of communications through the cutting of the wires was becoming very annoying, indeed almost unbearable. Our present methods were thoroughly inadequate. The enemy could dodge us every time, and slip up and cut the wires even before the retiring scouts were out of hearing. The only way to stop it would be to go out and lie for them, watch the wires and be on hand to intercept the mischief. Lieutenant Darrah[40] of Company A. had volunteered to lead a party of this kind, and he wanted only men who had seen previous service. Would I be one of them?

A service of this kind was not particularly desirable. "Lying in the brush" did not count for much, but the service asked was one of peculiar and extreme peril. Our neighbors across the line did not hesitate to conceal themselves and shoot down our troops, but they were greatly horrified if we should undertake it. The parties wearing the blue and doing that kind of thing would probably, if captured, be hung to the nearest tree.

While we were talking, our colonel, with whom I was well acquainted, rode up and insisted that there was no compulsion toward such a service, and rather dissuaded me from going. I told the messenger that if Lieutenant Darrah was going and wanted me, I would be one of his squad.

I returned to my tent, got my accouterments and was away. It was held necessary to keep the matter an entire secret, so I said nothing to my tentmates except that I was on duty. We were gone nearly 36 hours, and when we returned my comrades merely supposed I was on an extended term as picket somewhere.

We left camp about one o'clock in the night or early morning of the 2d. We marched to Brandon Church, an abandoned Episcopal church about five miles out, then quietly worked our way out along the line to a crossroad some three-quarters of a mile further on, reaching there just as day was breaking. Here we concealed ourselves in the brush.

There was a house just across the road, not more than six or eight rods from where we were concealed. We could hear the humming of the spinning wheel all day. In the morning, the children came out in the road, and seeing our footprints in the dust wondered how so many footmarks got there. We, not more than 50 feet off, almost held our breath till they went away. We lay there all day, and not an inmate of that house had the least idea that a soldier was nearer than the fort.

At night, guards were told off and the rest lay down to sleep. But now another problem presented itself. We had left the fort hurriedly and with the greatest secrecy. Hence, provisions were running low; indeed, they were scarce when we started. We had no wish to return without accomplishing something, so a couple started out to find a colored family whom they knew, to get corn-pone for the crowd. There were 13 of us. At eleven o'clock, I went on guard. I was ordered to be very careful until our foragers came in, after which I was to challenge no one, but shoot at anyone who should come along. Soon our boys came in with the word that they had been successful, but would have to return about two o'clock, as the "Auntie" would have to bake the pone.

It was raining a little and was very dark. The company was all asleep, but the corporal (Joe Gregg, my tentmate)[41] lay by my side, telling me to wake him if I heard anything or at the expiration of my time.

Between twelve and one o'clock, I heard the sound of horses approaching from the direction of the church and fort.

I pushed Joe, and we were ready. Two men came on horses to the cross-roads where we were lying, and turned off the telegraph road into the one running west. They checked up at once, and one said, "I guess there are no scouts out tonight."

"No, it is a bully night for us!"

They now turned back upon the telegraph road, and Joe fired. One man threw up his hands and cried out, "Oh, my God! I'm shot! I'm killed!"

The other spurred up and caught and held him on his horse, crying out, "For God's sake, men, don't shoot! You are firing on your own men."

During this time, I held my fire. It is a serious thing to shoot a man, and if that man was one of us it would be calamitous.

"Friends to whom?" shouted our lieutenant.

"Friends to the Southern flag."

Then I fired; but the horses were plunging, they were further off, and the aim was not true. The horses galloped back toward the church, and we gathered up our traps and got ready for action.

The lieutenant decided that as we were now located our position was perilous, and we had better move. It would not do to start directly for the fort. The horsemen had gone that way, and we would probably meet a force too strong for us.

In the pine woods of the South there are few fences, and the roads or driveways are numerous. This was fortunate for us. We struck out eastwardly from our ambush. As we went out that road, the enemy returned along the telegraph line toward the point of ambush. About a mile east, we struck another road running west toward the church and fort. We turned into this, the enemy following on the road east. As we passed along one side of the triangle, they followed us on another.

We finally reached the church, and as it adjoined a swamp we concluded to lie there until daylight. There were woods all around us. We lay close to, east of the church in some tall grass and under the boughs of a tree. The enemy had probably some 30 or 40 men, but in the darkness they had no way of learning our strength nor exact position without more risk than they cared to assume. We heard them on three sides of us at once as they reconnoitered, but after an hour or so everything grew still.

Before long, the lieutenant, hopeful and yet suspicious, ordered me to cross the open space north to a ravine running out from the swamp, to see whether I could find anything. He had probably forgotten that my turn as guard had expired.

I am frank to confess I was afraid. In crossing that space of perhaps 100 yards, I did not take one step. That was the only time in my life that I emulated a snake and sighed for greater thinness. Bless the man that invented tall grass! I made the trip, investigated among the trees, satisfied myself that the enemy had disappeared, and then, lest I might become satisfied that he had returned, I got down and crawled back, utterly oblivious of the fact that it had rained and that tall grass when wet does not add to one's appearance.

We lay there till towards day, then shifted our position and in the morning marched back to the fort. Parties coming in during the day brought word that the man shot had died and his body had been left in the old mill.

One well-grounded preference was stamped on my mind. I had been under fire, been in battle, gone on scouts, and I would rather do them all (at once if possible) than to play bushwhacker. It is not pleasant in itself, and the outlook if captured is miserable.[42]

One thing more I am sure of: Soldiers can, if necessary, be quiet. For nearly 36 hours our band did not speak above a whisper. One other reminiscence is in place. We missed our cornpone. It never hunted us up, and we charged it to profit and loss.

The campaign continued through a series of fights and the disastrous Battle of the Crater,[43] *through the hundred days, and months after the Ohioans had returned home. It would not end until just days before Lee's surrender at Appomattox Courthouse. Petersburg was the longest siege in American military history.*[44]

9 | Fourth of July

DESPITE THE WAR, *July 4th was still a holiday of picnics and fireworks across the North. Even in their long summer of army duty, many hundred-days regiments were able to enjoy the day. For the 157th Ohio, guarding rebel prisoners at Fort Delaware, it featured a 32-gun salute from the parapets at noon and a band playing "Yankee Doodle." Along the Ohio River in its home state, the 172nd Ohio paraded in Gallipolis "and made quite a fine appearance."*[1]

Even along the thunderous James River, Ohio hundred-days men managed to celebrate the holiday in their own fashion—with the noisy participation, planned or otherwise, of the enemy. In the mountains of West Virginia, rebel raiders and cavalrymen provided an altogether different sort of celebration, both threatening and unpredictable, and one that foreshadowed the danger brewing in the Shenandoah Valley. We begin the 4th of July, 1864, beside the James at Fort Powhatan.

Sylvester M. Sherman, first sergeant, Co. G, 133rd Ohio:

We celebrated the day by having regimental review and erecting a flagpole in the fort, on which was run up the stars and stripes. A salute of 34 guns was fired, and the boats in the river were decked out with flags and bunting in honor of the day.[2]

A newspaper correspondent was so soundly asleep that he did not hear the salute, and wrote home to his paper that there was no demonstration at the fort.

We were continually reminded that war existed in our vicinity by the heavy firing up the rivers in the direction of Petersburg and Richmond, and we anxiously waited for the time when we would have to repel a rebel attack on our post. Quite frequently, the rebels would station themselves on the river bank above or below this place, plant a battery and begin firing on every boat that passed up or down.

On the Fourth of July, they appeared with a battery at Wilcox's Wharf, between three and four miles up the river on the opposite side, and began firing on some transports that were passing up loaded with hay and grain for

Grant's and Butler's armies. There were nine of the boats, three abreast. The rebel aim seemed poor, for many of the shots fell into the water around the boats but did not do much damage. Only one hole was made of any consequence, and the boat's crew soon patched that up.

The rebels were in plain view from the fort, and as soon as they began firing we wanted to be at them. But it was out of our reach, for by the time we could land a force on the other side of the river and march to where they were, they could have the boats sunk and be gone. Our commander ordered Captain Von Shilling[3] to try the cannon of the fort on them.

He said, "I don't believe we can reach them, but I will try."

We had two guns, one a brass 32-pounder, the other a steel gun much larger. The brass piece was tried first; the shot struck the water in direct line toward the rebs, but only about two-thirds of the way to them. The steel gun was then loaded, and the shot went nearly to them. The colonel said, "Put in a double charge, Captain."

"I am afraid it will spoil the gun," was answered.

"Will it hurt any of us?"

"Oh no! But it will likely crack the gun."

"Well, try it! Uncle Sam will get us another."

So a double charge was put in with a shell. When the gun was fired, those who had their eyes on the rebs saw men, horses, and cannon suddenly fly into the air; then in wild confusion, they lit out for other parts. The shell had gone under the gun platform, and exploded just at the right time to be most effective.[4]

The gunboat stationed below the fort had started up the river to attack this battery. But to the eyes of the anxious and excited soldiers at the fort it seemed to hardly move, and many were the exclamations of disgust at its slowness. Our shots drove the rebs away before the boat got halfway there. These gunboats soon routed the rebels when they happened to be on hand, but the Johnnies took advantage of their absence, as the boats had to patrol the river up and down for several miles.

* * *

At nearby Fort Ohio at Spring Hill, on the Appomattox River, the 138th Ohio started its celebration, appropriately enough, with a reading of the Declaration of Independence by Private John Hancock, Company E, and a band playing "Yankee Doodle."

Gilbert L. Laboytreaux, private, Co. F, 138th Ohio:

Col. Fisher, being loudly called for, mounted the rostrum, or rather a washtub turned upside down, and commenced by reading a communication just received from [General] Sherman, who, by a flank movement, had captured Marietta,[5] and was still driving the enemy and destroying railroads. This was good news for the boys, and what followed was enjoyed equally well.

The Colonel was in excellent spirits; his sentences came out rapid and distinct, clear and clean as the hammering of steel upon steel—eloquent, forcible and argumentative in itself, compelling the loud applause it received. Thus have we celebrated the Fourth of July, if not *in* Richmond, at least in the neighborhood of it, on the "sacred soil of Old Virginia."

I will close with the following address to the "old lady":

Virginia! Old Virginia!
   How bears your pulse today?
We come up here to greet you,
   And, lo! you run away.
We heard you long'd to meet us,
   And when we come to see,
You lock yourselves in Petersburg—
   But Grant has got the key;
And is knocking—gently knocking—
   You have heard his "rap" before;
So you'd better come and open,
   Or he'll batter down the door.

* * *

At Fort Bunker Hill outside Washington, the holiday took a tragic turn for the haughty 150th. This brief account of it appeared in a letter later published in the Cleveland Plain Dealer.

William R. Reid, private, Co. C, 150th Ohio:

An accident happened to a member of our company this afternoon. The facts of the case are as follows:

Corporal W. H. Wyman, and four boys from the company, started to go to Bladensburg, about three o'clock this afternoon. They had almost arrived at the east post of our line when they were discovered coming by the picket guard. A friend of the Corporal said to the boys on picket, "I will snap a cap at Wyman, and scare him." He picked up a musket without a cap—he did not know it was loaded—put on a cap, and snapped it, discharging the piece at him. The ball struck him in the right side, and passed through his body. He only lived long enough to say, "My God, boys, I am shot." It is wonderful the ball did not kill another one of the boys. They were all together in a crowd. The body was sent to the hospital to be embalmed. It will be sent home soon.

* * *

Near Bermuda Hundred, on the James outside Petersburg, another Ohio soldier recorded in his diary the passage of another difficult day. The whiskey ration he mentions was medicinal, not recreational.

George F. Bailey, private Co. G, 132nd Ohio:

Morning warm and cloudy. Fell in for the whiskey at five A.M. At 6, I took seventeen sick soldiers to the hospital for the quinine. About half the regiment is unfit for duty. Am suffering now with a sore throat no doubt caused by laying [in] the trenches 22 nights in succession.

This is Independence day but no demonstration is being made in the way of celebrating the event. It was rumored in the camp last night that fifty cannon would be fired along the line at midnight. But nary [a] gun was fired. My Lord how dry—no signs of rain—wind from the north. At noon Gen. Butler ordered a National Salute all along the line. Even ordered to fall into the ditch fearing the firing would be responded to by the rebs in front. We marched to the trenches but instead of falling into the trench our brave Captain thought we would be more out of danger by drilling us half an hour or so—while the balance of the regiment were reposing gracefully in the trench. Were then marched to the Colonel's headquarters. At twilight we sallied for the trenches. Am getting about tired of laying in the ditches.

* * *

As the hundred-days men celebrated the Fourth of July in the East, either peacefully or under fire, the storm that had gathered in the Shenandoah Valley now rumbled more ominously. At its center as it swept north down the fabled valley rode Lieutenant-General Jubal Early. In a brilliantly disguised campaign to relieve pressure on Petersburg, Early was about to burst from the Valley with almost no Federal opposition between him and either Baltimore or Washington.

At Greenland Gap, West Virginia, the 154th Ohio was looking forward to the holiday. But these expectations, too, were dashed by the advancing Confederates.

Joseph A. Stipp, private, Co. B, 154th Ohio:

July 4th was now drawing near, and our love and reverence for the day had not diminished in the least. Our field and staff officers, always kind and considerate, proposed to vary the monotony of camp life, scouting and picket duty, and to that end steps were taken to provide an old-fashioned 4th of July celebration.

We were going to have a barbecue—save and except the roasted ox. However, we were well supplied with "mule meat," "salt horse," "sowbelly," beans, hardtack, coffee and rice. Pies, "sewed or pegged," could be obtained from the neighbors residing in our immediate vicinity.

Our drum corps could enliven the occasion by rendering the national airs, selections from *Norma,* and incidentally remind us of the *Girl I Left Behind Me.* The Union-loving people in and around the Gap were invited to participate in the festivities of the day. Everyone was progressing nicely and all were filled with the fondest anticipations; but a sudden change came over us. The promised holiday was deferred. All kinds of rumors concerning the presence of the enemy and his movements in our immediate vicinity were being circulated.

A large force of the enemy was in the South Branch Valley under command of General Imboden,[6] and reported to be moving on Greenland Gap. Our anxiety and suspense were now further increased by the arrival of mounted messengers bearing orders from General Kelley:[7]

"Send a scout of 200 infantry and all your available cavalry on a scout to Moorefield and Petersburg.[8] You must keep yourself advised of the whereabouts of the enemy and report to me often."

In obedience to General Kelley's orders, dated July 1st, a scouting party numbering 200 men was sent out by Colonel Stevenson. The scout was conducted in the greatest possible secrecy. Our detachment was conducted over the mountains and foothills by a trusty guide, traversing paths hitherto unknown to us, and in due time we reached a mountain known as "Charlie's Knob." We began our ascent, climbing its rough and rugged sides with great difficulty and fatigue.

Upon reaching the summit of this mountain, we found a rebel signal station, from the top of which we could look down upon the beautiful little town of Moorefield and survey, by the aid of a field glass, the country for miles around, obtaining at the same time a very fair glimpse of Petersburg, a neighboring town. We remained upon the mountain for some time, but finding the air so cold, and no signs of the enemy, we gladly retraced our steps to the valley below.

Upon our return to Greenland Gap, we reported our experiences to Colonel Stevenson, whereupon the following dispatch was sent to General Kelley:

". . . Nothing was discovered up to the time they left, which was 7 o'clock A.M. today, 3rd inst. I will keep scouts in that direction, also in the direction of Petersburg, and keep you advised."

At Greenland Gap, the situation was alarming, made doubly so by the constant and incessant arrival of mounted messengers, whose horses showed evidence of hard and fast riding.

"Colonel Stevenson, Greenland Gap:
"If you are approached by an overwhelming force you will retire on New Creek, via the Moorefield and Allegheny pike, to the junction. The rebels are reported in large force between Winchester and Martinsburg, and an attack on the latter place is momentarily expected.
"B. F. Kelley, Brigadier-General."

"Genl. B. F. Kelley, Cumberland, Md.:
"Scouting party of twenty men sent out in the direction of Ridgeville and Burlington have just returned, 6 o'clock P.M. They report McNeill has been reinforced by 400 men, making his full number 800, who were encamped two miles below Moorefield, near Romney pike, on Friday night. This, they say, is reliable. They report also that Imboden's force is in part a short distance from Moorefield.
"R. Stevenson, Colonel Commanding."

Our situation at Greenland Gap on that memorable Sunday, July 3rd, can better be imagined than described. Our force at that time consisted of eight companies of infantry, numbering probably 700 men, a detachment of the 2d Maryland infantry, mounted, probably 20 men, and two pieces of Battery L, 1st Illinois Light Artillery, 40 men. Deduct from the enumerated forces our men on picket duty, and those out on scouting parties; our actual force was reduced to a mere handful for defense in the event of an attack. The line of communication between General Kelley and General Sigel at Harper's Ferry, where severe fighting had been going on for some time, was destroyed.

Sunday night, July 3d, the entire force at Greenland Gap, save the picket force, was concentrated on the hill above our camp, a favorable and commanding position, and was under arms the entire night, expecting an attack at any moment. About midnight, the entire force was put to work with pick and shovel, throwing up a line of entrenchments; we performed this work with our accouterments on, our arms lying on the ground near at hand. The work continued until about 9 o'clock A.M., when three messengers came in bearing orders from General Kelley:

"Colonel Hoy, New Creek:
"Send messenger[9] and order Colonel Stevenson to fall back on New Creek by route indicated.
"B. F. Kelley, Brigadier General."

We have not forgotten the scenes enacted on that eventful day, July 4th, 1864. No barbecue at Greenland Gap on that day. Upon receipt of orders from General Kelley, we immediately repaired to our camp and began preparations for the evacuation of old Greenland Gap. Our personal effects were soon gathered up, packed and everything made in readiness for a hasty departure. Our quartermaster had just received a large quantity of supplies for future use, and being unable to remove them, they were destroyed by fire. By 12 o'clock, noon, the entire command was in motion.

Our destination was New Creek, and our route to that place just the opposite usually taken for that point. We marched out the road leading to Oakland and Altamont, until we came to the backbone of the Allegheny Mountains, thence along its crest until we reached the junction of the Romney, Moorefield, Burlington and New Creek roads.

In consequence of the continued scouting indulged in during the month of June, our boys were tired and footsore. The mountain road in many places was completely blockaded, which rendered our progress slow. We trudged along in the darkness of the night, the stillness broken only by the rumbling of the artillery and wagon train, the crack of the driver's whip and the clatter of horses' hoofs. In the meantime the long column had straggled to a considerable degree, and about midnight the command halted and our gallant Colonel Stevenson could be seen riding up and down the line speaking a kind word here and there and offering encouragement to the tired, weary and footsore soldier boys.

At the dawn of the day, we were again halted and the 2d Maryland mounted infantry was dispatched to the front to ascertain if the way was clear. We resumed our march, arriving at New Creek about 8 o'clock A.M., July 5th, having marched 32 miles. Here we learned the situation at Washington, Baltimore and Harrisburg was alarming in the extreme.

* * *

In the Shenandoah Valley, events before and during the holiday had been even more alarming and hazardous than those at Greenland Gap. Surprised and poorly commanded Federal outposts were knocked back, swept aside, or captured, and panic was in the air. At Martinsburg, the 160th Ohio found itself squarely in the middle of Early's advance.

Rev. Simeon Siegfried, captain, Co. E, 160th Ohio:

Towards the latter part of June it became apparent that the rebels intended an advance down the Valley. Hunter had been through Staunton on to Lynchburg, but worsted in his campaign returned, taking out the Kanawha Valley, leaving the way wide open for a rebel raid into Maryland and Pennsylvania.

We saw daily evidence of coming trouble on our picket posts, in the number and character of applicants for papers, in the impudence and assurance of rebel sympathizers, until the 28th of June, when a company of rebel cavalry dashed upon Duffield, a R.R. station some nine miles to the east of us. The enemy came on thicker and faster, until on the night of the first of July, the roar of Mulligan's[10] artillery tell us of skirmishing along the front.

Saturday morning, July 2d, the enemy enter Winchester and hold it in force. Saturday night the excitement runs high in Martinsburg. The promenade is thronged with excited citizens, and the shoulder-straps congregate in squads. Citizens of Union proclivities pack their valuables, merchants wish to secure their stock, the locomotives whistle with unusual frequency and vigor, the cars are loading, orderlies gallop from headquarters; everything looks like a "skedaddle."

Daylight of Sabbath morning, July 3rd, dawns upon our camp to find all astir. The Reveille has brought us up in obedience to last night's order to march. We cook a little breakfast, sup our coffee, and fall in line, and move out to the Winchester pike; half a mile out we form line of battle. The 160th, part of the 135th and 161st Ohio, a battalion of dismounted cavalry, and a battery of the [1]35th N.G. Artillery compose our force. Col. Reasoner is assigned the command, and is thus unexpectedly become a brigadier. We deploy a heavy line of skirmishers, take the most advantageous position we can, and with 80 rounds of cartridges, await the enemy's advance.

After five hours in this position, a courier arrives from Bunker Hill, eight miles this side of Winchester, and assures our commanders of the number and appointment of the enemy, and soon we are ordered to fall back to town. Gen. Sigel and his staff are mounted, Colonels, majors, etc., ditto, the wagon train moving off; we too fall in and move off out the Shepardstown road toward Harper's Ferry.

The enemy in force approaches from Winchester. Some of our forces have been captured at North Mountain,[11] and west of us on the R.R. Part of a train sent towards Williamsport has been captured and burned, and Mulligan is fighting the enemy at Leestown.[12] It looked a little as though the Johnnies had flanked us, north, south, east, west, but [we] will see. If Mulligan can drive them back where they assail him, we may get through to Harper's Ferry. We set out for that place with reinforcements.

Having traveled some two hours in extreme heat and through clouds of dust which sometimes obscured the file next to us, in which we marched, we halted in a shady wood to snatch a little rest and refresh ourselves with a draft from some bubbling spring. But we can't rest long. A company of rebel cavalry, seen through a valley a mile or more away, clash ahead on our right flank, and call us up for action, decided and vigorous. We form in line of battle across a large cornfield, deploy a line of skirmishers and scouts, plant our batteries, unfurl our Star Spangled Banner to the breeze defiant though retreating.

The rebels not liking appearances on our side of the woods, skedaddle so vigorously that even our sharpshooters can't get a shot at the last horse or rider. They're all gone—gone out of sight and hearing. A few shots were all they dared to venture before they bid us good bye. Had they remained we would have given them a reception that would have been worthy the occasion.

Nightfall finds us beyond Shepardstown (where we had many kindly greetings from Union citizens), and on the bank of the Potomac River. The wagon train is crossing and we must wait and secure it a safe crossing. We have no pontoon, and we must "take water," i.e., wade the river. We plunge in and march over in solid column, the current quite rapid, enveloping us to the lower portion of our blouses. We'll keep our powder dry. It was a scene we will always remember—that silent crossing of the Potomac on the night of July 3, 1864.

Crossing the Potomac the road lies immediately between the river and the canal, and is quite narrow. The bridge which crosses the canal is broken down. We lie down to rest till morning. Now we appreciate "the situation," the cavalry, wagon train, artillery, infantry are here altogether. Should the rebs gain the heights yonder, they could rake us terribly, and we could scarcely reply. But to our relief Mulligan commands the heights, and [is] holding them till the bridge is repaired; we cross in safety, forming a line of battle on an eminence commanding all outdoors. To our front and flank, the smoke of a hundred little fires tell of the coffee and soldiers' breakfast eaten. We are up and off again.

Arrived at Sharpsburg, we rest in the streets, being ordered to receive three days rations. But before the rations are issued, or even a knot of red tape untied in the way of requisition, the 160th Regiment is ordered on quick time to the heights in line of battle to protect our train from an attack of the enemy's cavalry, who are reported to be advancing upon them. We lay here an hour and a half, until the train is securely on its way down the Pleasant Valley road, and we are assigned to the rear to prevent the train from threatened attack.

We pass the stone bridge over Antietam creek, renowned in McClellan's battle as the place so violently held by General Burnside against the tremendous assaults of the evening. On the mountain to the left we can distinctly see the position occupied by McClellan's signal corps, and batteries, where he rained a shower of death upon the reeling columns of the rebels, which decided victory for the Union arms.[13]

About 3 o'clock P.M. of July 4, while resting by the roadside, John J. Steward of Co. E, this worthy young man, was killed by the accidental discharge of his gun. He died almost instantly. It was a sad calamity, and many a tearful eye turned from him, as the company and regiment to which he belonged filed by him on that dreadful march.

The regiment reached Maryland Heights about 9 o'clock at night. This mountain rises out of the Potomac on the east, is opposite Harper's Ferry, and is one of the strongest natural positions fortified as it is, in this or perhaps any other valley. It has four forts. Besides these a large 100-pound Parrott gun has a position on the top of the heights; garrisoned by 10,000 troops, and corresponding light artillery, perhaps ten times this number would find it extremely hazardous to attempt its reduction.

When we reached the Heights, Harper's Ferry was in the hands of the rebels. Our forces were burning the bridge which connected us with the village. We could see the rebs as we passed by to our destination; but no shots were exchanged, each party preferring to defer until the coming day the contest for the position. The mountain ascended to the forts and rifle pits, we lay down to rest. Some loose mules got up a stampede in the night which alarmed our brigade, which springing up in the darkness, one man from the 135th Ohio was killed by the discharge of a gun.

* * *

The alarm over the rebel invasion of Maryland spread slowly in Baltimore. A corporal recorded the events at Camp Bradford in his diary.

Samuel McCoy Bell, corporal, Co. D, 159th Ohio:

This is the ever memorable day of 1776, Independence Day. It is easily seen that it is held as a holy day by all business houses being shut up and our old beautiful banner waving in the breeze from so many windows. Shooting of firecrackers and firearms of all kinds over the city. At night a good display of fireworks.

Had a big dinner in the hospital with plenty of fair waiters about the table. Supper—O, my!—too poor to be appreciated even by a hungry stomach. Had to put a man in the guard house as using "Red Eye" too strong. Saw five deserters marched along with bracelets suited to kind.

Have had orders to march out to see the elephant. Do not know whether we will go or not. If we do, hope we may go with strong arms and brave hearts to meet the foe so long trampling on the rights of freedom. May God help to overthrow this wicked rebellion now having so long existed in this land. Western trains have not come in today on account of trouble on the railroad by insurgents.[14]

10 | Monocacy

Having swept the Federal forces from the Shenandoah Valley, General Jubal Early, West Point graduate (Class of 1837) and veteran of the Seminole and Mexican wars, was now poised to launch a Confederate invasion of the North for the third consecutive summer. The huge, unanswered question: What was his target?

Tall and sarcastic, irreligious and generous, "Old Jube" was a peacetime lawyer and politician whose reputation had risen steadily within the rebel army. With his II Corps, Early had slipped away from Lee's army near Richmond and marched almost unnoticed into the Shenandoah, where he had assumed command of the Army of the Valley. Thus reinforced, the rebels had expelled generals Hunter and Sigel from the valley. That left Early free to operate unseen behind the flanking mountains. Under Lee's orders, he now burst out of the Shenandoah.

Only one Union general, Lew Wallace, commanding the VIII Corps, Middle Department, sensed Early's flanking movement and its disastrous potential. Warned by the president of the Baltimore & Ohio that all the signs of rebel invasion were again present, Wallace began shifting troops forward. These included three companies of the 144th Ohio, which the rest of the regiment saw rolling past on the Baltimore & Ohio.

Tommy Shanks, private, Co. F, 144th Ohio:

Annapolis Junction
July 7th, 1864

We are still in camp here yet, but I don't know how long for there is quite an excitement here. The Rebs has got into Maryland. We got a telegraph dispatch on Sabbath night about 11 o'clock to have 3 days rations cooked so we might be ready to march at five minutes' warning. So we got all things ready to march on Monday morning, but we have not got any further orders yet. When we move we will go in the direction of Harper's Ferry for the Rebels is coming in there pretty strong. The report was that Harper's Ferry was taken but I think not. There is a report that they are going to destroy the Railroad betwixt Baltimore and Washington, and if that is true we will have to be on the lookout. This morning before we got out of bed someone said that our 3 Co. from Annapolis was come up.[1]

So we got out of bed and quick as we could and went up to the Junction and it was our Boys. They were coming to meet us. I was very glad to see them but we had to make short stories for the cars did not stop long. We saw all the boys that is in Company I. They are all well and in good spirits. George[2] is well and looks pretty well. I would have liked very well if our Co. had went with them. It does me good to have a good shake of an old Friend's hand and have a talk with them. Where they were going they did not know, but I think they are going in the direction of Harper's Ferry. They just had their guns and blankets. I think they will return in a few days for the news was favorable last night.

* * *

Samuel McClain was among those troops passing through Annapolis Junction. A former adventurer who had looked for gold and met his wife in California, McClain was now a 33-year-old farmer, father of four, and a drummer in Company I. In a long serial letter to his wife, Lucinda, he told her (with some confusion) of his latest adventure.[3]

Samuel McClain, musician, Co. I, 144th Ohio:

July 7

We left Camp Parole this morning at 2 o'clock. We arrived near Harper's Ferry at 12 o'clock. We are in battle line at this time awaiting the attack. The Rebs have not made their appearance yet.

I write this on my drum. We expect to lay on our arms tonight. I'll send this the first chance I get. I think the Rebs will not fight. I'll write soon again. When you write, add the words "Follow the Reg." Good bye.

July 8

4 o'clock. We can hear the battle. We can see them fighting at Harper's Ferry. Our men are driving the Rebs. We are 4 miles from the battlefield. If they come here we will give them the best we have in the shop. We are stationed in a small fort on the Baltimore & Ohio Railroad near Harper's Ferry.

We started after Johnny Rebs at midnight. We marched 14 miles before daylight. I am writing this while we are in battle line. I guess the Rebs are gone. We can't see them. We are at Fredricktown[4] now. We are all well. I write this on my knee. You need not be scared. We will be all right I think. I'll write as soon as I can.

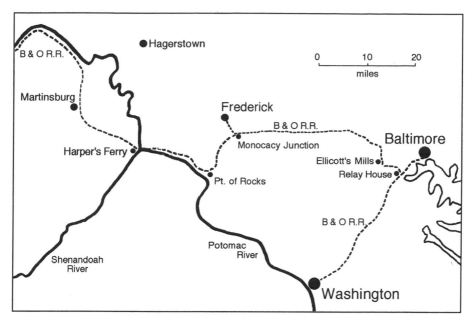

Baltimore-Frederick area

July 8

Ten o'clock. We are yet in line of battle. We are drawed up in a corn field. We are near Fredricktown in Maryland. I think the Rebs are on the retreat now. I will send this as soon as I can, for I expect you are anxious to hear from me.

3 o'clock. We were in battle line all day until 3 o'clock. Then we were ordered to fall back. The Rebs are afraid to give us battle. We could see them all the time. We are going after them now. I don't know as we will catch them or not. I am writing a little every chance I can get. I'll mail this as soon as I can. The communication is cut off now. We can't send a letter. Good bye to-night.

* * *

Lew Wallace had left his VIII Corps headquarters in Baltimore early on July 5th to investigate the reported rebel movements. An Indiana attorney in peacetime, he was now a romantic, charismatic, controversial soldier. Early military success at Fort Donelson was tarnished at Shiloh, where his division had been late in reaching the field; he would win enduring literary fame, however, nearly twenty years from now as the author of Ben-Hur: A Tale of the Christ.

Wallace's command was a paper corps, an occupation force whose few regiments (including hundred-days men) were scattered across Maryland.[5] On reaching Monocacy Junction on the railway near Frederick, without orders or approval from Washington, Wallace had begun assembling a makeshift force to meet Early's advance. Briefly euphoric after what he termed "the best little battle of the war" on July 7th, he soon realized that the real and unprecedented crisis still lay ahead of him. From a private's viewpoint, drummer McClain had no way of knowing that his general could no longer defend Frederick. Wallace withdrew to stronger defensive positions along the Monocacy River outside the city.[6]

On the morning of July 9th, commanding a handful of Ohio hundred-days men and Maryland home guards (under Brigadier-General Erastus B. Tyler),[7] and newly reinforced by regiments of Brigadier-General James B. Ricketts's veteran VI Corps division,[8] Wallace waited for Jubal Early's tough little Army of the Valley.

On the Federal left stood Ricketts's veterans, who would bear the brunt of the attack; on the right were the Ohio hundred-days men under Colonel Allison L. Brown, manning a stone bridge over the Monocacy and protecting Wallace's line of retreat. In the center stood an iron railroad bridge and a wooden covered bridge. Although heavily outnumbered, Wallace was determined to delay Early as long as possible. For this imaginative general, the possibility of a rebel army falling upon Washington was almost too horrible to contemplate.[9]

We continue with excerpts from Wallace's vivid report, which provides context for the battle and the hundred-days troops' vital supporting role in it.

Lew Wallace, major-general, U.S. Volunteers, commanding VIII Corps, Middle Department:

About eight A.M., the enemy marched by the pike from Frederick, and threw out skirmishers, behind whom he put his guns in position, and began the engagement. His columns followed a little after nine o'clock. Passing through the fields, just out of range of my pieces, without attempting to drive in my skirmishers, they moved rapidly around to the left, and forced a passage of the river at a ford about one mile below Ricketts. From nine o'clock to 10:30 the action was little more than a warm skirmish and experimental cannonading, in which, however, the enemy's superiority in the number and caliber of his guns was fully shown. Against my six three-inch rifles he opposed not less than sixteen Napoleons. In this time, also, the fighting at the stone bridge assumed serious proportions.

Colonel Brown held his position with great difficulty.[10]

About 10:30 o'clock the enemy's first line of battle made its appearance,

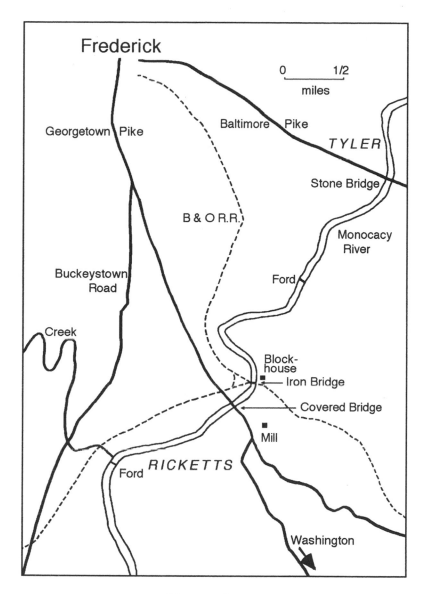

Monocacy Junction

and moved against Ricketts, who meantime, had changed front to the left so that his right rested upon the riverbank. This change unavoidably subjected his regiments to unintermitted enfilading fire from the batteries across the stream. So great was the rebel front, also, that I was compelled to order the whole division into one line, thus leaving it without reserves. Still the enemy's front was greatest. Two more guns were sent to Ricketts. Finally, by burning the wooden bridge and the blockhouse at its further end,[11] thus releasing the force left to defend them, I put into the engagement every available man, except Tyler's reserves, which, from the messages arriving, I expected momentarily to have to dispatch to Colonel Brown's assistance.

The enemy's first line was badly defeated.[12] His second line then advanced and was repulsed, but after a fierce and continuous struggle. In the time this occupied I could probably have retired without much trouble, as the rebels were badly punished. The main objects of the battle, however, were unaccomplished—the rebel strength was not yet developed. At one o'clock the three reinforcing regiments of veterans[13] would be on the ground; and then the splendid behavior of Ricketts and his men inspired me with confidence.

One o'clock came, but not the reinforcements; and it was impossible to get an order to them. My telegraph operator, and the railroad agent, with both his trains, had run away.[14] An hour and a half later I saw the third line of rebels move out of the woods, and down the hill behind which they made their formation; right after it came the fourth. It was time to get away. Accordingly, I ordered General Ricketts to make preparations and retire to the Baltimore pike. About four o'clock he began the execution of the order.

The stone bridge held by Colonel Brown now became all important; its loss was the loss of my line of retreat, and I had reason to believe that the enemy, successful on my left, would redouble his efforts against the right. General Tyler had already marched with his reserves to Brown's assistance, but on receipt of notice of my intention, without waiting for [Maryland colonels] Gilpin and Landstreet, he galloped to the bridge and took command in person. After the disengagement of Ricketts' line, when the head of the retreating column reached the pike, I rode to the bridge, and ordered it to be held at all hazards by the force then there, until the enemy should be found in its rear, at least until the last regiment had cleared the country road by which the retreat was being effected. This order General Tyler obeyed.[15]

A little after five o'clock, when my column was well on the march towards New Market, an attack on his rear convinced him of the impracticability of longer maintaining his post. Many of his men then took to the woods, but by his direction the greater part kept their ranks, and manfully fought their way through. In this way Colonel Brown escaped.[16] General Tyler, finding himself cut off, dashed into the woods, with the officers of his staff, and was happily saved.[17] His gallantry and self-sacrificing devotion are above all commendation of words.

The enemy seemed to have stopped pursuit at the stone bridge. The three regiments in Monrovia[18] joined me at New Market and afterwards served a good purpose in covering the march of the weary column, which bivouacked for the night about 12 miles from the battlefield. It would be a difficult task to say too much in praise of the veterans who made this fight. For their reputation and for the truth's sake, I wish it distinctly understood that, though the appearance of the enemy's fourth line of battle made their ultimate defeat certain, they were not whipped; on the contrary, they were fighting steadily in unbroken front when I ordered their retirement, all the shame of which, if shame there be, is mine, not theirs.

The nine [veteran] regiments enumerated as those participating in the action represented but 3,350 men, of whom over 1,600 were missing three days after, killed, wounded, or prisoners—lost on the field. The fact speaks for itself. Monocacy on their flags cannot be a word of dishonor.

It is now well assured that General Early attacked me with one whole corps, not less than 18,000 strong, while Breckinridge, with two divisions, remained during the battle in quiet occupancy of Frederick City.[19] It is also certain, as one of the results, that notwithstanding the disparity of forces, the enemy was not able to move from the battlefield, in prosecution of his march upon Washington, until the next day about noon.

As to the casualties, I regret that the speedy movement of some regiments of General Tyler's brigade made it impossible for him to perfect his report as he himself desired. The aggregate shows a heavy loss, illustrating the obstinate valor of the command.[20] I am satisfied, however, that the casualties of the rebels exceeded mine. To reach this conclusion one has only to make a calculation based upon the fact that the day after the battle over 400 men, too seriously wounded to be carried away, were captured in the hospital at Frederick City.

Orders have been given to collect the bodies of our dead in one burial ground on the battlefield, suitable for a monument upon which I propose to write, "These men died to save the National Capital, and they did save it."[21]

* * *

The man Wallace entrusted with protecting his line of retreat was a 29-year-old farmer and veteran. "Ally" Brown had earlier served as a sergeant in the 73rd Ohio, then as a captain in the 89th before resigning due to ill health. Now he was the colonel of the 149th Ohio.[22] Brown's older brother, Austin, was the 149th's quartermaster sergeant.

Allison L. Brown, colonel, 149th Ohio:

I reported that part of my regiment that remained under my command, consisting of Companies B, E, I, and K, to Brigadier-General Tyler at Monocacy Junction, at 3:30 P.M. July 7, 1864. I here found Companies C, D, and G of my regiment, which had been on duty at Annapolis, Md.; Companies B, I, and G of the 144th Regiment Ohio National Guard were, by order of Major-General

Wallace, commanding, attached to my command, amounting in aggregate strength to 660 men.

On the evening of that day, by order of Brigadier-General Tyler, my command was sent forward to take post at Frederick, which it did at daylight on Friday morning, 8th. I remained in position at Frederick during the day; [I] threw out skirmishers to watch the enemy, who were in force in my front a considerable portion of the time.

At 4 P.M. on the 8th instant, [I] received orders from the general commanding to withdraw my men and fall back on the Baltimore pike toward Monocacy bridge, which I did. Before arriving at the bridge, I was ordered by Brigadier-General Tyler to assume command of the 11th Regiment Maryland Volunteers and my own regiment, to move my command across the river to Monocacy and take position at that point. Soon after I had taken post at this point, an order came from Major-General Wallace to the colonel commanding the 11th Maryland Volunteers to take his regiment and the detachment of the 144th Ohio National Guard under my command and report to General Tyler at Monocacy Junction without delay, leaving me the seven companies of my own regiment with which to hold the position.

I posted my command in such a manner as in my judgment to most effectually hold the bridge and guard against a surprise, either in front or on my flank. From information gained from sources I considered reliable, I had reason to think the enemy would attempt to cross the river at a ford about one mile above the Monocacy bridge. I therefore posted one of my companies at that point with orders to hold it at all hazards. There was no alarm on my lines during the night.

At daylight on the 9th, I caused my skirmish line to be deployed on the crest of the ridge on the Frederick side of the river, and made every preparation in my power to hold the position as ordered. The enemy made his appearance at 6 A.M. and threw out his skirmishers, who soon became engaged with my men.

About 10 A.M., I discovered from a point overlooking the field the rebel cavalry making disposition to turn my right and cross the river at the ford before alluded to. I sent Company E, Captain Jenkins, to reinforce Captain McGinnis,[23] who held the ford; also a company of mounted infantry,[24] commanded by Captain Lieb, U.S. Army. The enemy were handsomely repulsed in the attempt to cross the river at the upper ford, and withdrew his forces, leaving only a light skirmish line.

I now discovered that an effort was being made to attack my left in force. I sent immediately for reinforcements. Companies B, I, and G, 144th Ohio National Guard, were sent to my relief. I had sent five men of the mounted infantry force to my left, to watch the movements of the enemy and report immediately should he make any demonstration in that quarter. These men I heard nothing of until some hours afterward, having been fired on and re-treated, leaving me without information as to the effort that was making against my left. As it was extremely uncertain at what particular point he would make the demonstration, I was compelled to keep three companies in reserve at the bridge in order to be prepared to meet him at any point he might choose.

About 11:30 A.M., the attack came; a heavy force of infantry had been deployed on the extension of my line of skirmishers and marched by the flank to within range of my extreme left. All this had been done under cover of the ground, which at that point was very favorable to the enemy for that purpose. The superiority of his numbers enabled him to push back my left and take position so as to enfilade my line.

In order to dislodge the enemy from this position and restore my line, it was necessary to have recourse to the bayonet, which in this instance proved very effective. I ordered Company B, 149th, to charge the enemy's position, which it did, but was repulsed. I then took Companies B, I, and G, 144th, reinforced, drove the rebels from their position and re-established my lines. During this charge my loss was quite severe, owing to the fact that the enemy was posted behind the fence, while my men were compelled to charge across an open field, up the hill in fair view, and within short range of his guns. We took 2 prisoners, and the enemy left 2 dead on the field.

I now extended my line so as to command this position, which I held throughout the day, until my force was withdrawn. Between 4 and 5 P.M., I received an order from Major-General Wallace to hold the bridge over the Monocacy at that point to the last extremity, and when I was pressed so hard that nothing more could be done, to command my men to disperse and to take care of themselves. At this time the firing had ceased at the Monocacy Junc-tion, and being satisfied that the enemy would make a desperate effort to ob-tain possession of the bridge, and thus cut off my retreat as well as gain the rear of the army, I made such disposition of the forces under my command as I thought would enable me to hold out as long as possible.

I contracted my skirmish line, thus strengthening my center, and covered all the commanding points I could with my forces. I ordered the officer in command of the cavalry to take such position with his men as would protect my left flank on the east side of the river and prevent the enemy from get-ting possession of my rear. Immediately after this, and about 6 P.M., a heavy attack was made along my entire front, and at the same time my left flank was turned. I now discovered that the enemy had gained a position in the woods, on the east side of the river in my rear, and was preparing to take possession of the bridge, thus cutting off my retreat entirely.

My command in front was withdrawn in confusion, owing to the extent of my lines and the knowledge that the enemy had gained possession of the woods in the rear and was attempting to cut off retreat. I attempted to rally my men, who were well disposed to obey orders under the circumstances, when the enemy brought his artillery to bear on the bridge and threw several shells, one of which struck it while my men were crossing it. I rallied a portion of the men in the orchard overlooking the bridge, and fired several rounds at the enemy, who were pressing from the west side, and also those in the woods and wheat field south of my position. This checked the pursuit, and enabled the main part of the command to gain the road on the hill. The enemy now opened fire on my flank from his skirmishers on the east side of the river, which added to the confusion. This fire was returned by a portion of the men stationed in the orchard, and the enemy's progress was checked.

The men now learned from citizens that the main body of the army had moved out some two hours before, and this, with the increasing fire of the enemy on my flank, produced considerable confusion, during which the men broke and threw away their guns and accouterments and attempted to save themselves. This information received, and that they were surrounded and would be made prisoners, caused them to break their guns to prevent them falling into the enemy's hands. I succeeded however, in bringing off about 300 of my command, with which I joined the main body at New Market about 8 P.M.

I feel justly proud of the manner in which the men conducted themselves during this first engagement, holding, as they did, an extended skirmish line for 12 hours in the face of vastly superior numbers of experienced troops. They exhibited a coolness and determination which gives promise of great usefulness in the service of the country.

I am unable to give the losses sustained by my command, on account of my surgeon being captured. Many of the missing will doubtless rejoin the regiment, and a greater portion of the wounds received are but slight. Up to the time of retreat I had six killed and 14 severely wounded, besides a number slightly wounded.[25]

As to the conduct of the officers—field, staff, and line—on that day, where so many did well, it is invidious to particularize. I cannot, however, close my report without referring to a few whose duties required them to expose themselves to more danger than others. Maj. E. Rozell,[26] who had command of the left wing for several hours, deserves particular mention. The aid rendered by my adjutant, T. Q. Hildebrant, in conveying my orders and cheering and encouraging the men, deserves grateful mention. He did his duty well.

I regret to say that Surgeon W. A. Brown, who throughout the entire day was at his post, attending promptly to the wounded, was left behind on the retreat and became a prisoner. He nobly refused to abandon his wounded men, and thus displayed a heroism worthy of emulation.[27]

* * *

The mounted hundred-days men were led not by their own officer, but by a cavalry regular.

Edward H. Lieb, captain, Fifth U.S. Cavalry, commanding a detachment of the 159th Ohio:

I left with my command of mounted infantry[28] on the sixth instant for Monocacy Junction. I arrived and reported to General Tyler, who immediately ordered me to move to the front and report to Colonel Gilpin, of the Third Potomac Home Brigade. I reported to him and was ordered to support Alexander's battery of artillery. About 12 o'clock at night, I was again ordered to move to the Monocacy pike bridge and hold it.

On the eighth, I was ordered again to the front with my command, to report to Lieutenant-Colonel Clendenin of the Eighth Illinois cavalry. He ordered me to move to the extreme front and turn out my men, which I did. I remained in position all day; at dusk I was relieved by a regiment of the Sixth corps, with orders to feed my horses and procure rations for my men.

I met General Tyler in the road, who ordered me to move out in the Buckeystown road and feel the enemy. I moved out about five miles, and was moving on when I was ordered back to Frederick. I arrived there about 12 o'clock at night and, in conjunction with the Eighth Illinois cavalry, brought up the rear guard to the Monocacy junction. From there, [on the ninth] I was ordered to move up the Monocacy River one mile to the Baltimore pike bridge to a ford and hold it. I was also requested to assist the colonel of the 149th Ohio (100 days' men) to hold the bridge.

I arrived at the ford and drove the rebels off, placed my men in position, and then returned to assist the colonel to hold his position, which, at that time, was being hard pressed. The rebels made a charge on the left of the line, and drove the left in, within 100 yards of the bridge. I immediately rode up and rallied the men, and drove the enemy back, captured some prisoners, and retook the old ground. I then assisted Colonel Brown to establish the line, and he threw his whole force over.

The position was a very good one; the enemy tried hard to take it, but at every point were driven back. My men on the extreme left held their position, and were not troubled by the enemy. I relieved all my mounted men and placed a company of the 149th Ohio in their old position; [I] took my command to the bridge for the purpose of holding it until our forces fell back on the Baltimore pike.

General Tyler requested me to draw the 149th Ohio over the Monocacy bridge, as soon as possible. I reported the intention of the general to Colonel Brown, and started to carry out the order. The men commenced moving to the bridge, and were crossing, [when] the enemy arrived in force on the opposite side and attacked our men on the left flank. I pushed all the men over I could, and when I started to cross I found the rebels in strong force in my front, and when I started to move to the rear [I] found it impossible to move in that direction.

The rebels were coming in rear and on all flanks. The way open was up the river, and I started in that direction. The rebels closing in in all directions, I could not strike the ford, and was compelled to ride my horse down a very steep bluff into the river. I crossed the river and directed the officer commanding a company of the 149th Ohio in what direction to move. He commenced moving before I left.

I started to the point where I had left my men to cover my crossing over the bridge, but found all had gone, and the rebels in possession of the ground.[29] I met a few men of the Eighth Illinois cavalry, and took to the woods. At twelve o'clock at night I arrived on the Baltimore pike, two miles this side of New Market, and found that the enemy had not been on the road further than New Market. I brought up the rear guard with eight men to one mile on the other side of Ridgeville, and there met my command.

I reported to Lieutenant-Colonel Clendenin for orders. He ordered me to act in conjunction with himself in bringing up the rear of our forces. I must here state that Captain Allen, of the 159th Ohio Mounted Infantry, repelled the rebel cavalry, killing six and wounding quite a number. The enemy did not follow after he drove them back.

At Ellicott's Mills I threw out pickets and remained under General Ricketts' orders. I sent out small parties to scout the country to the right, rear, and left, and drove the rebel cavalry back on the different roads. I sent Captain Allen out on the Elysville road six miles. He came up in the rear of a few rebel cavalrymen, killed two, and wounded the officers in command. All that could be found on my flank were a few rebel cavalry.

On Monday evening, the eleventh, I was ordered to bring up the rear of General Ricketts' division, and move to Baltimore on the pike. I arrived in the city about seven o'clock in the evening, immediately reported to the commanding officer for orders, and was ordered to go into Camp Carroll, and rest my men and horses.

I arrived in the city with 66 men. I [had] left with 98 privates and two officers. Since that time all had returned except ten; a few of my horses were shot, and I could not bring them off the field with me.

I am pleased to state that Captain Allen did all in his power to assist me in carrying out my orders. All the orders I gave he promptly carried out, and to my entire satisfaction. I am pleased to state that the mounted men under my command did well, more than I expected from men that have been in the service so short a time and not used to riding. The whole time I was absent, I could not find time to procure forage for my horses and rations for my men. Not a man complained; all stood the hard marches like faithful soldiers, and in battle I cannot find fault with one of my men; all did well.

* * *

One of the last men off the field sent a letter to his sister in Chillicothe two days following the battle.

John Earl, private, Co. E, 149th Ohio:

General Wallace sent word to Col. Brown to hold the Bridge at all hazards, which we did until an hour and a half after the left [flank] had retreated. When we commenced falling back, Company E covered the retreat. We had not got to the river when the rebs had crossed the [railroad] bridge and got on our flank and rear, firing on us in every direction. We held them for a few minutes until most of the regiment had crossed the bridge and passed us, and when we started on the double quick, the rebs still pouring it into us from every point. The Adjutant told us that if it had not been for Company E, the whole regiment would have been lost. As it was many were captured. Our company did not lose any killed that we know of. We are 21 men short, most of whom are captured.[30]

In the retreat I was in the rear. When the reb crew charged on us we broke for a wheat field, where I laid till dark, when I started for Baltimore. I overtook the army next morning, but did not see any of our boys until we arrived at Ellicott's Mills, when we found them on the cars.

* * *

In Baltimore, where its Union supporters were as alarmed by Early's raid as its Southern sympathizers were heartened, the 131st Ohio first saw the movement toward the shaping battle, then its aftermath.[31]

Henry H. Vail, sergeant, Co. C, 131st Ohio:

At sunrise on the morning of July 8th, we saw a great fleet of vessels anchored in the harbor below the fort, and we saluted it with the proper number of guns. It was a part of the Sixth Army Corps that was sent to aid Gen. Wallace in checking the movement of General Early toward either Baltimore or Washington. The troops and supplies brought up by these boats were landed and sent to Monocacy and some of them arrived in time to take part in the battle.

The Union army was driven back toward Baltimore, and for two days and nights the streets in sight of our fort were filled with army wagons and droves of cattle guarded by cavalry.

Stragglers from the field of battle found their way into our fort, having the smear of gunpowder still on their faces. From one of these runaway heroes we learned that one regiment of the "Hundred Years' Men" held a place in the Union line, in the battle of Monocacy, and as they received no order to retreat, nearly the whole regiment became prisoners of war. They were in Confederate prisons long after their term of service expired. Our informer said, "The damned fools didn't know enough to run."[32]

* * *

But the three companies of the 144th Ohio knew enough to run—and did—when the battle was lost and they were ordered to retreat. Here drummer McClain continues his dramatic July 9th letter to his wife.

Samuel McClain, musician, Co. I, 144th Ohio:

We marched to [the] Junction, got there at midnight. We lay on our arms all night. We are attacked this morning. The battle is going on while I am writing this. The shells are flying all around us. It's a very severe engagement.

2 o'clock. The battle is raging fiercely.

4 o'clock. The Rebs are driving our men, oh my God we have to retreat. We are striking for Baltimore. Our men are getting cut all to pieces. The artillery have left. I must go. Every man must save themselves. We have 45 miles to retreat. The Rebs are following us, throwing shells.

July 11.

We have arrived in Baltimore, or a part of us. We have retreated 45 miles. We marched all night & until 2 o'clock the next day. We have had a hard march. My feet are all raw. There are a great many of our men missing yet. Some are wounded and some are taken prisoners and some missing. We are expecting some more in every moment. Our Capt. McKee[33] is slightly wounded in the thigh. Wm. Barton[34] is wounded in the leg. They are in Baltimore Hospital. We have had a hard time. We don't know where we will be ordered to go yet. I will write as soon again as I can. You must excuse this short letter. The boys are still coming in. Fin Barton[35] is all right. I am well, all but sore feet. My feet are all raw.

There are none of our boys killed, but some are taken prisoner. You bet I had to git to save my bacon. I saw the battle. I was in [it] full all the time. I [saw] the elephant tail. The Rebs had four to our one. The battle was fought at Monoply [*sic*] Junction. We had to throw all our baggage away & guns. I stuck to my drum and grub. We got no sleep for three nights. I will write until we have to start, then I'll put this in the office. Just as soon as we get to our destination I'll write again and give the particulars.

* * *

As McClain, Vail, and others point out, many retreating Federals weren't lucky enough to reach Baltimore.

William R. Browning, private, Co. I, 149th Ohio:

I was captured July 9th, 1864, at the battle of Monocacy, after fighting from early morn until 4:30 P.M., when, being hard pressed and nearly surrounded by the enemy, we received orders for every man to save himself.

This order scattered our organization, and we broke for the rear. The rebels were fast closing in on us, leaving only one road open for our retreat. I took that route to escape and went through all right, but many of the boys were captured before getting through. I followed the main body of the troops who were in full retreat toward Baltimore.

I will not go into detail in regard to the capture of Philip Frank[36] of my company and myself by a body of rebel cavalry, but will relate one incident. The cavalry who had captured us met the infantry, who demanded of them that they turn over the prisoners to them because they had done all of the fighting and were entitled to take charge of the prisoners. A fierce quarrel arose; they drew guns on each other, and a fight was about to take place when a cavalry officer rode up, ordered the infantry to march on and the cavalry to take us to the rear.

After marching a short distance, they halted us and said that they would have to give us up soon, and that we would be searched when they turned us over. As they had captured us, we were their prisoners and it was their first search. They began and took away what we had that they wanted—combs, knives and some silver money that I happened to have—but they did not get rich, for we did not have much for them to get.

We marched back to Frederick City and were halted in the main street, where we were turned over to the infantry. While there, some of the loyal ladies of the town came with a basket of food and gave some to us. It tasted very good, as I had only two hardtack and a pint of coffee that day. They would not give our guard any of it, so they became angry and drove them away.

While here, more prisoners were brought in and we marched through the town, and went into camp for the night in a field outside the limits. The next morning we marched back through the town and on about four miles to Monocacy Junction. At the junction we were joined by 500 prisoners who had been captured and brought there the night before. These men had drawn two days' rations from the rebels, but we did not get anything. However, there was no help for it.

We started on the Rockville road toward Washington, passing through part of the field of battle of the day before. The dead and the wounded were still lying on the ground where they had fallen. Some of the wounded were lying by the roadside and begged us piteously for water. My canteen was filled with water, and I stepped out of ranks to give the poor fellows a drink.

A rebel guard drew his gun on me and swore he would shoot if I did not get back into line. I told him I only wanted to give the wounded men a drink. He said, "Let some of the Yankee citizens round here give them water." At that, I took off my canteen and threw it over to the wounded men. My guard at that said I was a fool and that I would "need a canteen before I got one." This was true, for I never had another but often needed one.

We marched on to Rockville, where dead horses were lying in the street. There had just been a fight here. We went into an orchard surrounding a house and got water from the well. A lady came out and said, "If any of you boys want to write home, I will mail your letters for you. The rebels will soon retreat, and then I will send the letters." W. W. McCracken[37] wrote a letter telling our folks at home all the particulars of our capture. He left the letter with the lady, and it reached its destination.

I told her I had no rations and that I was very hungry and wanted something to eat. She gave me a big slice of homemade bread and butter. I will never forget that loyal lady, and have often wished that I could go to Rockville to repay the kindness done to a poor boy, only 15 years old and a prisoner of war. We were then taken out to another road on our way toward Washington, and camped in a field for the night.[38]

11 | Fort Stevens

*A*FTER THE FIGHT *at Monocacy Junction, Jubal Early's tough but bloodied veterans hadn't the strength to pursue Wallace's defeated Federals. Instead, the army paused, then marched the next day toward the capital.*

Washington that summer of 1864 had the appearance of being heavily defended.[1] A fortified perimeter some 37 miles long ringed the capital with 53 forts and 22 batteries, including several hundred guns and mortars. These should have been manned by at least 35,000 men. But this was an illusion, as most of the trained men had been shifted to Grant and the Army of the Potomac. Washington, as Wallace knew, "seriously menaced, was incapable of self-defense."[2]

A U.S. artillery lieutenant later recalled that by May "so many troops had been withdrawn and called to the field that the dismounted batteries and 'veteran reserves,' or 'invalid corps,' constituted about all of the old soldiers on duty there, whilst the addition of hundred days men and other troops brought up the total strength to about 13,000 men, less than 4,000 of whom were on the north side of the lines."[3]

As the danger posed by Early's army became horrifyingly clear and the capital came close to panic, experienced VI and XIX Corps troops were ordered up to reinforce it.[4] But as a motley collection of hundred-days men, militia, invalids, and government workers manned the defenses, none really knew whether the veterans could arrive in time.

Waiting anxiously at Fort Stevens on the capital's far northern outskirts were the soldier-students of Company K and Oberlin College.

James H. Laird, orderly sergeant, Co. K, 150th Ohio:

A common soldier is expected to know little more than he sees, so our first intimations that we were likely to have a chance to fight came from the passing of cavalry scouts northward July 9. Singularly enough, some of these cavalrymen were led by General A. B. Nettleton,[5] afterward an assistant secretary of the treasury, who had once been orderly sergeant of Company K.

Sunday, the 10th, about noon, the Black Horse Cavalry escort of the President dashed up to our postern. Lincoln hastily left his barouche, entered the fort, and passing from gun to gun, looked out upon the field it covered. In his long, yellowish linen coat and unbrushed high hat, he looked like a care-worn farmer in time of peril from drought and famine.

Company K was put in line to salute him as he passed out. His hat was drawn down upon his ear in recognition, but he was too anxious to smile at the men.

In the evening of that hot Sunday we took it kindly to be moved from our board-bottomed bunks in the barracks to bed on the grass in the fort.

When the morning of Monday, the 11th, dawned bright and hot, we in the fort seemed to be "waiting 'round" until 10 o'clock; then came the excitement of battle. The commandant of the fort, standing on the lookout, called loudly, "Charge the guns!" Pointing up the turnpike, he added, "See that cloud of dust. The enemy will be down upon us in half an hour."

There was a scurrying to the magazines, with a confusion of calls: "I want shell;" "24-pound;" "30-pound;" "I want solid shot," etc.

This was the hour when the Confederate general, Jubal Early, disclosed a force on the 7th Street road near the Lay or Carberry house, quite within the range of our guns. This was, as we learned, Rodes'[6] division of infantry, flanked by cavalry. Early, it is said, rode in the front, saw the fort, and ordered Rodes to advance and take it.[7] When the guns were charged, we had time to see our pickets in the distance firing and falling back. For some of us, this was the first powder we had seen burned in battle.

Wagons loaded with house furniture, chicken coops and excited women were coming within the lines. Some of our boys with torches stood beside the houses near the fort, to burn them in case of the enemy's near approach. Some of our picket men came into the defenses and were assigned places at guns, but they were not all there.

There had been talk among us about a chance to go to the front, but now the front had come to us. We were conscious that our defense was inadequate.[8] We knew little of the reinforcements that were centering in upon us. We did not know that Wright and Emory[9] were near at hand with their tried veterans. Like Elisha's frightened servant, our surprised eyes were soon opened to see men filling the breastworks that united the forts and forming for advances upon the rebels.

Word came from the skirmish line that ammunition was needed. An old buggy was loaded. Four men were to push it down the pike past the old tollgate house. This was exposure to which few men in that action were called. With sad apprehension I read off the detail, "Morgan, Todd, Van Antwerp," and another who cannot be recalled. George K. Nash, late governor of Ohio for two terms, told me not long since that he drew a big breath of relief when I stopped reading, for the next name was his. The boys came back unscratched, but that buggy was riddled, bed and spokes.

* * *

Another member of the Oberlin company remembers the tumultuous events at Fort Stevens.

James C. Cannon, private, Co. K, 150th Ohio:

Rumors of the advance of Early to Harper's Ferry, and of his march toward Baltimore, caused some excitement, and the guards were all ordered to be vigilant, for the enemy was possibly making for Washington. Saturday, July 9, Corporal Ryder[10] took out another picket detail, and on the 10th Lieutenant-Colonel Frazee ordered all picket posts to keep extra watch all night.

The cavalry scouts reported Early's men coming in on the Rockville road, but they were later seen to turn eastward with the evident intention of reaching Seventh Street.

Sergt. Fackler[11] had made picket headquarters at the Blair Place out on Seventh Street, also known as Silver Spring, and placed Corporal J. F. Hudson at Chestnut Tree Post with three men; on the post between were Geo. R. Morgan and Dick Holland. He also posted a vidette[12] of three men, Bedient, Chidester and Beech,[13] on a hill about a mile further out on Seventh Street. At the fort, the men were all stationed and kept in readiness to take their places at the guns at a moment's notice.

President Lincoln, with some members of his cabinet and military officers of high rank, visited the fort and received the reports of the enemy's approach with evident anxiety. Very late Sunday night, the 25th New York Cavalry arrived and camped in rear of the fort.

Sunday night was a very lively time out on the Seventh Street road. A stream of fugitives poured in along the road all night, and the men at the vidette post were expecting every moment to receive the fire of the enemy's skirmishers. By morning, Bedient had three prisoners.[14] Corporal Ryder and his men were relieved at 8 o'clock Monday, 11th, and went back to the fort, where after a few moments' rest they were put on duty at the guns.

At Silver Spring, the picket had finished their breakfast when a cavalry officer with his command came down the road on a run, and told Sergt. Fackler that the enemy's cavalry were coming on fast and that his vidette on the hill refused to come in without orders.

The sergeant started at once to order them to retire, but when he came in sight of the post he saw the men just climbing a fence and disappearing in a cornfield. A moment later, a gray and dusty cavalryman appeared on the hill and opened fire on the fugitives. Sergt. Fackler fired at the cavalrymen, then turned and ran back to the post with bullets whizzing over his head, and ordered a retreat to the fort.

At the next post eastward, Morgan and Holland were fired upon, but escaped into the brush, from which Morgan, looking out, soon saw a greycoat mount a fence and look around. He at once drew his rifle and fired at the rash skirmisher, then retreated to the fort. After the battle, Morgan went to that spot and found the rebel's body just where he dropped from the fence.

* * *

At the "Chestnut Tree Post" near Seventh Street, a young corporal and three privates[15] had listened anxiously to the approaching skirmishing. They had nonetheless obeyed their orders to stay at the post until attacked.

James F. Hudson, corporal, Co. K, 150th Ohio:

Between eleven and twelve o'clock, the day being hot, Leach asked if he could go back to the house and get fresh water for our canteens. I authorized that, and he started out. A few moments later, becoming somewhat uneasy by the fact that the sound of the skirmishing seemed to be getting to our left rear, I went through the scrub growth to see if I could discover the state of affairs.

Getting through to where I could see the open ground, I discovered that the rebel skirmish line had gone in along the Seventh Street road until it was one third nearer the fort than we were. I saw that its advance, if continued, would cut us off from the fort. I was a good deal disturbed by this, but as I started back toward the post, reflected that if we were cut off by that road we could fall back toward Fort Slemmer.[16]

Just then I heard an outcry from the road down which Leach had gone for water. Running out to the road, I met the other men there, and then running down the road we found Leach shot through the thigh and bowels. Down across the fields at a considerable distance were the rebel skirmishers leisurely advancing, not directly towards us, but towards the fort. As they had fired across at Leach and hit him, it did not seem safe to stay there with a wounded man.

The cavalrymen, or one of them, was still with us. I asked him if he would take Leach on his horse in by the road to Fort Slemmer, which was clear, and he said he would if Leach could ride. Leach was very certain that he could ride. So we put him on the horse, and started them, first going out to the front away from the fort, and then by a circuit to the right, getting back to Fort Slemmer where Leach died the next day.[17]

After getting him cared for, we looked across to the rebel skirmishers and saw some of them advancing toward the house on our left rear, where another cavalryman was giving them a lively fusillade with a revolving carbine. We got down behind a pile of rails, three of us, and gave the rebels a volley with our Enfields, the only effect of which seemed to be to turn a line of skirmishers in our direction.

At this we got back into the scrub growth in our rear, and coming to a fence, I concluded that I would stand on top of it, where I could see over the short trees and reconnoiter. When I got up I looked across to the road where we had just been and there about 200 feet away or less was a group of half a dozen rebel skirmishers. I have often thought since then that those rebels must have thought it was too bad to kill an innocent youth who would get up on a fence within point-blank range of them, and for that reason they hesitated a moment.

About the time that they made up their minds that I must be disposed of it seemed to me that I had better get down off that fence, and I dropped with the bullets whistling around me, one of them scoring the lock of my rifle, and if my recollection of the way I held the gun is correct, its glancing on my rifle prevented my being shot through the chest.

When I picked myself up from my rapid drop from the fence, I heard my late companions charging for the rear through the bushes, and as I followed them I reflected that though they had not been ordered to take direction to the rear their movement was entirely justified by the circumstances. I got back into the rifle pits of the fort just about the time that Early's first line tried to rush the fort, in the hope that it was so weakly held that they could take it, and so open the way for his main force to get into Washington.

* * *

With the capital threatened, Fort Stevens was suddenly overrun with worried brass and government figures.[18] *After the pickets were driven in, several men in Company K saw Abraham Lincoln standing on the parapet under fire. This astonishing event quickly became legend. More than six decades later, at age 91, Corporal Elihu C. Barnard still recalled seeing him step out of a closed carriage and "stand at one point of the works on the afternoon of the battle. Mr. Lincoln wore a long linen duster."*[19]

One account of the battle has Lieutenant-Colonel Frazee anxiously telling his commander-in-chief, "there are plenty of Colonels about, but no such President as you," and General Wright ordering the president down.[20] *Lincoln survived the experience, if narrowly.*

James H. Laird, orderly sergeant, Co. K, 150th Ohio:

During the battle, I was in command of a gun at the angle between the old and new parts of the fort. In connection with the separating wall of the parts was a lookout, joined to the wall on its west side and to the parapet on the north or front. A small group of persons stood upon this lookout, which was about ten feet from our gun and perhaps eight feet above it. The central figure was President Lincoln. Near the President was a uniformed man whom we afterward learned was an army surgeon. The party were looking out upon the battlefield. Minie balls were singing about us.

Bedient, hot with excitement, had just come in from the picket line with a bullet hole in his cap. Scarce knowing what he said, he called out: "President Lincoln, you had better come down; the rebels will shoot you."[21]

A few minutes later, I saw the surgeon fall. They picked him up, and drew up his trousers. I could see the blood flowing from the calf of his leg. Those upon the lookout hurried down and disappeared.[22]

This casualty seems to have occurred in the early afternoon of the 11th. Some of our boys who brought in prisoners said the captured men told them Lincoln was seen from the cupola of a house, was recognized and fired at. He may have been seen through a field glass, and recognized on account of his stature and peculiar form.

Edgar H. Hinman, private, Co. K, 150th Ohio:

President Lincoln visited the fort accompanied by Senator Zack Chandler of Michigan. The enemy was firing lively from the bushes in front of the fort, and it was dangerous for any person to look over the parapet. Chandler hugged close to the parapet, but the President was bound he would look over and see what was going on.

Soon a sharpshooter fired at him and he dodged, [and] in doing so tipped over the pass box on which he was sitting and tumbled down. The ball fired at him struck one of the large guns, glanced back and went through a surgeon's leg on the look-out. Lincoln gathered himself up and laughingly said: "That was quite a carom."

I was standing back of him at the time, and was curious to know what a carom meant, and so asked one of the boys; in billiards he told me that it was when you shot at one ball and hit another. Some of those standing by thought the President was given to a little too much levity and that the remark was a little too jocose for the occasion, but he did not realize what had happened until after he said it.[23]

* * *

The young Ohioan captured at Monocacy Junction had a view of the battle from the rebel perspective.

William R. Browning, private, Co. I, 149th Ohio:

About noon we began to hear heavy firing in front, and the rebel stragglers began passing us hurrying to the front so that they might be among the first to enter Washington and loot the city. One of the guards told me that the roar of the cannons was the sweetest music on earth to the rebels. I answered, "I think before you take Washington you will be accommodated with plenty of sweet music."

We marched on for three hours under heavy fire from siege guns. The stragglers who had rushed to the front in order to be the first to enter the city began to come back. We taunted them, asking, "Why didn't you go on into Washington?"

They replied, "We would, only the cursed Yankees are throwing flour barrels at us."[24]

We were marched up until in full view of Fort Stevens, where we could see the stars and stripes floating above the fort. They placed us in an orchard so close to the fort that the shells would crash through the tree tops above our heads. This was not of long duration, until a rebel line of infantry came out of the woods and charged the fort.

The fort reserved their fire until the rebels got close up to it, and I began to fear that it would be taken. All at once, it let loose with artillery and a galling infantry fire from a line of troops that we had not seen. Such a noise I never heard. The smoke and the gathering twilight hid all the combatants from view, but we could tell from the sound of the guns that the rebels were falling back and that the Union infantry was following them up. Directly all firing ceased, and we knew that the enemy had been repulsed.

At this time we drew two days' rations of beef and flour, but before we had time to cook it we were ordered to fall in and under a heavy guard began marching to the rear. The whole rebel army came pell-mell, almost a stampede. The cavalry and artillery filled the road, the infantry going through the fields. The cattle they had stolen in Maryland were also driven through the fields, the drivers yelling and swearing, making the air hideous with the din. A fine residence of a United States Senator[25] was burned to the ground.

All this made an impression upon my mind. I learned afterward that after their repulse at Washington, the word was passed that General Hunter was advancing from Harper's Ferry to attack them in the rear.

* * *

The timely arrival of the veteran VI and XIX Corps reinforcements meant that Early's audacious attempt to enter the Northern capital was finished. His tired troops could no longer hope to burst through feeble defenses manned by hundred-days men, convalescents, and government volunteers. But fighting continued through the day, and that night each side settled down uneasily, waiting for whatever dawn would bring.

James C. Cannon, private, Co. K, 150th Ohio:

The morning of the 12th opened with the singing of bullets as they flew over our heads and plunged into sod on the bomb-proof. Our guns were trained on two remaining houses in front of the works, and they were soon burned to the ground. Firing was active between the lines through the day, Early being apparently disappointed by the effective fire of the fort, and especially by the appearance of the 6th Corps. However, he decided late in the afternoon to advance his line, and the 6th Corps made arrangements to give them battle.

Of the following engagement, Brigadier-General Wheaton[26] says in his report:

"At 5 P.M., the 7th Maine and the 45th and 19th New York were formed in rear of the line. A signal was made when they were in position, then fire was opened from Fort Stevens. As had been previously arranged, after the 36th shot had been fired from Fort Stevens, a signal was made from the parapet of that work, and we dashed forward, but found the enemy stronger than expected and ordered up the 77th and 122d New York and 61st Pennsylvania. The enemy were forced back into the former skirmish line when orders were sent our men to attempt no more, and the fight was therefore over. In this battle there were 19 officers and 243 privates killed and wounded."[27]

During the heat of the engagement a call was made for more ammunition, and a detail was ordered from Company K to take a load of ammunition out on the field in an old buggy. On the 12th, the guns of Fort Stevens fired 67 shots.

Alongside the barracks on the morning of the 13th was a long row of the enemy dead and dying. Before noon, 28 dead were buried in their uniforms, uncoffined, under a sycamore tree.[28]

James H. Laird, orderly sergeant, Co. K, 150th Ohio:

About 5 o'clock in the afternoon of the 12th, we were told to fire five rounds from the fort, mostly at two houses, the Carberry, or Lay, on the west, and the Reeves on the east of the turnpike, about three-fourths of a mile from the fort. For some time before the firing, we saw a movement of troops in the grove to the northeast—officers dismounted and men hidden mostly by the shrubbery. It was at the time when Bidwell's[29] detachment of the 6th Corps was ordered to move toward the rebel lines.

Soon our lines of men drew out to the open and crept along the slope northwestward and lay upon the ground. The time had come for our volleys. A shaking roar went up from Fort Stevens, and also from Slocum[30] on the east and DeRussy on the west. Shell and shot flew over the heads of the prostrate men of our battle line.

The Lay house was soon in flames. The forces of the enemy massed behind it were seen scattering in disorder into the open field beyond. The 6th Corps men sprang to their feet, and in orderly ranks loaded and fired as they charged upon the rebel line. The musketry continued until after nightfall.

In the darkness, I went to the barracks in the rear of the fort. Ambulances were coming in. A man was limping out of one of them. I gave him my shoulder to help him down. As we came into better light, I noted that his uniform was gray. He begged that I would not allow his leg to be taken off. "I have a wife and six children in Carolina."

We stretched the struggling man on the table. "No help for you," said the surgeon. "If it were one of our own soldiers, we should do the same. The knee is shattered." Sadly, I consented to hold the sponge to his face. A stretcher pressed against my limb. I looked down and saw a brave fellow in his last gasp. By the walls, dead men were piled like cords of wood. The tables were filled with mangled men under surgeons' hands.

By 11 that night, the conflict ended.[31]

In the morning of the 13th, Corporal Lucien C. Warner and I went over to the Reeves house to see the effect of shells he had fired. One, which we could trace to his gun, had passed through the building without exploding, and on its way cut off the leg of a piano.

One sad "after-the-battle" sight was the men of the gallant 3rd Brigade gathering their dead comrades from the field and laying them in their gory garments in a trench, cut near our fort. One-fourth of their number, we were told—a quarter of the men of that little brigade—had fallen in the charge upon Early's forces.

Our men of Company K were, in a sense, raw troops, yet in this battle they bore the aspect of calm courage. Of this company were the central picket lines when the enemy approached. I remember the heroism of the plea some of them made to be allowed to enter the ranks of other bodies of soldiers which were advancing to meet the charge of the Southern men. Several of them served in this way.[32]

12 | Back to the Valley

FROM WASHINGTON, Federal troops pursued Early's little army back into the Shenandoah Valley. Again, fighting spilled over into West Virginia and Maryland, embroiling the hundred-days men once more. After its fight at Monocacy Junction, the battered 149th Ohio, rejoined by most of its missing men and the companies from Baltimore, entered the chase into the Shenandoah.

George Perkins, private, Co. A, 149th Ohio:

We were just boys of from 15 to 18 years of age. But we were having too good a time in Baltimore for it to last. The last opportunity we had to go downtown was on the evening of the 4th of July, when there was a grand display of fireworks.

On the 12th day of July, Companies A and F under marching orders left Fort No. 1 and Baltimore for Washington City, where we arrived early the next morning. We lay at the depot until ten o'clock, when we were ordered to "fall in" and with the balance of the regiment marched up Pennsylvania Ave., greeted by the cheers of the crowds who lined the sidewalks and filled the windows of the buildings. We marched past the White House and the Treasury buildings. At the latter we saw President Lincoln on the steps waving his high hat as we marched by.

We went over into Georgetown, where, after a short rest, we joined the 19th Corps in the chase of Early, who, after being repulsed at Fort Stevens, retreated to the Shenandoah Valley.

The first day's march nearly used us up. During our march the boys began to pick up from the fields various articles that they considered valuable as relics, intending to carry them home. Bayonets and cannon balls seemed to be favorite articles for collection. After carrying them for a few miles they began dropping them one by one. We found out in a very short time that the less we had to carry the better we could march. Our feet were blistered as we hobbled along. Our accouterments were heavy, our guns a burden. But a canteen filled with water seemed heaviest of all; the string over the shoulder felt like it would cut clear through.

The next morning early the march was resumed and we went into camp at Leesburg, Va., where we rested the balance of the day and night. We were ordered to guard the wagon train, and by easy marches reached Snickers Gap[1] on July 17. Our train was halted about a mile back of the gap and our regiment camped on a mountainside.

Once on our march toward Snickers Gap, I saw a squad of soldiers taking a cow from a farm lot. They had tied a rope around her horns; two were tugging at the rope, and others were pushing. The woman of the house and her children were crying and begging them to let her alone. The argument was still on as we marched along.

On this same march, we passed a field where a fight had taken place a day or two before. The dead had been buried and the wounded removed, but the field was full of dead horses. The stench from the swollen carcasses lying under the sweltering rays of the hot July sun was terrific. We hurried past as fast as possible, breathing a sigh of relief when we came again into the pure air of the mountains.

The army advanced to the gap, and in crossing the ford the enemy opened fire upon them and a brisk engagement followed. From our position we could hear the cannon and see the smoke of the battle. This continued until sunset. We were ordered out on picket and took our posts in the woods, being cautioned to keep a sharp outlook. Our troops began to fall back and our second sergeant brought in the pickets, exclaiming in breathless haste, "The army is cut to pieces and in full retreat."

We hurried back into ranks, drew 40 rounds of cartridges, and guarding the wagon train started on the "double quick" for Washington. This was at nine o'clock at night. That night, in passing through burning pine woods, the train was fired upon from ambush and some were wounded. During this hard night march the men walked along nearly asleep on their feet, and if there was a temporary halt they dropped in the dusty road, asleep instantly. We marched without a stop until eight o'clock the next morning, when we halted at Leesburg.

After a short rest at Leesburg, we pushed on and went into camp near Chain Bridge at Washington. We arrived at night, completely worn out from our long forced march. The regiment stacked arms, spread blankets on the ground and lay down to sleep. We lay upon our gum blankets and covered with the woolen ones. During the night, it turned quite cool and rained hard. We were soaked through when we awoke in the morning. We started fires, made coffee, ate some hardtack, then wrapping our blankets around us sat down in the mud to silent meditation.

It rained hard until about noon, then began to break away. By night it was clear. We occupied the crest of a hill or ridge that sloped gradually to the south, making an ideal camping ground for the army. As night drew on, camp fires were kindled and twinkled by thousands over the slope while the soldiers prepared their supper. Stories of their adventures and songs served to pass the evening. When the time came for "lights out," a drum corps on the right began playing *The Girl I Left Behind Me*. A brass band in the center struck up *Home Sweet Home*.

These were all the tunes we recognized, for every band and drum corps in camp began playing. Pandemonium seemed to have broken loose as the great volume of sound came up. Tunes could not be distinguished; the discord was terrific. It gradually died away as band after band ceased playing. A deep silence came over the plain, the stars blinked in the summer sky. The army was asleep.

The next morning, July 21st, we drew new shoes, formed ranks, crossed the bridge and followed the Sixth Corps who were just breaking camp as we came up. We marched through Maryland via Rockville to the battlefield of Monocacy, which we passed over. We saw there the signs of the fierce fighting, the high fences full of bullet holes, and the grain stacks that obstructed Gordon's advance.[2] We forded the river and marched on through Frederick.

From Frederick, the army marched on to Harper's Ferry. Crossing the pontoon bridge, we passed through the town and went into camp at Halltown. We reached this camp on July 23d and remained there two days. The Sixth and 19th Corps had passed up the Shenandoah Valley in pursuit of Early. Gen. Crook's[3] forces engaged Early at Kernstown but, losing heavily, had been forced back to the Potomac. This reverse caused our forces to fall back to Maryland Heights. On July 25th our regiment fell in on the left and began what is known as the terrific "hot march."

The sun was blistering. The heat seemed concentrated in the valley, while the dust rising in clouds was suffocating. As we plodded along on this short march of four miles, men could be seen dropping from sunstroke; I saw an officer throw up his hands and fall backward off his horse. Comrades pulled them to the roadside and did what they could for them. It was reported that 35 men had suffered sunstroke on that hot afternoon.

We crossed the Potomac and began the ascent of Maryland Heights, arriving at the summit about sunset. The view from the top of the mountain was grand: tier after tier of blue mountains fading away in the distance, while a rebel wagon train moved slowly up the valley, shrouded in a cloud of dust that looked a mile high. That night there came a welcome shower. The next morning we were ordered down and again took up the march back to Monocacy Junction. Our commanding general made the remark, "The boys were taken to the top of the mountain to see the sunset."

Our appearance after two or three marches would have made Rip Van Winkle on awakening look like a dude in comparison. We were ragged, tattered and torn, our shoes worn out, and the sacred soil of old Virginia was ground into our system from the dust that we continually lived in. We thought the turnpikes of the Shenandoah valley were the hardest in the world. But they were not too hard to sleep on when the weary soldier dropped in his tracks the moment a halt was made. I have seen the men marching sound asleep only awakened when their heads came in contact with the tail board of the wagon in front. I heard one of the men of the 19th Corps say, "We have served for three years, but have never seen campaigning like this."

While we were rushing frantically up and down the valley of the Shenandoah trying to find Early, his forces were marching through Pennsylvania marauding at their leisure.[4] At this time Gen. Grant came over from Washington to consult with his generals. While standing on the station platform, I heard the following conversation between Generals Grant and Hunter.

Grant said, "General Hunter, where is the enemy?"

Hunter replied, with a tremor in his voice, "I don't know, General."

At this Grant in anger exclaimed, "Move your troops back to Harper's Ferry, cut off his line of retreat and you will find out."

Orders were immediately given to return to the Ferry. The infantry boarded a freight train and were rushed back to Harper's Ferry. Every time we passed through this town it was on a Saturday, so we nicknamed it "Harper's Weekly." McCausland in the meantime retired from his raid and escaped to the south. We marched to our old camp ground at Halltown, arriving there July 28th. We remained quietly here for two weeks.

At this time dissatisfaction with Hunter's policies became acute, and he tendered his resignation. Gen. Grant had for some time been contemplating organizing a new department to be known as the Army of the Shenandoah with Gen. Phil Sheridan at its head. Fears had been felt that Sheridan was too young for such an important position. Grant, however, had confidence that the right man had been found for the place. Accordingly, Sheridan was placed in command on August 7th and at once began organizing his army.

General Sheridan's force was an imposing army of young men, numbering 30,000 infantry and 10,000 cavalry. On the 12th of August, Sheridan moved up the valley, passing along the road near our camp. The General and his staff rode at the head of the column. The cavalry came next riding in columns of four, followed by the Sixth and 19th Corps, the army of West Virginia and the artillery. Our brigade was detailed to guard the wagon train.

The mere statement gives no idea of the magnitude of this force. But when I say that it took an entire day to pass our camp, the cavalry and infantry in column of fours, some idea may be had of the grandeur of this army. They were moving against Early, for the authorities at Washington had become tired of the harassing raids of the rebels into the north through the Shenandoah, which had almost become "the valley of humiliation" to them.

On this march [later] occurred one of those events that made an impression never to be forgotten. It was nine o'clock at night on a beautiful summer night. The moon shone brightly through the dark pines on the mountains and glistened across the guns of the great army that marched down the turnpike into old Charlestown.[5] The men were weary and footsore from their long marches and were swinging along carelessly. Suddenly someone started singing *John Brown's body lies a moldering in the tomb.*

Companies, regiments and corps took up the refrain; tired bodies straightened up and took step to the music. The grand chorus rang out *Glory, glory hallelujah* until the mountains gave back the echo *Glory, glory hallelujah,* as though the hosts of Heaven were joining in the refrain *His soul is marching on.*

It was the song of triumph, and if the spirits of the departed know of things on earth, surely the shade of old John Brown was gratified. Here he was hung, and in the graveyard his body was lying "moldering in the tomb." But his soul was marching on in the ranks of the 30,000 soldiers who on that night marched through Charlestown, keeping step to the grand chorus, *Glory, glory hallelujah.*

* * *

Following its arduous trek in the Shenandoah with the wagon train, the 152nd Ohio eventually returned to nearby Cumberland, on the upper Potomac. From there editor Nichols reported a battle fought by the 153rd Ohio. Since many men in that regiment hailed from Springfield, Nichols's hometown, his sources were likely reliable.

Clifton M. Nichols, corporal, Co. E, 152nd Ohio:

Cumberland, Md., August 3d, evening.

On Sunday night, July 31, 1864, Colonel Stough of the 153d Ohio, whose command was distributed for 50 miles along the Baltimore & Ohio railroad, was ordered by General Kelley to gather up his men and report with them at Cumberland for the defense of the city.

The Colonel was here on Monday, but intelligence having been received by the General from Averell[6] that Bradley T. Johnson, with 3,000 rebel cavalry and a heavy battery, was advancing on Oldtown, in order to cross the north branch of the Potomac into [West] Virginia, the order was countermanded and the Colonel directed to take his men, 450 in number, to Green Spring, just across the river from Oldtown, and cut off Johnson's retreat.

The Colonel went out on Monday afternoon, and at 3 o'clock lay in ambush for the rebels at a point, on a hill, two miles north of Oldtown. The rebels were expected to arrive at 5 o'clock, but instead of advancing directly to Oldtown they marched upon Cumberland, and upon being fired upon by our artillery and held back by the cannon and Hundred Day Infantry and a few companies of Virginia Infantry, for several hours they fell back and proceeded along the mountain road to the point for which they had started.

Colonel Stough lay in wait for the foe until 4 o'clock on Tuesday morning, when the rebels came in on his pickets on a road on his left flank, and at once the whole force came up in splendid order, with lines of skirmishers in front and full regiments following closely. Our men held their fire until their foes were within rifle range, and then arose from a reclining and covered position and gave them a well-directed volley. This threw their advance back in confusion, and a hearty "tiger" went up from our men.

A party of rebels soon attempted to cross the locks of the canal,[7] but four of them were shot dead and the rest retreated. The engagement lasted from 5 o'clock A.M. until 9, when the rebels commenced flanking our force with their greatly superior numbers—3,000 men—advancing with a 24-pounder Parrott gun, a 12-pounder howitzer, and four three-inch regulation guns. Colonel Stough gradually fell back across the river with his command, with every man in his place during the entire movement notwithstanding the heavy and continuous fire from the foe.

Having crossed the river, Colonel Stough put 40 of his men in the Green Spring blockhouse and placed the remainder behind the railroad embankment. He was here supported by an ironclad train, which was soon knocked in pieces and therefore gave him no assistance. A ball pierced the locomotive and let out its wind in an instant, and another went into a porthole and knocked one cannon into flinders.

Our men fought from the railroad half an hour, rising to fire and then falling behind the embankment again. But the rebels advanced and their concentrated fire could not be withstood. The larger portion of the force with Captain Harry C. Cross got on board of the train lying near and, supposing Colonel Stough was on board, pushed off to Cumberland. The Colonel then repaired to the blockhouse and with just 79 men fought the whole rebel force until 11 o'clock, at which time our last shot was fired.

The rebel shots and shells were tearing the blockhouse down over the heads of its brave defenders at this time, when the firing ceased and a party of well-dressed men in Confederate uniform made their appearance with a flag of truce, and inquired for the commander of the blockhouse.

Colonel Stough at once stepped out on the embankment and the following note was handed to him:

AUGUST 2, 1864.

Commanding Officer in the Blockhouse:
     You will immediately surrender the post in your command. If you do not you will not receive any terms.

BRADLEY T. JOHNSON,
Brigadier General Commanding Confed. forces.
Official. G. W. Booth, A.A.G.

The Colonel then stepped inside and consulted with his officers, and after going out and being allowed to view the rebel force, which had completely flanked him, and the artillery so posted as to destroy the last vestige of the blockhouse in five minutes, he wrote and delivered the following message in reply:

AUGUST 2, 1864.

General Bradley T. Johnson:
    I have the honor to acknowledge the receipt of your note of this date demanding the surrender of the blockhouse and forces under my command. I will surrender on the following conditions only:
    1. That my men and I shall be immediately paroled.
    2. That our private property shall be respected.
    3. That the men will be allowed to retain haversacks, canteens and blankets.
    4. That I be allowed to transport my wounded by handcar to Cumberland.

I. STOUGH, Colonel Commanding
Squad of the 153d Ohio N.G.

This note was immediately sent by the flag of truce party from the commander of the *squad* to the commander of the rebel *division,* and an officer came dashing back at once, announcing that the terms were accepted. Colonel Stough and his men, they with haversacks, canteens and blankets, then came out of the blockhouse, and Generals Johnson and McCausland came up. The latter wished the haversacks, etc., to be given up, but Colonel Stough claimed that they were his by the contract. The General then asked him if he ever belonged to the 44th Ohio.
    Colonel Stough replied that he did.
    "Were you a Captain?" asked McCausland.
    "I was," was the reply.
    The General then asked: "Were you not the leader of the scouting parties who used to capture my pickets on the Greenbrier River every two weeks?"
    The Colonel replied: *"I am that very man."*
    The General then said: "We are old acquaintances. You are all right. You can have your haversacks, canteens and blankets."
    Upon being asked about the Chambersburg affair, General McCausland showed his orders to burn the town unless $100,000 in specie or $500,000 in greenbacks were paid him in half an hour. Colonel Stough saw the signature of General Early to the document. General McCausland said he rang the courthouse bell and called the citizens together, giving them the terms, *"and they simply stood and laughed at him."*
    General Johnson then conversed with the Colonel and asked him about the forces in Cumberland. Colonel Stough told him: "Enough to whip you; but

you had better go and see for yourself." He also asked about the forces east, but the Colonel told him if he wanted information he had better send out a reconnoitering party.

The Colonel's firmness and wit, added to the great gallantry he had previously displayed, favorably disposed the rebels toward him, and both generals commended him and his men for their bravery. The Colonel told them he desired to be exchanged at once, and to fight them under more equal circumstances.

The Colonel then sent off his command by the tow path to Cumberland, the wounded being on the handcar mentioned, he accompanying them; and the rebels actually cheered him as he came away, knowing him to be a man of pluck and military science although an enemy, and one whose command had, by their admission, killed 20 of their men and wounded 40 more.

Captain Cross and his company fought splendidly. Of Captain Cross's men, young Taylor, son of Jonathan Taylor of New Carlisle, and young Coffield, son of Esquire Coffield, of Enon, were mortally wounded.[8]

As the officers came in with the flag of truce, they told Colonel Stough that they had taken one of his men, who was mortally wounded, under a tree in the shade and left four of their men to administer to his wants. These men, it was afterwards learned, covered the ghastly wounds with alder leaves to protect the brave but unfortunate hero from the annoyance of flies. The young man lay there until after the surrender was accepted.

Colonel Stough then went out, and the rebels having given him a stretcher, removed young Coffield to the house of two excellent Union ladies in the village of Oldtown. As the party approached, the warm-hearted women came out weeping to receive him. He was so badly wounded that he could not be brought into the city on a handcar, and the Colonel had to leave him. He was in terrible pain, but was calm and resigned, and ere this has undoubtedly died like a true soldier.

Young Taylor was in the hospital here, and died today.[9]

It was reported in the city that Colonel Stough was killed, and it was supposed a matter of impossibility that he should escape. When, however, he made his appearance, his men and the citizens sent up a cheer the like of which was never before heard in Cumberland. The Colonel is now the hero of the hour, and great attention is paid to him by all classes of people. General Kelley commended him very highly for his skill, courage and pluck. He has been in our camp all day and we have been enjoying his presence.

The rebels thought so much of him that, during the engagement, they took off a lock of the hair on his right temple with a bullet, leaving a white spot the size of a dime, and there are two bullet holes in the front part of his blouse.

* * *

After the fight with the 153rd, Confederate cavalry and irregular forces continued toward Cumberland. The town was now well defended, however, and the rebels made no serious attempt to take it.[10] *Smaller, more isolated outposts such as Greenland Gap and even New Creek were more likely targets. The 154th Ohio had returned to its mountain pass after its July 4th retreat.*

Joseph A. Stipp, private, Co. B, 154th Ohio:

The situation at Greenland Gap, upon the receipt of the information of General Crook's defeat at Winchester [on July 24th] and his retreat upon Harper's Ferry, can neither be imagined nor described.

All kinds of reports were being received and circulated. Our anxiety and suspense were hourly increased by the arrival of mounted messengers, and when we were ordered to make preparations to fall back on New Creek the second time in less than 30 days, we were totally unable to comprehend the state of affairs in any light whatever. We immediately proceeded to gather up our "traps and calamities," and made a forced march upon New Creek.

We were soon made acquainted with the conditions existing throughout the department, and we further learned that we would soon be called upon to defend our position to the last extremity.

The alarm and consternation that prevailed elsewhere now became contagious, and the forces at Cumberland and New Creek soon became infected. The excitement that prevailed in consequence of the movements of McCausland and Johnson was further increased by the active operations of McNeill, Harness and Jones in our immediate vicinity.

The enemy, having leisurely moved on Springfield,[11] where they were enabled to rest and obtain supplies off the country, now moved in the direction of New Creek, via the Romney road to the junction of the Allegheny road, then down the New Creek Valley.

The ridge crossing and terminating the New Creek Valley commands it and the Potomac Valley, forming a strong position. The summit is occupied by a work—Fort Kelley—of moderately strong profile. From this work could be seen the approach from the south—the New Creek Valley—for a distance of about two miles; it also overlooks the Valley of the Potomac on the north. In this fort were four large siege guns, two 12-pounders and one six-pound rifled ordnance gun.

The force at this time consisted of nine companies of the 154th Ohio Volunteer Infantry; two companies of the 6th West Virginia Infantry; one company of the 2nd Maryland Infantry, mounted; one section, Battery L, 1st Illinois Light Artillery; and one section, Battery H, 1st West Virginia Light Artillery, manning the fort. The camp of the 154th was in the Potomac Valley, between the railroad and the North Branch of the Potomac River and about one mile distant from Fort Kelley. The artillery was parked on the ridge just outside the fort, and the company of the 2nd Maryland, mounted, on the slope of the ridge about halfway between the fort and the railroad.

About one o'clock in the afternoon of the fourth day of August, firing was heard in the direction of our outpost, situated out about two miles on the Moorefield and Greenland Gap road.

Our boys had partaken of their allowance of bean soup, hardtack and sowbelly, and not a few of them had quietly stolen away to their tents to indulge in a little afternoon nap. In a very short time, an officer mounted on an iron-gray horse was seen coming at full speed in the direction of our camp, and he rode up to the headquarters of Colonel Stevenson. Before the long roll could be sounded, the boys could be seen buckling on their accouterments, and, with Enfield rifles in hand, forming in the company streets.

The command *fall in* could now be heard on every hand. The companies formed in a very short time, and with the command *right face, forward, double quick*, nine companies of the 154th were soon on the dead run for the fort on the ridge. Our gallant Colonel Stevenson, mounted on his black charger with his hat in hand, signaled us on. Upon our arrival at the fort, we were met by Colonel Stevenson and his staff.

Companies A and B were at once thrown out on the right and left and were soon advancing as skirmishers, while the detachment of the 2nd Maryland, mounted, was sent out to develop the strength of the enemy. In the meantime, our outposts and inner line of pickets were being driven in.

In a short time, the 2nd Maryland, Co. F., was driven back by an overwhelming force of genuine "Johnny Rebs." There seemed to be no end to their numbers. They advanced steadily in solid column until they reached a point about one mile from the fort, where they formed in a line of battle stretching from the foothills on our right to the mountain range on our left.

Colonel Stevenson in the meantime had sent General Kelley the following: "We are attacked. The force is more than McNeill. They have infantry, cavalry and artillery."

Flank movements were now being attempted by the enemy on our right and left. The right was at once reinforced, and the fighting for advantage ground now became hot and furious. The artillery in the fort had a sweeping effect on the center, and made that ground very dangerous for an advance by the enemy; the very rugged and uneven ground, with fallen timber, on the left, seriously retarded any progress the enemy was disposed to make in that direction.

In response to the dispatch sent General Kelley, the following was made: "Put your force in position and fight them to the last. I will send the Eleventh to you."

About two miles up the New Creek Valley, a wagon road had been made, leading to the summit of the mountain range on the east side—our left. Upon the highest point of this mountain stood the remnants of old Fort Piano, a work built at an early period of the war but long since abandoned on account of its high elevation. A strong force of the enemy had taken this mountain road, and had made disposition of infantry and artillery for the purpose of turning our left flank.

Having gained the crest of this mountain, they advanced about halfway down its steep and rugged sides, when they were met by our troops. A hot engagement was waged by both sides. The contest was decidedly uneven, owing to the superior force of the enemy.

A general engagement now ensued and the fighting became general all along the entire line from right to left, and was waged in the most furious manner. We were now fighting three brigades of the enemy's war-worn veterans, under the command of rebel generals McCausland, Bradley T. Johnson and Ransom[12]—a part of the same force that had contributed to the defeat of General Crook at Winchester, engaged General Lew Wallace at Monocacy, compelled General Sigel to evacuate Martinsburg and fall back upon Harper's Ferry, and completely flanked General Averell after the destruction of Chambersburg.

The enemy was further reinforced by the forces under the command of McNeill, Harness and Jones, and were being piloted into New Creek by that noted guerrilla chieftain, McNeill.[13]

Our left was now being hard pressed, and for a time it seemed as though the enemy would succeed in their design. But we held our ground, and occupied relatively the same positions as at the beginning of the battle.

About four o'clock in the afternoon, a line of boys in blue was seen coming from the direction of New Creek station, following the valley road. They proved to be a detachment (four companies) of the 11th West Virginia Infantry. They were ordered to go in on the left, and in a short time joined our boys on that rugged mountainside. Cheers and shouts rent the air and made that old valley ring, to be re-echoed by the hills across the valley on the right.

The enemy, who had been very aggressive, now seemed to be in a quandary as to what movement they should make next. We did not have to wait very long, as their fire was opened with renewed vigor. Their line advanced with a spirit and determination that seemed as if success must crown their efforts. The artillery and infantry fire now became general all along the line. The shriek of the shell and the rattle of musketry was heard, and not infrequently, over and above all, the bellowing and booming of the large iron siege guns in Fort Kelley. The enemy returned the fire in the most vigorous manner. Their artillery—five pieces—were worked with surprising rapidity, while their infantry and cavalry put forth every effort to drive us from our position. The scene was grand and inspiring.

Darkness finally came upon us and put an end to all operations for the night, except an occasional shot fired by the advance skirmish line. Our forces maintained the positions occupied during the afternoon, with the exception that the skirmish line was advanced under cover of darkness. The entire command was under arms during the night, and the utmost vigilance exercised. The 156th O.V.I. was sent from Cumberland to reinforce us during the night, but too late to render any service.

The heat throughout the day had been most intense; our hunger and thirst forbade sleep, while our tired and worn-out condition invited the same. It was a night of intense anxiety and suspense.

> *Watchman tell us of the night,*
> *What its signs of promise are?*

The very first dawn of the morning's gray light found us all on the alert, waiting for demonstration on the part of the enemy. Our feelings can better be imagined than described when we found the enemy had retired from our front and were nowhere to be seen. They had been most gloriously repulsed and defeated, and were now seeking a more congenial clime.

* * *

At eight o'clock in the evening two days after the battle, thinking of his family in Ohio, Isaac Hambleton sat down to write a few reassuring lines. That message would pass his wife's anxious letter to him in the mail.[14]

Isaac Hambleton, second lieutenant, Co. C, 154th Ohio:

Dear Wife & Family,

I thought I would pencil you a few lines this evening to let you know that I am well. Jane, we have had a small Fight at last. The citizens came in Tuesday & told us that there was a force coming to attack us in a day or two. But we hardly credited it for we had been fooled so often.

It happened to fall to my lot to inform the Camp of it. I was on the Grand rounds that day with Cap Swanston.[15] The Pickets on the Greenland Road are out three miles from Camp. We had just got to the outer Post as the advance got to there. Five of them fired on them. The outpost are cavalry. The rebs were all cavalry [estimated] from three to five thousand. They didn't hit any of us, so you see we broke for Camp & they after us. I happened to have the smartest horse & got in camp first.

They drove the pickets within a mile & a half of camp & then they took to the woods thinking to surround us, but we couldn't see it. They attacked at half past one & fought us till sundown. They thought we had but three hundred men but they found out their mistake. We had between eleven & twelve hundred besides six pieces of Artillery. We come off pretty well. There was but one of our company wounded, that was Andrew Kepler, a flesh wound in the arm.[16] We were stationed in the Fort to support the Battery, but few of them fired. They didn't come close enough.

James Arnett & John Watson were captured. They were picking blackberries.[17] But four wounded in the Regt., one is thought mortally. He has had his arm amputated. A part of the eleventh [West] Virginia was in it. They suffered considerable, nine killed & nineteen wounded. The rebel loss is not ascertained. They left four dead on the ground & five wounded at a house. The neighbors say they admit of losing between sixty & seventy. We captured three prisoners. [Of] our Regt., six is supposed to be captured.[18] The rebels were commanded by General Bradley Johnson & McCausland. They retreated in the night. No more at present. Your heart's friend.

* * *

In August, the battered 144th and 149th Ohio escorted a wagon train into Virginia, unaware they were heading toward the hundred-days force's worst and most costly encounter with any guerrilla band. Drummer Samuel McClain was still writing his long serial letters to his wife.

Samuel McClain, musician, Co. I, 144th Ohio:

Aug. 9.

All quiet on the Potomac this morning & all well. We are laying in camp near Hall Town, 4 miles west of Harper's Ferry, Timothy Valley. 20 thousand cavalry come into camp today. This army is under General Sheridan's command.

This is the day that we were to start home, but I can't see it. My tent is right in front of the General's headquarters. You bet I watch him close to see if he is making preparations for us to go home. Can't see any yet. We have only 9 days to serve yet. Our company has to go out on picket tonight. I guess I'll go out with them tonight.

Evening. I just received 2 letters from you bearing date July 19th & 25th. Believe me, I was glad to hear from home & to hear of your good health and success on the farm. Our Lieutenant-Colonel came to see us today. He brought the letters to us. Will & Wils Brown[19] is with us. They are well. Isaac Vanhorn[20] just heard of the death of his little babe. He takes it very hard. I pity him. He says if he had only got to seen it he would have been satisfied.

The Rebs is retreating is the news tonight. I think we will start home in a day or two.

Aug. 10

All well. Quite a stir in camp this morning. The troops are all on the move, but our brigade & we are in camp yet. I hope we will get to move toward home. We sent a petition to the General to relieve us. I don't know if he will or not.

If we have to go on to the front again, I'll mail this to you if I can. I got your photograph in a letter. It looks well. I would rather see you if I could, but I'll have to look at the pictures a while yet. I look at your likeness very often & also at Annie's and Willie's.[21] I have carried them along with me this far & I will carry them as long as I can. It is almost impossible for me to keep them dry, for I have to carry them in my pocket and I sweat so much. I think more of those pictures than I do of my money.

Fin & me is all alone tonight. The boys have all gone out on picket. We are getting dirty and ragged. I hope we will soon det[ach] where we can get some clothes & get to wash and clean up a little, for we have got more gray-backs[22] than greenbacks. We have not had our pants off for 36 days & nights. I'll not finish this until morning. Good night.

Good morning, Aug. 11. All well. Fin & me are keeping house. He has just eat breakfast. I got breakfast this morning & I let my "wife" sleep. We had coffee & hardtack. I have washed my shirt & socks this morning. I gave them a cold water rinse, for I despise nastiness, you know.

It is rumored this morning that we are to report to General Lew Wallace in Baltimore tomorrow. I hope this is so. If the report is true we may expect to be on our road home soon. I'll mail this letter today if I get a chance & write again soon & let you know the news. You must excuse poor writing & spelling, for I have to write on my knee & there is all kinds of noise going on to bother me, so I have to do the best I can under the circumstance & you must try and read them if you can & if you can't, just wait until I come home & I'll tell you all the news.

I remain yours truly for ever & ever.

* * *

Company I left camp at noon the following day, escorting the wagon train to Winchester. McClain had earlier soothed his wife's fear that he would "get catched in a trap. Now don't fret about me & Fin, for you know it is hard to catch an old bird with chaff. We will take care of No. 1."

On August 13th, unable to write another letter, he made this entry in his diary: "Saturday. Got up this morning & was eating when Mosley's [sic] command charged on us and took quite a number prisoners. We were ordered to mount mules & then to double-quick. Went thru Snickers Gap & encamped all night."

Among the hundred-days men captured along with McClain by John S. Mosby's feared Partisan Rangers were Fin Barton, the Brown boys, and Isaac Vanhorn.

Following is a view of the disaster from the companion 149th Ohio.

George Perkins, private, Co. A, 149th Ohio:

Our brigade was distributed through the length of the train [on August 12th], each company in charge of 30 wagons. The day was pleasant when we started. We marched through Charlestown, where they had hung John Brown. The place seemed deserted, the only sign of life being a negro woman peeping at us from a half closed door. We pushed on; we had orders to make Winchester by the next morning, for the army needed supplies.

Soon after dark, in spite of warning from the officers, the men began to straggle, dropping out of ranks. Some were getting into wagons, others climbing the fences and sleeping in the fields, expecting to overtake their command by morning.

My chum James Ghormley and myself, after marching until eleven o 'clock at night, concluded that we were too tired to go any longer that night and that a good sleep was just what we needed. We were within two miles of Berry-ville[23] when this notion entered our heads. When we awoke, daylight was just visible. We hurried on to overtake our regiment, expecting to boil coffee at the first fire we came to. We walked on, and soon came to where the train had "parked" for the night and was just pulling out.

It has been said that this stop was made without orders from our officers, but that the rebels, riding along during the night dressed in our uniform, saying they were aides, had given these orders, their object being to cut off the train and attack it for plunder. Our little squad soon came to where a company of the 144th Ohio were cooking breakfast. We asked permission to boil coffee at their fire. This was readily given.

We stacked arms, and our coffee had just come to a boil when "bang! bang!" came two artillery shots at us, scattering the limbs of the trees above our heads. These shots were followed by a volley from a clump of woods. Then they charged, yelling as they came.

They were Mosby's Guerrilla's, 400 strong, raiders who disbanded when too hardly pressed and became the innocent farmers of the valley. We grasped our guns, leveled them over the stone wall, gave them one volley. Then the captain in command gave the order to scatter and save ourselves. Well, we ran. In the confusion, Ghormley and I became separated and I saw him no more.[24]

I was with the most of the company going up a steep lane toward a farm-house, about half a mile from the road through a patch of corn and an orchard. A man was sitting on the porch, and he told me to run to the barn. I took his advice. The barn was a mow on stilts, open on every side, and stood on high ground. I stopped for a moment and looked over the field. The raiders were shooting our men down in every direction. I climbed into the hay mow. I was like the man who was asked if he had run at the battle of Bull Run: "Sure I did. Them that didn't run are there yet."

The fight was hot for a little while, but Mosby hurried for fear of the army ahead. He captured 200 prisoners and 600 head of cattle and burned 70 wagons. He expected to get the paymaster who was with us with money for the army. The paymaster was shrewd; he had packed the money in a cracker box and placed it in a wagon, keeping his strong box in his own vehicle. During the fight, this cracker box was tumbled down the banks of a little creek that ran through the field. I saw it lying there, and after the skirmish the paymaster came back and got it.

This attack was a complete surprise and a great loss to Sheridan's army. I joined our boys who were gathering together on the field. As I passed through the house lot, I saw lying on its face the body of a handsome young lieutenant who was shot by one of our company. The ball entered his forehead and scattered his brains. He was Lieutenant Eddy[25] of Mosby's men, a member of one of the good families in Richmond, Va. Gen. Mosby lamented his loss greatly, he being one of his most trusted men.

Our colonel and adjutant came riding back in full gallop and hastily reformed the men, formed a skirmish line and scoured the field, picking up discarded arms and compelling an old man who had come to the field with a mule and cart to pick up what he could and to haul it on to Winchester. We guarded the wagons that were left on to Winchester, where we found the regiment.

That night we slept on the stone pavements of the town, and on the next day were sent out on picket south of the town. We remained there two nights and a day. On the 15th of August, we started on our return early in the morning. Before starting Colonel Brown made a speech to the regiment in which he berated us for straggling in the enemy's country, and said he "would punish severely any disobedience of his orders." We reached Berryville at noon and camped at the farm where the fight had taken place.

Two wounded men of the 144th were lying on the porch of the house. They informed us that almost every man of their company had been captured. The 144th lost 130 men in this engagement. Lieutenant Eddy had been buried in a shallow grave in one corner of the house lot. We kept a sharp outlook for our missing comrades, hoping that they had made their way back to Harper's Ferry. A captain in our regiment brought home a beautiful sword that belonged to one of Mosby's men and was found on the field after the fight. It was a beautiful piece of work, ivory hilt, gold mounted, with a scabbard inlaid with gold and silver designs. It was highly prized by the captain, and no doubt would be more highly prized by the man who lost it at Berryville.

We marched on and went into camp on Bolivar Heights, near Harper's Ferry. Here we were joined by John Cook and Jeff Martin of Co. A, who had been captured by Mosby but escaped the same day.

They told us the story of the capture, how the others had been taken south and they had escaped. Mosby's men, after gaining the shelter of the mountains, began to examine their plunder and stopped to array themselves in new Union officers' uniforms. They were marching over a steep mountain road, guarding prisoners, when a portion of them stopped while those in front passed on out of sight. This left the road clear without a guard in sight. The two boys took advantage of the opportunity and made a break for liberty. Down the mountainside they ran, stumbling and falling, but straining every nerve for freedom.

They were not missed apparently, for the rebels did not pursue them. For three days they wandered through the mountains, only approaching the negro cabins by night, where they always found friends ready to feed them and help them on their way. Finally they reached Harper's Ferry and waited until we came up.[26]

13 | Prisoners of War

Few histories from the Civil War are sadder than those of prisoners. Earlier in the war, captured men were routinely paroled or exchanged. By 1864 this system had largely broken down, and wouldn't be renewed until shortly before the war's end. In Federal prisons, rebels died in shameful numbers of disease; in Southern prisons, such as Libby and the notorious Andersonville, sickness was abetted by starvation rations. Dozens of hundred-days men fell into Confederate hands during the summer. Many wouldn't return in their 100 days or ever. Here, Private Browning resumes his march toward imprisonment after his capture at Monocacy Junction.

William R. Browning, private, Co. I, 149th Ohio:

[During the retreat from Washington on July 11,] we marched all night and forded the Potomac at Edwards Ferry early the next morning. We waded the river, which came up to my armpits, I being small. We camped near a big spring not far from the river, where we rested and cooked what little we had.

The next morning, two days rations were issued and cooked. We again took up the march, passing through Leesburg, Va., and on through Snicker's Gap, getting to the Shenandoah River after dark. Here we camped for the night. The next morning, they allowed us to bathe in the river. We resumed the tiresome march and pressed on to Winchester, where we halted in the edge of the town. While here we drank from a spring, the coldest water I ever saw.

We then marched to Kernstown, where we encamped for two days. Here Joseph Rowland and Joseph Hays[1] of my company made their escape. This left eleven of our squad still prisoners: Sergeants James Nichols and Reeves McCall; Corporals James and William Harrison, brothers; and Privates W. W. McCracken, Thomas Broaders, Philip Frank, Wm. Houser, James Cruit, Peter Garratt and myself.[2] The stop here gave us a much-needed rest, and we again drew our two days' rations of beef and flour. Two days' rations may sound big, but a hearty man could eat it all at one meal without discomfort. It was not near enough to satisfy our hunger.

We again resumed our march, bound for Staunton up through the beautiful Shenandoah valley, passing through New Market, Mt. Jackson and Willow

Springs. At Staunton, we boarded the cars and rode to Charlotte. Here we went into camp and drew what they called rye bread and tainted salt beef. The bread was the worst I ever saw. It was dough inside, with a thick hard crust that could hardly be broken; when it was broken, the dough rolled out. The next morning we were again taken by the cars to Lynchburg. Here we were placed in a tobacco warehouse. The floor was covered with dried tobacco juice and licorice, at least that was what the boys said it was. I did not use the weed. We remained here a few days. I only recollect the stinking meat issued to us.

While here, I passed my sixteenth birthday, the 26th of July. On the 27th, we went on to Petersburg and Richmond Junction, thence to Danville, arriving there on the 28th. We were assigned to Prison No. 7, an old tobacco warehouse. The first floor was used as a hospital, the second, third and fourth stories for prisoners' quarters. I was put in squad No. 7 on the second floor. We were 50 men to a squad, in charge of a sergeant whose duty it was to draw rations for the men and to detail two comrades each day to carry water from the Dan River, about 200 yards from the prison. Here the hard prison life began.

There was a cookhouse near the prison, the cooks being Union soldiers. The rations were cornbread made of corn and cob ground together, sometimes with salt, often without. Once in a while we had bean soup made from black peas, with a little bacon in the soup full of skippers. I could not eat it, it was so filthy; I only ate a small piece of the cornbread each day.

I cannot go into detail. Each day was like another and very monotonous. We suffered from the heat when we first went into this prison. There were five squads of 50 on our floor. When we all lay down at night, there was no room to spare; we were packed like sardines in a box. To economize space, we would lie in rows across the building and when we turned over all would turn. On a hot night, the stench was fearful.

We remained here during July and August, using water from the Dan River. This was stagnant, in pools, for the river had almost dried up in the summer. The rebels would march us past as nice a spring of good cold water as ever flowed, and would not allow us to get it but take us to the river, where we skimmed the green scum from the surface with our buckets and dipped water from the hot, stinking pool. The hot weather created thirst, and the prisoners drank it as fast as it was carried to them and cried for more. If our guards were not in the humor, we would have to wait until they were ready; consequently there was great suffering from thirst.

About the last of August, Smith Miller of Company E of our regiment became suddenly insane and was taken to the hospital, where he afterward died.[3] Philip Frank of my company was also sent to the hospital, where he died. Many of the men became sick, and we were all growing weaker day by day. In September an order came to exchange a certain number of the sick.

When the doctor came to examine them, I took Samuel Jones to him. Jones could not walk, so Joe Shepard[4] and I carried him down. The doctor passed him, and then asked me, "Now what is the matter with you?"

I told him, "Nothing, only I want something to eat."

The doctor replied, "If you would say so, I will pass you."

I said, "No, take some poor fellow that was sick. I am not sick, and I do not intend to die in prison."

The boys of my company that were released at this time were James Nichols, Reeves McCall, James and William Harrison and Peter Garratt. The two Harrison boys died at Annapolis, Maryland, on their way home.

Disease and exchange now cut our number down, but our condition did not improve. We were growing weaker every day for want of food. In October, I was sick with diarrhea and went to the hospital. The sick were better cared for, and the nurses were detailed Union soldiers. The doctors were rebels, and did not have much regard for the prisoners. I remained in the hospital but did not get any better. In October, Thomas Broaders was brought into the hospital, paroled on sick leave, and afterward died at Annapolis. Later in the year, William Houser was brought over to the hospital, but only lived a few days.

Between Christmas and New Year's Day, I took the pneumonia, and the doctor told me, "Well, little Yank, you will have to die."

I told him, "I will never leave my bones in the southern confederacy."

He put a fly blister on my chest, and the next morning I was better. Then I had inflammation of the bowels, and he swore I would die. He had no medicine to give me, but put another fly blister on my stomach. The blisters broke in the night and the water ran all over me. In the morning, I again felt better, but soon erysipelas set in where the blisters had been. He then said I must be painted with iodine. This the nurses refused to do, saying that I would die and they did not see the use of torturing me, but let the boy die in peace. The doctor said it must be done.

They asked me about it. I told them if they would let Edgar Hulbert of the Twenty-third O.V.I., who was a nurse, paint me I would never say a word.[5] He did the job and I kept my promise. About a week later, I was up and walking around. I improved rapidly, and on the 25th of January I was returned to the prison. About this time the United States sent some clothing to us, but not enough to go 'round. I drew a blouse and my comrade McCracken a blanket.

It was now very cold in the prison. Some would sleep under blankets while others marched around to keep warm. We kept this up until becoming exhausted; we would rouse the sleepers and take their places. This was kept up continually day and night, as long as we remained at Danville.

About the 10th of February, we were placed in the cars and carried to Richmond, Va., and put in Libby prison. We suffered terribly from the cold on this trip. We were weak and our clothes were worn out. I was dressed in the blouse, remnants of a pair of trousers and a pair of socks that I had taken off a dead man. My pants were so badly worn that I would not be presentable in good society. But McCracken had his blanket, and we snuggled under it in one corner of the car and did the best we could until we landed in Libby.

There has been a great deal said about Libby prison, and truly too. But it was the best one I was in; we had a warmer place to stay and a greater variety of food, although the rations were extremely small. Here we talked about being exchanged. We thought we had been brought here for that purpose.

On the morning of February 20th, a rebel officer came to the prison and told us to get ready for parole. There was a glad lot of poor boys; all was excitement. The officer went away until afternoon, when he returned with other officers and clerks and called us up in line. We took the oath of parole to do no duty for the United States Government until regularly exchanged. This we gladly took. That night we had a big time. Nobody slept; in the morning, we were going back to God's country and home. McCracken sold his blanket for fifty dollars (confederate), and bought six pounds of flour with it. We made flapjacks, baked them on a stone, ate and talked about what we would eat when we got home.

In the morning, we were taken on board the rebel flag-of-truce boat. I was very weak, but Joe Shepard, the good Samaritan of our regiment, helped me aboard. We started down the James River to Harrison Landing. Someone shouted "there is the old flag."

In an instant everybody was alert, and on looking down the river we caught a glimpse of "Old Glory" through the treetops on one of the boats of our fleet. Such a time I never saw; we were the happiest boys on earth. We cheered, we shouted, we cried, we prayed, we were so happy. Many were going back to die, but they were glad to get where they could die under the dear old flag.

We landed at Harrison Landing, where the 25th Corps (colored) was stationed. It looked queer to me to see them on the skirmish line opposing the rebels. Each fellow had his "gopher hole" to dodge in. One big black fellow picked me up like a baby and carried me back through the lines. They all came running to us with something to eat, those great black fellows. My man carried me as far as he could go, and I walked a short distance to the river, where the transport *New York* was waiting for us.

We went aboard and had a good meal of soft wheat bread, pickle pork, coffee with sugar and condensed milk. I thought I had never tasted anything so good. We arrived at Annapolis on Washington's birthday, February 22, 1865.

I have tried in my own feeble way to tell something about my prison life. I have written it from memory and there may be some errors of dates, etc. An old man's memory is sometimes faulty. I have not told of all the horrors that I have witnessed. No tongue can tell nor pen describe what I have seen in these hells. To tell all would make a book. What I have told is true. I was discharged March 29th, 1865, at Tod Barracks in Columbus, Ohio.

* * *

A detachment of the 153rd Ohio was captured on July 3rd below the Maryland border in West Virginia while hunting bushwhackers. Its captain kept a diary of his captivity.

Thomas W. Rathbone, captain, Co. A, 153rd Ohio:

Saturday Oct. 1st, 1864.

And yet a prisoner in the "Roper"[6] in the old and dilapidated city of Charleston [S.C.], the Cradle of Treason and Rebellion. I was sick nearly all night with inflated stomach and this morn it resulted in Diarrhea, feel weak. No news of note this morn. Our messes were equalized by putting Leeds[7] in ours making four in each. The other mess had got tired of his whims I think —he is not very agreeable in a mess but we will get along with the case. Rained quite hard during the night. Mosquitoes very troublesome, flies about the same as in Ohio. This is Ration day, but only flour brought in late. Our last 10 days' rations lasted about 5 days, so we had to go on our own pockets. Eat but a light supper and laid down about 9 P.M.

Wednesday Oct. 5, 1864

While eating breakfast, an order came for the prisoners in "Roper" to pack up and be ready to go to Columbia in an hour. Hurried things together and when called upon marched into the street. Caps. Glenn, Day and myself and Lt. Baird and Harrison[8] agreed to make our escape from the cars on the way.

Train started at 12 noon. Reached Branchville at dusk and at 8 P.M. five jumped off unseen by the guards. And a mile or two further, as near as we could judge, about 20 miles North of Branchville, we took our everlasting leap. It would be useless for me to attempt a description of my feelings— suffice it to say that for some time I was in no condition for knowing anything. However we gathered ourselves up and put the pieces together and started on a country road leading north westward on our 500 miles tramp. But who won't do a great deal for Liberty, no matter how short the enjoyment. I thanked God for sweet freedom as I had it and may Providence prosper us. How much more will I be thankful.

Soon after starting on foot, Captain Glenn was taken very suddenly with bilious colic. I gave him an opiate so that we did not lose more than a couple of hours. We walked on till about 4 A.M., when we crossed a small river running across our route to our left. Our general course was nearly north slightly west. We selected the most secluded place and lay ourselves down for a short nap. Waked at daylight and moved across the stream into a swamp thicket, distance about 12 miles. The river above spoken of is the North Edisto, and we are on the state road leading to NW corner of the state. How Providential!

We have a little bread, about 3 lbs, one half of which we used today, Oct. 6th, while we lay in Camp Edisto. 5 ounces of bread to a man a day! Oh we live even live! on that, but then it is the best we can do as yet. Our expectations are to get corn and sweet potatoes from the farms, but have found none yet. The farmers and their *cattle* are making molasses from sorghum, and we saw their lights and heard the songs of the simple-minded negroes in their attempts to drive dull care away. Our greatest danger is from being hunted down by their Bloodhounds. But so long as they don't see [us] nor our marks (which we don't intend they should), we are safe. We being new hands at the biz are un-usually cautious, but 'tis for the best. The dogs barked at us last night as we passed along the road just as they would if anybody passed.

The white men are about all gone to the war, so that is favorable for us. The road is very good, but very sandy. At dusk it came on to rain hard, so we moved from our swamp retreat sooner than intended in order to cross the stream on a tree before it was too dark.

We soon got on the road, and it rained and lightninged until we were about saturated. Met a man on horseback. The signal was given and to the bushes we went, so he was none the wiser. We next concluded to flank a plan-tation house, which took about an hour through the woods and brush. Halted to rest about every mile, for we find that our powers of endurance are not improved much by confinement on Rebel diet. Turned out for three wagons had come. Slept an hour by the road side at about 4 A.M. 12 miles.

Friday Oct. 7th, 1864.

Selected a site to stay till daylight, so that we could secure a good camp site. Slept soundly till day when I waked the boys and Lt. Harrison selected the site for our 2d Camp of Escape (Camp Harrison).

The first night we had great difficulty in getting drinking water, but last night was different. The copious rain gave us drink, but Mother Earth nor negro labor gave us no corn or potatoes. So we will lengthen out our 5 ounces bread till perhaps morning. The mosquitoes are not bad, so that is quite a re-lief.

About 3 P.M., had quite a scare and a narrow escape of being discovered. Some darkies were driving a herd of mules along the road going North when some of them (mules) got into the brush and darkies after them. So we went into [the] swamp on hands and knees and lay down for about 3 hours, when we ventured back to our old camp and lay down on our brush beds and had to lie close to get warm. Went to sleep and waked about 9 P.M., and we started for the road. Got there and found the moon too bright yet to travel in safety, so we waited awhile and without much danger of interruption.

Daylight found us within about 4 miles of Columbia, which we intended to pass 20 miles distant. The Saluda River and pickets at Columbia bridge however stopped our course in this direction. We got some corn during the night so we can go for a day or two longer. 15 miles.

Saturday, Oct. 8th.

Broad daylight and no hiding place secured, so we stopped near and among some oaks & bushes on a ridge near the road. Lt. Harrison went out to look around and is missing. We suppose he is lost. Cool day. Slept some in the sun, but could not in the shade. Columbia is in sight and we can hear the darkies sing plainly.

Making our supper on raw corn and taking a nap to wait for citizens to get off the roads, we started through the brush and in a half mile came to a road running nearly west, which suited us for direction, so away we went, but had to stop frequently to rest. Capt. Glenn, poor fellow, he will never be able to go through. Made 15 miles and camped on the south side of the road in a small swamp thicket about 5 A.M.

Sunday, Oct. 9th, 1864

Tried to start but could not, for the reason that Captain Glenn had a chill and vomited repeatedly. At about 9 P.M., we started. Capt. Glenn concluded to return and give himself up. So Capt. Day, Baird & myself went on, passed Lexington C.H. in about three miles, flanked it by passing round to the right. Got away from the main road and among the plantations roads which run in every direction. Tied up at daylight (after making a cup of coffee) in an open woods. Capt. D. and I lay down in a fence corner and partially covered ourselves with leaves. Lt. Baird secreted himself behind a large rock. I had fallen into a creek at daylight and got wet to the waist and was very cold.

Early in the forenoon, a little girl in passing discovered us and, scared, she ran. Soon four men came on to Capt. D and I, one armed with a double shotgun, and arrested us and marched us back, and halted at a farmer's, where the women brought us out some breakfast. Wheat bread, corn bread, bacon, and sweet potatoes pie and sorghum syrup. So we made a hearty breakfast and after talking with the proprietor were marched on to Lexington C.H. and were put in jail by the enrolling officer (a mean cuss).

Day, Baird, and Harrison were all recaptured; with Glenn, they all survived the war. On November 1, Rathbone escaped again, with four others from a prison camp in Columbia, S.C. They struck out for the sea, and on

November 12 were rescued by a warship on blockade duty. Rear-Admiral John Dahlgren invited them to breakfast.

* * *

Men taken at Berryville also suffered great hardships. The Scioto Gazette *in Chillicothe, home of the 149th Ohio, printed this letter to Mrs. Thomas Ghormley a month after her son wrote it. "This we believe was the first information received from our boys after their capture," the editor reported, "and will relieve the suspense of their friends."*

James Ghormley, private, Co. A, 149th Ohio:

Lynchburg, Va., Aug. 17th, 1864.

Dearest Mother:—

I suppose you have heard before this time of my being captured by Mosby's men, together with Wm. McCommon, E. F. Armstrong, Henry Benner, Eldridge Whipple of Co. A and Major Rozell, also Andrew Fix, of Co. H and Preston H. Sayre of Co. F.[9] The major was wounded in the arm.

We are all well, and will try to get along as well as we can do, so do not make yourselves uneasy about us. Rev. Z. D. Hickman, Co. B., was also taken at the same time.[10]

Your aff. Son,
James Ghormley

* * *

Ebenezer Rozell, major, 149th Ohio:

Some of us remember a little "scrap" with Mosby at Berryville on an early morning (the 13th of August, '64). I have only to look at my left arm to remind me that a rebel bullet went crashing through that arm and paralyzed it for the time. I had to grab rein of bridle with sword hand, but was soon surrounded by "Johnnies" and started for the "sunny" south. I was separated from the "boys" at Lynchburg, and never saw them more, except as they passed Libby a few days later.

I was in luck to get out about a month later, and home about a month after the regiment got back. I had, while in three-year service, been shot through the left lung, in right shoulder and face, and was discharged in the summer of 1863. The wound received at Berryville was enough to place me in what was called the hospital in Libby, and an order was made to examine inmates of [the] hospital, and all who were considered permanently disabled were ordered paroled. I "fell back" on old wounds, and got out on that order; a very happy man I was, when at Aiken's Landing I passed from under the rebel flag into our lines and under the "stars and stripes."

* * *

William McCommon, private, Co. A, 149th Ohio:

I was taken prisoner at Berryville, Va., on August 13th, 1864, at 4 A.M., together with James Ghormley, Edward Armstrong, Eldridge Whipple and [Andrew] Fix, with one man by the name of Sayre of Co. F.[11]

We were cooking coffee by the roadside when all at once we heard the report of a cannon and the shell burst just over our beads and came down through the branches of the trees we were under. At that moment, 400 of Mosby's mounted guerrillas came down on us demanding our money, watches, jewelry or anything else of value we had on our person. I had one dollar and 40 cents. They told me to give them the dollar and I could keep the 40 cents as I would need that before we got back, which I found was the gospel truth. That rebel was honest, anyhow.

They ordered us each to mount a mule and carry a six-pound shell in each hand until we crossed the Shenandoah River, and then they would provide some other way to carry them. I was riding a small mule and when about the middle of the stream myself, mule and shells dropped into a hole, and the shells are now lying on the bottom of the Shenandoah River. When we got across a rebel sergeant asked me where my shells were. I told him I did not know. He replied "I will report you to Col. Mosby and you will have to pay for them."

That would be the first whack at my lone 40 cents. I heard no more about it until noon, when they drew us up in line to count us. The sergeant asked "who is you all men that lost the shells in the river?" Nobody knew anything about any shells and he did not recognize me. He said to me, "You look like the man," but of course I did not know anything about his old shells. That is the last I heard of them.

Our dinner the first day was one loaf of bread cut in four pieces for four men. I can say that none of us had to let out our trouser straps. We marched 30 miles the first day and were pretty well tired out by night, when they issued to each of us one pint of flour. This we mixed with water and slapped it on a flat stone, which we propped up opposite the fire and baked. This tasted good to us, but I am afraid it would not pass muster at the Waldorf Astoria.

Armstrong said he could not eat his without butter, but we told him his complexion would be better if he would abstain from butter. Finally, he concluded that we were right and let it go at that. A lieutenant came along and asked how we were making out. We told him that we were perfectly delighted with the menu. He said, "I am glad you have nothing to complain of."

The next day's ride took us to Culpepper C.H., the bracing air of Virginia still keeping our appetites in fine shape. No breakfast this morning, but we had a bounteous feast at noon. They cut a loaf in two for two men. It tasted good while it lasted, but the time seemed so short.

That afternoon Ghormley said he was going to make a break into the bushes and get away. He jumped off his mule and had not gone more than ten feet from the road when a guard spied him and fired six shots into the bushes. Ghormley came back in a hurry. He told the guard that he only wanted to get some blackberries. He watched him closely after that, and told him "the next berries *you* get will be lead berries."

At the end of the third day we reached Lynchburg, Va., where we were put into an old tobacco warehouse. There were 300 prisoners there when we arrived. We were quartered on the dirty floor, covered with tobacco dust. You could hear the men sneeze in all languages. Our fare was still one loaf of bread for two men. At this place our largest and strongest man, Henry Benner, a wagon maker from Chillicothe, said, "Boys, we will never get out of this alive."

He began to weaken right there, and in three weeks from that time he died of homesickness. We tried to shame him out of it, saying, "You are the healthiest man in the bunch and you will live through it if anyone will." One morning I found him lying dead on the ground, the first one of our little party to go.[12]

They kept us at this place for four weeks and then moved us to Richmond, Va. As we marched past Libby Prison, we heard someone calling from an upper window, "Hey! there! old 149th." It was Major Rozell, who had been captured the same morning that we were. In the fight at Berryville the major was wounded in the elbow and had been taken direct to Libby. We were not allowed to speak to him.

We remained in Richmond one night. Then they took us across the river to Belle Island, where the hardest part of our prison life began. It was a bleak spot, bare of trees. Some few of the prisoners had tattered tents; the majority had none. It rained every day while we were there and the fog was so thick you could almost cut it until about noon, when it would fix for another rain. We had no protection whatever from this weather, and we would walk around in the night in the rain until we fell asleep on the muddy ground. We would lie there until awakened by the intense cold, to get up and walk again.

Here they fed us on wild pea soup, flavored with ox tail, without dressing. No napkins went with this course, and the meals were never on time, as it took the cooks an hour or more to skim the maggots off the soup, as they wanted our meals to come to us perfectly clean so we could not tell our folks at home that they did not understand their business.

Here is where Armstrong told us, "Boys, we are never going to make it."
We answered, "Now you commence and you will go like Benner."

All the sick men at Belle Isle were to be transferred to City Point, an order having been issued to that effect. Whipple was not feeling well, so I told him that I would try to get him off on the boat. I told him as we neared the boat for him to fall down and I would call the officers' attention to him. As we had not rehearsed the part, he fell down too soon. I said "You fell down too soon. Wait until I give the word and then fall."

We came near making a mess of it, as it was. He began to laugh about the time for him to fall, but the officers did not see him laugh. The doctor asked me, "What is the matter with that man?" I told him I did not know but he was awful sick. He finally passed him to City Point. I heard after getting home that he got as far as Annapolis, Md., and had died there.[13] I fully expected to see him when I got home, as I knew the others were dead. He was a baker by trade and worked in Chillicothe before his enlistment.

We remained for seven weeks on Belle Isle, when we were sent to Salisbury, N.C.[14] We thought Belle Island was awful, but this place no man can describe, only an ex-prisoner of war. The stockade contained 20 acres and was fenced with trees split in half, with several large gates. A large brick building occupied part of the ground, which was formerly the North Carolina Penitentiary. It had three stories, the upper story when we were there being used as a jail for rebel deserters and other outlaws from the rebel army.

If there ever was a more villainous looking set of men, I never saw them. The first night I was there I went up to this third story to sleep, as it was raining hard, not knowing anything about the place. A man came to me and asked me if I knew what kind of a place I was in? I told him I did not. He said, "Get out of here as quietly as possible or they would throw you out of the window." I went instanter.

Within a month, James Ghormley and Edward Armstrong both died. I was going around the grounds one morning—we had long lost all dates—when I saw Armstrong lying dead on the ground. I scarcely recognized him, he was so black from stooping over the little pine-knot fires. About a week later, Ghormley died.[15] I was talking with him the night before. He said, "I cannot last but a day or two." I tried to cheer him up, but it was of no use. This left me the only one of our boys alive that I knew of. The last I saw of Armstrong and Ghormley, they were piled on the dead wagon that came in twice a day to collect the dead. The corpses were piled in, one on top of another like so many logs, taken out and buried in trenches.

I remained there three months longer, and was just about ready to give up when one morning a rebel lieutenant came to me and said, "Here, you cussed Yank, get up to the gate, you are to be exchanged." I told him that was an old story. He said, "Stay there then." I told him I could not walk, so he had me carried to the gate. There were a thousand loaves of cornbread lying on the ground. They told each man to take a loaf, as that would have to last us until we got into our lines. We were three days getting to the Union lines and our loaves looked very small when we arrived at Wilmington, N.C., where we were exchanged.

We ran in on a foggy morning. One of our boys cried out, "There is our flag." You cannot realize how we felt, how we tried to raise a feeble cheer, when we knew that we were in God's country once more.

We were ordered to "pile off," which we did in short order. There were piles of broken crackers and scraps of meat lying on the ground, which had been tramped upon by men and horses. We began to eat it greedily, until we were stopped by our officers putting a guard around us. They told us not to eat that garbage, as Uncle Sam's rations would be ready in a few minutes. It seemed like a dream to us. We were in a heaven of happiness.

We were kept in a hospital at Wilmington for about a week, and then we were sent to Annapolis, Md., by transport. At Annapolis, we were put in tent hospital after burning all our clothes and the "varmints" that went with them. They then cut our hair close, turned the hose on us, gave each man a good scrubbing and clothed us in *night gowns,* as our uniforms had not arrived from New York.

We remained in hospital for two weeks, when we were sent to general hospital at Baltimore, Md., where our record was taken. My weight at that time being 85 pounds—having lost 75 pounds in rebel prisons, I could not well spare any more. I remained in hospital at Baltimore three months longer, when I was discharged and sent home. My own mother did not know me until I told her who I was.

* * *

Drummer McClain of the 144th Ohio faithfully kept a diary of his service and confinement. Captured at Berryville, he, friend Fin Barton, and others from Company I eventually reached North Carolina.

Samuel McClain, musician, Co. I, 144th Ohio:

[October] 15. Saturday. We are still in Salisbury, Rowan County, N.C. prison. Drew bread, molasses & rice. Very pleasant today. I got some squash seeds today. I [am] anxious to see my family.

16. Sunday. All well this morning. Bread, beef & rice today. 6 men died last night & a captain shot. Captain Davis of N.Y. Slept good. Dreamt that J. Roland's house burnt down.

17. Monday. All right. 6 men died last night. Drawed hardtack & rice soup. Pleasant today. Good news heard of the surrender of Petersburg.[16] Fin

sold one ration of bread for $4.00 & bought sweet potatoes. You bet they were good.

18. Tuesday. All right. Fin & me slept under the hospital like hogs last night. 6 men died last night. Drawed bread, molasses & rice s. Fin bought a pie for $2.00. Cool night.

19. Wednesday. All shivering around this morning. Fin bought a sweet cake for $2.00 in Confed. money. We have hard fare here. No tents or blankets yet. News the Yanks are shelling Richmond today.

20. Thursday. All well. Drawed flour, rice & molasses. 10 men died last night. Cool day. I slept in the convalescents hospital last night. Very cold sleeping.

21. Friday. All well this morning. Drew beef & bread. I sold my ration for $4.00 in Confed. money & bought a tin cup for $2.00 & 2 sweet potatoes for $1.50. 6 men died last night. Frisby[17] died of the 144th.

22. Saturday. Almost froze today. Cold & stormy, high wind. Great suffering among the prisoners. 6 men died. Drawed bread & molasses, rice s.

23. Sunday. All well. Slept in the prison all night. Crowded very much. 9 men died last night. Cool day.

24. Monday. I had a heavy chill last night. Drawed our rations at 9 o'clock at night. 8 men died.

25. Tuesday. All well. 9 men dead last night. Fin is sick. Pleasant today. Drew bread & rice s. & molasses.

26. Wednesday. Moved today to the other side of the lot. 13 men died last night. Drew flour & rice soup today.

27. Thursday. Pitching tents this morning in the rain. Very disagreeable today. 15 men died last night. 600 men came in tonight.

28. Friday. Warm today. 23 men died last night. Fin B. went to the Hospital today. Got no flour today. I got some of Uncle Sam's coffee today from a prisoner just captured.

29. Saturday. I had the heart burn all night. 25 men died last night. I am better. Sold a ration of bread for $3.00.

30. Sunday. All right today. Drew bread, beef & rice s. I sold a pint of flour for $2.50 today. Fin is better today. 27 men died last night.

31. Monday. All well. Fin is getting better. I made him a cup of coffee today. I washed socks today. I slept in the tent last night. 18 men died last night.

Nov. 1. Tuesday. I am sick today.

2. Wednesday. I am sick today.

3. Thursday. Findley Barton died today. I am so sick I can't go to see him.

4. Friday. I am sick today.

5. Saturday. I was laid out to die, but God spared my life a little longer.

6. Sunday. I am sick today.

7. Monday. I am sick today. Wilson Brown died today.[18]

8. Tuesday. I am gaining some, but very slow. I hope that I'll soon be able to be around again.

9. Wednesday. I [am] very unwell yet. We get but little grub.

10. Thursday. I am gaining some.

11. Friday. I feel better today. W. H. Wheeler[19] died today.

12. Saturday. All well. I am now on the mend.

13. Sunday. I am getting better. Got a bad cough.

14. Monday. Big talk of us being exchanged. I hope it's true. Hard work to keep the lice all killed.

15. Tuesday. I am on the mend, but very weak. I eat crust coffee.

16. Thursday.[20] Cool this morning. I bought a vest today for seven dollars in Confed.

17. Friday. I am some better today. Pleasant day. Walter Wood[21] died today. 12 hundred died since we come here.

18. Saturday. I am some better today.

19. Sunday. Wet day today. I am about the same.

20. Monday. Raining yet.

21. Monday. Raining yet.

22. Tuesday. I am getting better slowly. I thank god for it.

23. Wednesday. Cold night. Froze hard. I slept cold.

24. Thursday. Pleasant day. I feel better today.

25. Friday. Pleasant day. I am better.

26. Saturday. All got 1/4 rations today.

27. Sunday. I dreamt that I was home talking with my wife & got something good to eat. I got a letter from home today & was glad to hear from home.

The diary's final entry, three weeks later, is in another man's hand.

Dec. 16. This day poor Sammie bid farewell to earth and its sorrows.[22]

14 | The Other Enemy

R*ARE IS THE DIARY or memoir of a hundred-days man (or anyone else in uniform during the Civil War) that does not mention illness. Nearly every soldier suffered at some time, to some degree. Though the United States Sanitary Commission and similar organizations strove to maintain the health of the troops, disease stalked the camps.*

The 169th Ohio suffered most among the hundred-days regiments, losing 41 of its men to sickness during the suffocating summer at Fort Ethan Allen outside Washington. Its hospital register lists an appalling range of diseases, the deadliest of which were fevers.[1] Private S. M. Terry of Company B touched on the 169th's decimation in a poem he read at a regimental reunion 32 years later:[2]

> With saddened hearts we call to mind
>   A long extended list
> Of comrades who at dress parade
>   Were from their places missed.
> The horrid fever fired their blood
>   And burned their temple down
> And death's relentless messenger
>   Revealed his fatal frown.

These deaths didn't break the spirit of the 169th, but instead seemed to strengthen it. Many survivors revered their colonel,[3] and held reunions far into the next century. Troops knew the dangers of disease, and took what precautions they could. But like the unfortunate 169th, and most veteran units as well, hundred-days regiments lost many more men to disease than to enemy fire.[4]

Justin E. Twitchell, chaplain, 131st Ohio:[5]

Fort Federal Hill
Baltimore, Maryland, August 6

When our regiment was mustered into the United States service at Columbus, and we left for duty, it was remarked—"We shall not all reach home again."

No one could read the future, and I am sure no one thought that he should be the missing one on our return. We were reminded of this remark soon after reaching Baltimore, and now we have been reminded of the same again.

As we come nearer the time when our service would end, our hope of entire preservation grew stronger, and we began to say—"How remarkable, if, after near four month's absence, the last roll should be called, and only *one* fail to answer his name." This had come to be our hope, but God's ways are not our ways; and again our hearts have been made sad, as we sat beside a dying friend—saw him struggling on the outmost verge of life for twelve long hours; and then sink into that sleep, which knows no waking until the resurrection morning. Cornelius F. Young, of Company I, has gone to his long home.

I believe everything possible was done for him, the surgeon remaining by his side nearly all the time—but at one o'clock on Wednesday morning he died. Disease, neuralgia of the heart. Such hours for the soldier are sad; and there were tearful eyes that night from some men. In this kind of life we all feel like *brothers,* and the bond of our union here, away from home, is *strong.*

He moved to Ohio about one year ago, and had since been residing in Centerville, where he gained many friends. He was a true and faithful soldier, timid and shrinking from observation, but always at his post, securing the confidence and respect of all. We held our funeral services in the open court in front of company quarters, at 3 P.M., and the next morning his body was conveyed to his early home near Frederick, in this state. May that comfort which the mourner needs be vouchsafed to his sorrowing friends.

The health of the regiment is generally good, and has been remarkable since we left home.[6]

* * *

Although the 133rd Ohio near Petersburg had "mercifully escaped death from bullets, we have not been so fortunate in withstanding disease and mortality attendant thereupon," its chaplain reported.[7] The area was "acknowledged by the citizens as being unfavorable for health. Mid and late summer is their sickly season. Our sick list, despite the vigilance of our medical staff, has been largely on the increase."

Sylvester M. Sherman, first sergeant, Co. G, 133rd Ohio:

The rebels were not the only foes we had to contend with at this place [Fort Powhatan]. Toward the middle of July, a good many of the men were troubled with diarrhea, which was quite obstinate and rapidly weakened them. We also had another foe whose approach was more insidious, whose attacks were harder to repel, took more time to recover from, and was in every way more discouraging. The Malarial Typhoid Fever, peculiar to the James River, was this foe.

Nearly 300 men of our regiment were on the sick list with this terrible disease at the same time. At one time, only 333 were fit for duty. The men would first complain of feeling tired and stiff, muscles sore, headache and dizziness, much like ague coming on. Then a slight fever would appear in the afternoons, getting worse and lasting longer each day, till finally it would be continuous and the patient delirious. He would be a very sick man.

This would last for three or four weeks, when the patient would usually be able to walk about a little, looking like a yellow ghost, reeling as he went and feeling dizzy and miserable as could be imagined. He would of course keep on drinking swamp water from the spring which supplied the garrison, and would soon be down again with a relapse unless he took medicine as regularly as he ate his meals. If he did this, he might keep just about so. If he neglected his quinine, down he went. The usual bill of fare at this time was hardtack and sowbelly, with quinine for dessert (after blackberries were gone).

Several attempts were made to get better water by digging wells in several places. Some wells which were dug along the banks of the river gave a supply which seemed a little better than that from the spring. There was a fine spring outside the picket lines; but that was too far off and seemed too dangerous to be utilized, though several times barrels of the water were brought in by guarded parties.

The stoutest and most robust men in the command seemed to be the first victims of the fever. Among those we lost by it was Major Joseph M. Clark,[8] a most estimable man and a genial comrade, and Captain Thomas Lilley, a Mexican veteran, a very efficient officer and agreeable man.[9]

Major Clark was taken to Fortress Monroe, where he died. Captain Lilley had been sent to Bermuda Hundred to the field hospital there, but it was intended to remove him to Fortress Monroe.[10] He was taken on board the boat in the evening to start in the morning, but he died during the night. Many of the men went home from service about as miserable as they could be from the effects of these diseases, some of them being affected for years with chronic liver and stomach trouble and diarrhea.

When a man got too sick for duty or to eat his rations, and could only sit around and think of his ailments and wonder how things were going on at home, he was pretty apt to get blue and homesick. He had left home on short notice and did not have time to arrange his affairs; consequently, he had to leave his farming to his wife and children, or his store or shop in the care of clerks or apprentices. This fact and his sickness made him feel as if he was about broke up.

When they were well, all the members of the regiment—though conscious of the sacrifices they had made—accepted the situation cheerfully and manfully and stood up to their work bravely. They could not help thinking sometimes how nice it would be if they could only look in on the folks at home for a little while, and straighten up business matters somewhat; they could then come back contented to serve out the balance of their term, or longer if needed. But there was no chance for a furlough.

Among the kind offices to be performed for the boys when they were sick was that of writing letters to friends at home, and it was a duty which was done cheerfully by all who were called upon. But no one excelled our (Rev.) Lieutenant Whitehead,[11] whose letters carried such comfort to the friends of sick and dying comrades. Some of his letters were so prized that they were printed and framed by the families who received them.

About the latter part of July, the wives of Colonel Innis and Lieutenant-Colonel Ewing[12] came to the fort on a visit and stayed a couple of weeks. This was a great pleasure to the whole regiment. Many were acquainted with the ladies and could thus obtain direct news from home. The others could hear in a general way how matters were at home, which was a good deal of satisfaction. Besides, the ladies showed a good many kindnesses to the sick, which were greatly needed, for at this time the malarial fever was at about its worst.[13]

The marshy country around the fort, heated up by the fierce rays of the sun through the day, rendered the air almost unfit to be breathed, and the sick were reported by the dozens.

The sickest men and those who were likely to be sick for some time were put on steamboats and sent to the hospital at Fortress Monroe,[14] where more convenient and permanent arrangements had been made for the care of sick and wounded than could be had in the field. Our own field hospital would, of course, accommodate only a small number; it is not customary to keep on hand any great amount of medicines, so that our supply got pretty low. Another good reason for sending away the sick was that we were liable to be attacked at any time.

* * *

Surgeon Eames described the neglect of his hospital in a letter to his wife, before his regiment moved on to Fort Delaware.

William M. Eames, surgeon, 157th Ohio:

Relay House Md.

Our Hospital is nearly ready to receive the sick and we have a supply of bedsacks that would astonish you—viz. 15 old ones. There are now 20 sick men in the Hospital besides nurses, and we are having men come down with measles and fevers every day. They sent 10 old blankets also and about the same proportion of everything else. I wish the Sanitary Commission could know how shabbily Ohio soldiers are used in the Middle Department. They would send part of the stores which have been so liberally contributed by them and others to their aid.

We ought to have at least 50 beds filled up, as the measles and fevers and the great number of weakly men in this regiment will at least fill that number the whole 100 days. But they can get along in their "dog tents" on the ground—and on the floor of dirty barracks—tho' some may die. The poor fellow that died the other day here with spotted fever died on a hard board with a little hay under him. There is nothing to be got here unless I go to Baltimore and buy it with my own money. Don't imagine I am borrowing trouble about it—but the officers and men are looking to me to remedy the evil, and I have done all I can by going to Baltimore once and sending once, and when I do all I can I quit there—and sleep easy.

* * *

Jacob Souder Holtz, private, Co. H, 164th Ohio:

June the 26 / 64

Dear Father, Mother and Brother,

I thought I would write you a few lines to let you know that I am not very well. I had a very bad Cold and it settled in my head, and the weather is so warm and dry that it keeps me weak. I am in my bunk part of the time. I think I [will] get right in a couple of days. Mother, I got a letter from you yesterday. Our box is in Washington. Norm is going to get it tomorrow. When you write send me a little wormwood.

I must close for it is so warm it looks like rain.

Yours, J. S. Holtz

Norman D. Egbert, first lieutenant, Co. H, 164th Ohio:

Fort Woodbury, Va. June 28th

Mr. Holtz,

At Jacob's request I write to you. He has been sick for several days, not dangerous however. He has improved since yesterday morning rapidly, and can walk out some this morning. You may well rest assured, I will do all in my power to have the best care taken of him. I will write to you every day until he gets able to write himself, which I think will be in a few days. The Surgeon said this morning that he would be "all right in a few days." If anything, however, should turn up, he get worse or anything of the kind, I will Telegraph immediately to you.

I do not apprehend any danger. The air is cool and much more favorable to health than it was a few days ago. I will write tomorrow. Give yourself no uneasiness.

Fort Woodbury, Virginia, June 30th

Mr. Holtz,

I wrote you yesterday concerning Jacob's sickness, and Telegraphed to you last evening.[15] Jacob is worse, painful as it is to me, I will tell you all. I consider him dangerously sick tonight. When I wrote to you last evening he was quite smart, and could set up some. It is a hard matter for me to inform anyone of such a fact. But I tell you as I would like anyone to tell me, if I were in your place.

But you may rest assured he shall have the best of care. I will do everything in my power to make him as comfortable as possible. I will write again tomorrow's mail.

Respectfully, N. D. Egbert

Fort Woodbury, July 1st

Mr. Holtz,

Jacob is about the same, some delirious today. I was on duty yesterday and last night and could not therefore be with him but little. I am going to stay with him tonight. Also Mr. Lee.[16] He answers all questions as soon as you ask him them. He asked me if I was going to write to you today. Told him I would, says he, "Tell them I am about well, and will be able to write myself in a few days." I think he will get well, he will be very sick I fear. He is situated as comfortably as he possibly can be. Either I, or some of the boys are with him all the time.

I will write to you by every mail.

Jake Holtz died of typhoid fever later that day. Lieutenant Egbert was married to Jake's cousin and lived on a neighboring farm.[17]

* * *

Wallace W. Chadwick, private, Co. F, 138th Ohio:

Fort Spring Hill [Virginia], June 30th.

I have been in the hands of a doctor for a week past. The first three days were very severe on me, as it was the most uncomfortable hot weather I ever saw and the poorest accommodations for the sick imaginable.

My complaint was dysentery. It was pretty severe, and I felt weak as if I had had a short spell of fever. A good many of the boys are complaining, but most of them get better in four or five days. There are generally from four to eight men in the company at the hospital every morning for medicine, but there is hardly a serious case in the regiment.

While I was sick there were dewberries to be had. They were very small, but by cooking them we could make them very nice. We managed to get some tea and soft bread, but the latter we cannot buy now. There is little at the sutlers' within the reach of the common soldier. They charge 20 cents for a pound of crackers, 20 cents for a pound of ham, five cents for two sheets of paper, and other things in the same ratio. If a man has a little money, they will soon have it away from him.

July 2nd.

Among [the army's] sick the suffering is very great, although the Commissions[18] are doing very much. My health is some better, yet I still feel miserably weak and unfit for duty. That is one great trouble here, for they put the men on picket duty or at guarding prisoners as soon as they quit taking medicine, and then they are sick again in a day or two. We have as mean a colonel as a regiment could have. The rest of our officers are pretty well thought of, unless it is the quartermaster.[19]

July 6.

I expect to go on duty again tomorrow, for I feel as if they will look on me as a shirker if I am not at my post as soon as possible. Some six or eight of the boys are on the sick list, but no one is serious. For a while, we got orders from our officers for food at the post commissary, but they have shut down on that now. About one day in six, we get soft bread, and fresh meat we have twice a week.

July 10th.

I am on duty now. It is extremely unpleasant to be sick out there, yet our regiment is very lucky thus far, not having lost a single man by death.

Sunday, August 14th.

I hope that two weeks from today may find me home or as near home as Camp Dennison. I have been sick again with a bilious fever. I took some pills and then procured some camphor of the neighbors, and since then I have been getting better. I expect I shall be away from my company until the Colonel gets orders to start for Ohio. Our time is up one week from today.

I am sorry that we will have to leave one member of our company behind, as Mr. Poole[20] is no more. The rest of the sick are all better and will be able to travel with us, we hope.[21]

* * *

Gilbert L. Laboytreaux, private, Co. F, 138th Ohio:

The 138th regiment has lost two men by disease: Peter Poole, Company F, died of typhoid fever, August 10, and J. T. Jukes, Company H, August 11. They were both good men and good soldiers, and died in the service of their country; that is enough, they need no eulogy from me. Our regiment will leave for home this week.

> We buried them under the pine trees
>   That fringe the Chesapeake's shore;
> In the grave we gently lowered them,
>   And silently covered them o'er.
> Here the wind from the far-off ocean,
>   As it sweeps o'er the sparkling bay,
> Will sift through the evergreen branches
>   When their comrades are far away.
> The birds in the early spring time
>   Will carol their wild notes there,
> And flowers spring up in the evening
>   To sweeten the morning air.

* * *

Clifton M. Nichols, corporal, Co. E., 152nd Ohio:

Cumberland, Md., July 13.

It is our painful duty to record the first death in Company E since it left Springfield for 100 days' service. John Fitzpatrick, a native of Ireland, aged 19 years, died in the hospital in Clarysville, 18 miles from here, on the 16th of July from typhoid fever.

He was a member of the Central Methodist Church in Springfield. While in the service he proved himself a prompt, willing and reliable soldier, and he brought his religion with him into the field. We knew personally of instances where he "stood up for Jesus."[22]

* * *

Private Frederick Hood, 44, died of "inflammation of the Brain" on July 7 in the Washington forts. His 19-year-old son Freeland served in the same company.[23]

Freeland Q. Hood, private, Co. I, 151st Ohio:

Dear Mother Brothers and Sisters,

I set myself this evening after hearing from home to inform you of my troubles, which I have to bear. I am well and hearty, but the thoughts of parting with a father, I don't see how I can stand it. Well, Mother, I was by him from the time he took sick until he died. I took his red handkerchiefs from his poor old forehead and I have got all of his clothes in my knapsack and I am going to fetch them home with me, if I live to get home and I hope I will.

Freeland Hood mustered out with his company.

* * *

James C. Cannon, private, Co. K, 150th Ohio:

Several of the company were down with fever, and on the 15th [of July] Henry A. Cowles died. His death caused unusual sadness, both on account of his personal attractions as a friend and companion, and because of the sorrow it would bring to the home where his place would ever be vacant.

Sunday, July 31, Companies K and D moved into Fort Saratoga.

Fillmore[24] and Sergt. Keyes were sick, and Dr. Dutton[25] took them to the hospital. Todd, Frazer and Bennett[26] were also sick this first week of August. Edgar L. Beech died on the 1st, and on the 3d John Monroe passed away. Monroe was from Norway, and was not subject to military duty, but enlisted from pure love of the country he had adopted for his home. His body was embalmed and sent to Oberlin for burial.

On the fourth of August, Ells[27] died, thus making a vacancy in the senior class [of Oberlin College]. Sickness was now making serious inroads into our ranks. In the hospital at this time were Morgan, Burrell, Hudson, Johnson, Jackson and Partridge.[28] Morgan was so low that a telegram was sent for his father to come to the camp.[29]

But now the period for which we had enlisted was fast drawing to a close, and on Aug. 11, after 9 o'clock at night, orders came for us to leave for home. On the 12th we started, with 55 men in ranks. We rode up the Susquehanna Valley by moonlight, rejoicing that so many of us were safely through our time of service, yet with sorrowful thoughts for the five comrades who had given their lives to our country during this short time.

Some sick were taken home on the train, being considered strong enough to bear it. Morgan and Todd were left in Washington with Keyes to look after them.

* * *

James E. Borton, private, Co. C, 130th Ohio:
August 26, 1864

Dear Mother, Brother, and Sisters:

I set myself or rather prop myself to write a few lines to inform you that I am still alive, but I can't walk any nor haven't walked 2 rods at a time since the 5th of this month. I was taken on the 1st and have been bedfast ever since. And ever since I come here, my legs from my hips down have been cold and numb all the time. By a great deal of coaxing, I got them to rub them with alcohol but it don't seem to do much good. My feet turns all black and blue sometimes. They can rub with all their mights and I won't hardly know they are rubbing them. My appetite still stays good and I buy milk and crumb my bread in it. Our grub is toast without anything on it, slop coffee, and tea, water gruel made out of corn meal. The doctor took my name down yesterday to send me north. But the ward master when he sent names in omitted mine because I was a hundred day man.

Mother, don't trouble thyself about me. I am in a hard place, but I hope I will get out of it soon. Silas,[30] if I am sent to the state soon and I am no better, I should like you to come. Our regiment is expected along here every day. We will follow the regiment. All the regiments have gone home but ours. I must hurry up and mail this. I am in hopes you live peaceable and quiet. If not, do. I impeach you try and make it all up and resolve after this that all old things be forgotten and that you live a new and happy life. Our family is getting small and it does seem to me you might try. Mother, take none of this to thyself. I know thee and wish I was there under thy care. I needn't suffer so much. Good-bye. I hope to see you soon. My time was out the 20th of this month. I guess it is hardly worthwhile for you to write. Good-bye dear mother, brother and sisters.

J. E. B., Hampton Hospital, Ward 20
Fortress Monroe, Va.

Kingsbury House
Toledo, Ohio
September 12, 1864

Dear Mother, Brother, and Sisters:
I take the present opportunity of writing a few lines to inform you that I am this near home, at least. And am better if anything than when I left Hampton Hospital. I can walk a great deal farther but then I am very sore from the effects of riding in the cars. We rode in boxcars most all the way, and in coming over the mountains, I tell you, I shivered. I thought I'd freeze certain. We got into Pittsburg at 11 o'clock and lay on the wet and cold sidewalk until 5 in the morning, when they give us transportation cars. A little better than boxcars and not much either. We came through Alliance [Ohio] but I didn't know the place for some time. She has gone down awfully, looks hard indeed.

Silas, I have good care here, I tell you, and a middling good bed, good enough. And then the young ladies takes hold of my arms and helps me up and down the door steps. There is 3 of us here. The rest went home but are to be here today. Silas, Toledo respects soldiers. I can get all I want to drink or eat, most without a cent. I am entirely out of money. Silas, if he has any business or anything here, come down Wednesday on the morning train and help me home. Don't come unless he can leave handy.

The regiment will be here tomorrow, I guess.

J. E. Borton.

James Borton mustered out on September 22 and died before he could return home.[31]

15 | Johnny Comes Marching Home

BY THE END OF *the hundred days, the Army of Northern Virginia was still fighting tenaciously, the Army of the Potomac had yet to take Richmond, and the end of the conflict was nowhere in sight. Governor Brough's grand strategy for ending the war clearly had failed. The Ohio regiments had served well, however, and the tremendous value of maintaining an organized state militia that could be called for Federal service would not be forgotten.*

If the mood in the North was no longer buoyant as in the spring, there was nonetheless reason for hope. Sherman's army marched into Atlanta during the first days of September, and so opened a gate to the sea. The victory, coupled with a big soldiers' vote for "Father Abraham" in the fall election, would prove enough to end former general George McClellan's campaign for the presidency. John Brough, buffeted as always by political controversy and turmoil, would decide not to seek another term as governor, and would die in office a year later, a lame duck.[1] Some believed that he would have gone on to join the cabinet in Washington.

The torrid summer of 1864 faded, and the Ohio regiments began returning home, having served out their time and perhaps a little more. In the streets of their hometowns, at their train depots and courthouses, in meeting rooms and their own kitchens, the hundred-days men were met with the same warm emotion that had seen them off in May. Most would remember it the rest of their days, and as old men would recall the "boys" who hadn't returned beside them.

Benjamin R. Cowen, adjutant-general of Ohio:

It was interesting to note the steady change of public sentiment in the state after the Guard was sent away.

Before they were ordered away, the call was exceedingly unpopular, for reasons already stated. It was looked upon by many excellent men as an imposition on the state to require from her citizens this heavy additional burden, in view of what she had already done. The government was abused without stint for an alleged over-officious zeal in offering the services of the Guard without consulting them on the subject. Fathers were angry because their last son was taken away from the active duties of the farm and home, and protests were loud and deep from all quarters.

The Guard marched away in the first half of May. By the 1st of June, we began to receive reports from the regiments showing a most satisfactory spirit, many of them even of an enthusiastic character. Letters of the same kind came from the homes; the dear ones there caught the enthusiasm, and began to exult over the fact that their sons and brothers were with those who had brought renown to the state, so that by the time the 100 days had expired it was hard to find a man of any prominence who had not favored the call from its very inception, while the number of those who had advised it originally was something remarkable.

But the proudest and happiest parties to the call were the members of the Guard, who have never yet ceased to be thankful that they were recorded on the roster of those who fought in the great Civil War.[2]

The service was correctly and concisely summed up by Mr. Lincoln in the certificates he caused to be given to each member of the Guard at the close of its service. "The term of service of their enlistment was short," he wrote, "but distinguished by memorable events in the Valley of the Shenandoah, on the Peninsula, in the operations of the James River, around Petersburg and Richmond, in the battle of Monocacy, in the entrenchments of Washington and other important service. The National Guard of Ohio performed with alacrity the duty of patriotic volunteers, for which they are entitled, and are hereby tendered, through the governor of their state, the national thanks."[3]

What a glorious record to be comprised within so brief a period!

There were those who affected to sneer at the services of the hundred-days men of '64, but Lincoln and Grant and Stanton were not of the number. Grant knew very well that the reinforcements of 35,000 men which were sent him so promptly in May, 1864, enabled him to make his bloody battle summer of that year the prelude to the closing scene. He said he had never seen a battery more promptly and effectively supported on the battlefield than he was supported by the militia of his native state in May, 1864. And I have never doubted, for I know that Lincoln and Grant and Stanton did not doubt, but that the services of the Ohio hundred-days men shortened the war.

* * *

Like all soldiers, everywhere, Ohio's hundred-days men were eager to go home. They were also proud of themselves and their regiments. In Virginia, the poet laureate of the 138th disputed the claims of another Cincinnati regiment, the 137th, then at Baltimore.

Gilbert L. Laboytreaux, private, Co. F, 138th Ohio:

We do not brag—we never did brag—but neither Col. Fisher nor his men will ever admit that the 137th has done, or ever could do, what the 138th could not do. Look at the map, if you please. At North Mountain we were on duty several days; at Washington we manned three of the forts, could have defended them, too; at "White House" we not only guarded prisoners, but took innumerable pills and untold powders; at Spring Hill, in front of Petersburg, within range of the Rebel forts, and under a blistering sun, we did all that was required of us, and that was enough, in all conscience; it was drill, fatigue and guard duty all the time, still all orders were cheerfully obeyed.

Look for us when you see us, but

We are coming, we are coming,
    Throw your banners to the breeze,
Hang them out from every house-top,
    Let them float from all the trees;
We are only waiting orders,
    (Why, in thunder, don't they come?)
For sure our wives and sweethearts
    Are looking for us home.

* * *

The 154th Ohio, however, was kept on Federal duty at New Creek because of continued Confederate activity in the area after the recent battle. The regiment was neither happy about this turn nor slow to say so.

Isaac Hambleton, second lieutenant, Co. C, 154th Ohio:

New Creek, August 22nd 64

Dear Wife,

When I wrote the last to you I thought I would of been home before this, but this is the fortunes of war. I hardly know what to tell you now. We have been looking to be relieved every day for the last ten days.

The Colonel telegraphed several times to Kelley, but don't get much satisfaction. He says the emergencies of the case demand that we should stay a few days longer, but we can't see it that way. The Colonel telegraphed to Governor Brough this morning to see what he could do in the matter. I think it's doubtful if we are home before the first of September. We think the emergencies of the case demand that we should be at home now.

Our company is getting quite small. There is about twenty-five of them at home & more talking of going.[4] We haven't done any duty except camp duty for several days. The most of the men have refused to do duty, though they haven't been urged very strong. I guess they or the most of them will rebel if they are required to. For my part I am ready to do my duty under all circumstances, although I am as anxious to get home as any of them. I think it is my duty to obey my superiors, although I may not think the duty just. Well, no more on this subject. . . . [5]

* * *

The unfortunate 149th had better news than the 154th.

George Perkins, private, Co. A, 149th Ohio:

It rained hard all the time we remained at Bolivar Heights, but we did not care, we were going home. At last orders came from headquarters for our discharge.

Giving three cheers, we started for Harper's Ferry on a dark, rainy day. Here we found a train awaiting us, which we boarded and at night pulled out for Baltimore, getting there the next morning. We formed ranks and marched to the Northern Central depot, and took a train for home.

We returned over the same route over which we came, with the same accommodations. We had another good supper in Pittsburg, and reached Columbus, Ohio, at noon. We left our train, marched to Tod Barracks and remained overnight. The next day we rode to Camp Dennison, were assigned to the same barracks that we had left four months previously. Cooks were detailed, and we remained there a week, until Aug. 30th, the officers making out payrolls, discharges, etc.

While there, several citizens of Chillicothe came to see us, and we received many boxes of good things to eat from home. Several of the boys left camp, walked to the next station and came up home, returning to camp the next day. To say that we were happy but faintly expresses it. We were finally discharged from the United States service and paid off.

A special train was furnished, cars with seats in them, and we sped homeward. When we arrived at Chillicothe, we were met by a large outpouring of citizens who, to music furnished by the German Brass Band, escorted us uptown. We marched up Main Street, and we stepped proudly, but were saddened as we passed the homes of James Ghormley and Edward Armstrong. We were coming home, but these, our friends and comrades, never returned. They starved to death in Salisbury, N.C., prison pen.

The good people of Chillicothe had prepared a dinner for us in the market house, and we did justice to it. After dinner we "fell in" for the last time, marched up Paint Street and drew up in front of the courthouse, where after a few remarks by the Colonel we broke ranks, each went to his home, and the 149th Regiment, Ohio Volunteer Infantry, became a memory.

* * *

"Nickliffe," the 152nd Ohio's tireless Boswell, reported the regiment's return, as he had recorded everything else.

Clifton M. Nichols, corporal, Co. E, 152nd Ohio:

Cumberland, Md., August 12.

We had a tornado here yesterday. Your correspondent was lying ill, in the tent occupied by Colonel Doty, when the storm came on in full fury. It required the entire strength of the Colonel, John Bretney,[6] Charley and the "subscriber" to keep the tent from going up like a balloon with the inmates hanging on.

A very heavy rain came with the wind. Several tents in the camp were overthrown. In the city the Soldier's Rest, a long, wooden building, occupied by about 70 soldiers, was blown to the ground, one man killed instantly and several others wounded.[7]

Yesterday, the force—artillery, cavalry, and infantry—at this post was reviewed by General Kelley, and marched through the principal streets of the city, which were properly decorated with national flags. As the force was quite respectable in numbers and the men well drilled, the scene was one of considerable interest. The 152d, of course, participated, and made a fine appearance. Colonel Putman being in command of the entire force, Colonel Doty was in command of our regiment. The troops were favorably received by the citizens.

Camp Dennison, August 15.

We arrived here yesterday (Sunday) from Cumberland, with 70 sick men from the 152d Ohio, sent as an advance guard of skirmishers to clear the way for the remainder of the command.

General Kelley, before we left, gave assurances that the entire regiment would follow in a few days. The term of service (from the 10th of May) expires on Wednesday of the present week, and from all we can learn we can see no reason to doubt that the men will start for this point by that time.

We brought with us Sergeant Neill, Mr. Arbogast (the older of the two of the same name in the regiment), Wm. H. Kimball, Reuben Huffman, David Henrickson, and John C. Oldham, all of Captain Welch's company.[8] Kimball jumped from the cars while we were running at full speed this side of Grafton.[9] He was in a somnambulic state and made his "leap in the dark" (for it was night) without being wakened by the concussion. The only injury he sustained was a scratch on the face.

The "History of the Hundred Days" is now written. The 152d has now only to return to Camp Dennison by the route it went out to New Creek on the 12th of May, to be paid off, mustered out and the men returned to their homes.[10] Their battles are all fought, their marches accomplished, their short rations superseded by an abundance of food, and they are about to resume the pleasant home associations from which they were separated by the call of Governor Brough.

* * *

Delayed by red tape and inefficiencies, mustering-out for some regiments was a cruelly long and tedious process, as the 132nd Ohio could attest.

Sgt. George F. Bailey, Co. G, 132nd Ohio:[11]

Saturday Aug. 27

Farewell to Norfolk. At seven o'clock & twenty minutes we hauled out from the dock—passed Fort Monroe at 9 o'clock. Turned the head of the *Monohansett* northward. At ten o'clock a schooner struck us on the larboard[12] quarter carrying away the flag staff & upper railing—sweeping one man overboard & bruising several others. The steamer laid to trying to find him but in vain. He was a member of Co. A & had no doubt written home that he would be there in a few days. But alas he now sleeps in the Chesapeake Bay unless picked up by the Schooner, which is hardly probable.[13]

Thursday Sept. 1

Arrived in Columbus at noon [by train]. Are now in Tod Barracks awaiting dinner. Finally dinner was announced by a blast from the Bugle. We went in expecting to find at least soldier's fare. But "Oh God" the same eternal hard-tack & coffee. I downed one biscuit and half the miserable coffee allowed me. Made my exit from Brough's Hotel & hope to God I'll never see it again. Soon afterward we fell in for Camp Chase, where we arrived at sundown dusty and tired.

Friday Sept. 2

Eight Regts. are here waiting to be paid off. Our time will come sometime. Four months ago today we gave ourselves to our country for one hundred days—expecting to be discharged when that time expired. But here we are twenty days over our time with a week or ten days ahead of us.

Saturday, Sept. 3rd

At 3 P.M. we took our guns & accouterments to the Cap's quarters. Disengaged one piece from another. Passed them without shedding a tear. Nothing welled up from the heart. All seemed eager to get rid of the musket that we had carried two thousand miles or more.

Monday, Sept. 5

Rained tremendously through the night—this morning Camp Chase is as muddy as it was last May and from the appearance of things will be while we sojourn here, which we sincerely hope will not be long. The 135 left camp this morning to be paid off in Columbus. Another Regt. or two are to leave today, which will thin Camp Chase considerable.

Co. G has become demoralized. Not more than twenty five or thirty left. The balance that are here have come to the conclusion that it will not be worthwhile for us to go, as those that have gone will relate all the adventures that the 132's passed through. Some that have gone should be preparing things—or getting the papers ready to have us mustered out. But a man is nowhere unless he wears shoulder straps, which is the beauty of soldiering.

In a few days we are all going home—some say to stay no more—as the draft is waiting for us. If we are caught in the draft after being drove around as we have this summer, the powers that be will not get any support from us. Now we will try and make some coffee—if it stops raining. If it don't we will do without. Oh for a Lodge in some vast wilderness where mud is unknown. The camp presents a gloomy appearance. A few scattered soldiers here and there are hovering over a small camp fire with gum blankets around them trying to make a little coffee—oh who would not be a soldier? Now twilight comes & another day closes in Camp Chase & still rains.

Thursday Sept. 8

Camp Chase is navigable for light draft steamers this morning. The day was spent in cussing everybody generally that wore shoulder straps. We can learn nothing about being mustered out. We now have the assurance that we will be mustered out this week.

Friday Sept. 9

Morning clear & warm. A first rate prospect of staying in Camp Chase until Christmas. The officers say the matter is the mustering out officers are drunk all the time & cannot be persuaded to do anything.[14] If I was Col. of the Regt. I would march it to Columbus forthwith & tell Jno. Brough to muster it out today. Or I would furlough the Regt. until I saw proper to call them together again. By doing so we could all be home tonight. Some of us talked of going home last night. The Capt. said if we did we would be considered deserters & may be court martialed.

Saturday Sept. 10

At 10 o'clock the mustering out officer came squared around & we were mustered for pay. But the pay did not come. About that time Co. G concluded to go home & spend the Holy Sabbath. Then the order was to pack up & clean out.

Shouldered our traps & headed for Columbus arriving there at 3 o'clock tolerable wet with sweat—which I hope will be the last sweat I will take around Camp Chase or any other military camp. Left Columbus at 5, arrived in Urbana at 8. Took a small turn around town. Took the S.D.C.[15] train at 10 arrived at Liberty at 11 & found all at the depot awaiting our arrival. Martial music was playing. I did not stop to listen but leaned out for home.

Sunday Sept. 11

Arose rather late. Found breakfast ready & once more sat at my own table.

Spent the day in relating my adventures to my friends and they came to congratulate me on my safe return from the war. Retired at night but not on the soft side of a board.

Monday Sept. 12

Arose rather late. Took a turn up town. I left at noon for Columbus to settle up with the U.S. Arrived in Columbus at 3 P.M. Took a bus for Camp Chase. Found six of Co. G there awaiting the arrival of the paymaster, who had not made his appearance as yet. Evening came & another night in Camp Chase. Was found rather too cool to be comfortable. Got up at midnight and sat by the fire until morning.

Tuesday Sept. 13

This day closes my career as a soldier. We spent the fore part of the day in looking for the paymaster. Long assured that he would be there at 8 A.M., the men became impatient. Curses loud and long came down on his head. Finally at 2 P.M. he arrived & commenced paying. Co. G was paid at four. I immediately struck out for town without shedding any tear. Found I was too late for the train. Waited until 7 o'clock & took a freight train. Arrived in Urbana too late for the night train going north. Concluded not to wait until noon next day. Corporal Weatherby, Pri. Loudon & myself walked to West Liberty.[16]

Thus closed the campaign of our One Hundred days—consuming four months and ten days.

* * *

Sylvester M. Sherman, first sergeant, Co. G, 133rd Ohio:

We did not know how long we were to be kept in the service, but thought our time was nearly up and began to expect orders to leave [Fort Powhatan] at almost any time. When the order came, it was received with great satisfaction.

The colonel had reported to General Butler that we had so many sick that it would be very inconvenient to take them on a boat crowded with noisy soldiers, and asked for a hospital boat. Butler telegraphed to Baltimore, and the authorities in command there impressed a peach boat, the *Mina,* and sent her to convey our sick.

The captain was a rebel sympathizer and did not relish this service a bit, but dared not disobey orders. He, however, took every opportunity to make himself disagreeable, and carried it so far that the colonel ordered a squad of men to pitch him overboard into the James. He now realized the situation and begged for mercy, which was granted. During the rest of the trip he behaved himself, with some show of respect for everyone on board.

About 10 o'clock on August 11th, the steamers *United States* and *Mina* arrived at the fort with the 130th O.V.I.,[17] which was to relieve us. We were at once ordered to strike tents and pack up, which we were not slow to do. At once everything was hurry and bustle, and about 4 o'clock we went aboard the *United States,* the sick being placed on the *Mina.* When the boats got out into the river, the boys gave three hearty cheers and our fifes and drums played *When Johnny Comes Marching Home.*

The weather was very hot, but when we got down the river a piece the banks were low and the breeze got a chance to strike us, making it very pleasant. The country had the same deserted appearance we noticed on going up the river. We passed Fortress Monroe about 11 o'clock at night.

August 12th, at about six o'clock in the morning, we turned from the bay into the Potomac River. It was quite cool in the early morning, but soon got so warm that the boys stretched their tents over their heads—which helped a little, and yet it was so hot that the perspiration streamed from every pore. The night had been a very uncomfortable one, on account of being so crowded on the boat. The men lay in every possible shape to find room, some even letting their legs hang over the sides of the boat.

Our journey up the Potomac was uneventful, and in a few hours more we were once again in the capital of the nation. The boys' faces beamed with smiles at the change. For nearly four months we had scarcely seen anyone but soldiers, and these living in a rough and tumble sort of a way that does not seem at all like the way people should live. But now that we had got back from the seat of war and saw women and children again, it seemed more like civilization.

We disembarked and marched to the Soldiers' Home, where we got supper. Three of our sick men died on the boat coming up. All the rest who were not able to accompany the regiment home were sent to the different hospitals. In the evening we were drawn up to go to the White House, on the invitation of President Lincoln, but a furious rainstorm prevented our attendance.

We found the 150th O.N.G.[18] here, and they looked very clean and well kept. They must have had a very easy time as compared with our regiment.

The Sanitary Commission sent each company of our command a bushel of good peaches, which seemed delicious to us. The people of the North were full of patriotism and sent liberal donations to this commission to be distributed to the soldiers. Nearly every family in the land sent one or more of its number to the field, and the hearts of those who remained at home were filled with love for all who were in the Union army, and they were ever ready to do them a kindness. Postmaster General Dennison[19] was very kind to the members of the 133d, even going so far as to authorize drafts to be drawn on him for money that any member of the regiment might need.

After we boarded the cars for home at Washington City, a Quaker lady approached an officer of our regiment and said, "Thee looks as if thee had come from the front."

"Yes," was the reply, "we have come from in front of Petersburg and Richmond."

"Thee looks as if a little money might be useful to thee. I have $20 in my purse which thee is welcome to."

She offered a $20 bill, which the officer declined, saying, "No, I thank you! We are now where we can get all the money we need. Keep that for some one who may not be so fortunate."

On Sunday morning, August 14th, at 4 o'clock, we were ordered to pack up and be ready to move. We waited till 9 o'clock, when we got started, and at 2 o'clock we got to Baltimore. Here we were treated to a good dinner of corned beef and bread and excellent coffee, and then marched a mile and a half to the other depot. One man died on the train coming to Baltimore.

We boarded our train and pulled out of Baltimore just about dusk. The moon shone brightly and gave a beautiful appearance to the country as we glided along on the cars. All along the road the people turn out and greet us with cheers and all the usual signs of patriotism.

The morning of August 15th found us within 45 miles of Harrisburg, Pa. Here we were divided into two trains, having come so far on a single train. Passing through Harrisburg, we kept on and about noon arrived at Altoona. Here we got dinner and had two extra engines attached to our train, as the grades among these mountains are very steep and the road very crooked. It seemed sometimes as if we were going right back the way we came. After a while we got over the ridge of the mountains and reached the down grade and then made very fast time.

We reached Pittsburg about 7 o'clock P.M., got off the train and went to the Soldiers' Home, where in a clean, nice dining room they gave us the best supper we had seen since we left home. We had bread and *butter,* coffee, *good water,* dried beef, tomatoes, cabbage, pickles, butter crackers and an apple apiece. The boys showed their appreciation of the good things by giving three cheers and singing some army songs. We then marched about half a mile to the depot, and were given passenger cars to ride in this time.

It seemed that the nearer home we got, the better we found things. Then, as now, Ohio was the best state in the Union. We got to Alliance about 6 o'clock in the morning, and from here on to Crestline the country looked fine. Our colonel telegraphed to different towns ahead to know if they could feed the regiment, directing them to telegraph their answer to the next station ahead of us. Each place answered that they could not, until Crestline was asked. The answer now was, "Yes!"

We got there about 1 o'clock, and having had nothing to eat since we left Pittsburg, the men were nearly famished. Consequently, they did full justice to the dinner provided for us here. Boarding our train again, we proceeded toward Columbus, where we arrived about 4 o'clock with hearts beating with joy to be at home and among friends once more.

There were thousands of people at the depot to welcome us, and they fairly went wild with joy as we alighted from the cars. Everybody embraced everybody else, and then shook hands all round and cried and laughed, and gave other evidence of the emotion that possessed them.

There were some hearts though that were sad amid all this tumult of gladness. Twenty-seven of the brave comrades who went away with us had died, and to their families there was no glad homecoming. These friends could not participate in the general rejoicing, but could only mourn for the loved ones they had given as a sacrifice to preserve the Union. Some sick comrades had been left at Washington, but their friends were hopeful that they would soon come home too.

When greetings were over for the time, the regiment fell in and was formed in open order.

The food and delicacies brought by our friends was passed along the lines. The display of eatables would have tempted any hungry man, but unfortunately we were in no condition to do justice to the offering. We had nearly starved from Pittsburg to Crestline, and at the latter place had eaten so heartily that we lost our appetites. At the Soldiers' Home, which stood just south of the railroad on the west side of High Street, we were also invited in to dinner, but could not accept.

Fresh horses had been provided for the field officers. After supper, the regiment was reformed and a parade of the City Fire Department and the local military organizations took place in honor of our return. We then marched to the Statehouse, while cannon were fired and all the bells of the city clanged out their glad welcome. Here the State Treasurer welcomed us back in a stirring patriotic speech, after which the regiment was dismissed till morning, and scattered to their homes or those of their friends.

On the 17th, the regiment assembled and at 11 o'clock marched out to Camp Chase, to be mustered out as soon as the necessary forms could be complied with and papers made out. The men were not under much restraint now, and ran about almost at will. On the 20th we were mustered out, having been in Uncle Sam's service 110 days.

The boys had already prepared for their departure, and all that was left to be done was to bid farewell to each other. This caused many heart pangs, for though our term of service was short, it was long enough to allow that feeling of fraternity which is so strong between soldiers who have lived and marched together and stood with elbows touching in times of danger and death.

* * *

After Lee's surrender the following spring, the hundred-days men were largely forgotten. Some of "the boys" tried to forget their service, while others remembered it proudly for the rest of their lives. Colonel Leonard Harris's Cincinnati regiment held an annual reunion as late as 1925. Below are excerpts from a poem printed in the program of that occasion, 61 years after the summer in Maryland.

Charles R. Wild, private, Co. A, 137th Ohio:

> Call back sweet memory, that tramp of feet,
>   To Drum beats throbbing through the fife's fierce strain;—
> The tear wet faces, lifted fair and sweet,
>   To loving lips they ne'er may press again. . . .
>
> Call back the storm swept days:—The camp fires light—
>   The solemn stars that watch where sentries tread:
> The sweet sharp call of bugles in the night:—
>   The Victor's shout:—The tears for comrades shed. . . .
>
> Attention, Comrades! Forward March! The years
>   Stretch fair and few, along the shortening road.
> Behind them lie Life's Battles, Triumphs, Tears,
>   Lo! Just beyond, the Eternal Camp of God.[20]

Appendix A: Mr. Lincoln

In addition to the 150th's historic encounter with the president during the fight at Fort Stevens, and the 149th's glimpse of him at the Treasury, various other Ohio regiments also saw Abraham Lincoln during the hundred days.

One vivid eyewitness account was given decades later by First Lieutenant Edward R. McKee, of Company A, 149th Ohio. On duty in Washington when martial law was declared during Jubal Early's audacious raid, McKee was put in charge of a volunteer company of Treasury Department employees. He and his men proceeded to a position in the breastworks on Arlington Heights.

The anxiety of the great president (Mr. Lincoln) for the safety of the Capitol was evident when he insisted in being taken to the very outpost of the army in defense, giving a word of cheer to the soldiery as he passed along from one post to another, the president himself being actually under fire, as occasionally a bullet from the enemy's sharpshooters would whiz past.

General Ord in command urged his retirement to a place of safety, and finally under protest [Lincoln] was about to enter his carriage (his military escort in waiting). His attention was attracted to a young calf tied to a tree near a farmhouse, seemingly in great distress. The earthwork was built through a lawn surrounding a farmer's house, and is now the Arlington National Cemetery.

Mr. Lincoln's great heart was touched at the distress of the young animal, and stepping from the carriage he was about to enter, went to examine the cause. It was found that a small bullet had been embedded in the tail of the calf and [it was] bleeding from the fresh wound. Mr. Lincoln, taking out his pocket knife, cut the ball out, and with a gentle pat on the back of the calf, placed the ball in his pocket. Being again advised to retire to safer quarters, he reluctantly boarded his carriage and was driven back to the city amid the shouts of the army.

The Akron Guards, Company F of the 164th Ohio, were permanently assigned to Washington's defenses. A soldier who signed himself "H. W." recorded the scene when they visited the White House on Saturday afternoon, May 28th:

The Marine Band of 30 pieces began playing at half past four. For some time persons of and without distinction had been assembling; soon a tall, care-worn man stepped out upon the portico and took his seat. A thousand eyes at once fell upon him, and then there was hurrying to points of better observation. The countenance of the President when sitting alone was inexpressibly sad. To read the thoughts of his heart at such a time would require the skill of an immortal, rid of the blur and dim visions that attach to earth. He heard the music, saw the crowd, but his mind was evidently not there.

Part of the 164th saw Lincoln about a month later. "Some of the boys was over to town the other day and saw Old Abe," Private Jacob Holtz of Company H wrote home on June 18th. "He shook hands with them . . . and talked to them." The entire 164th saw the president one more time, at the White House on August 18th while on the way back home to Ohio.[1] Jake Holtz, however, had died seven weeks earlier.

The 130th Ohio, raised primarily in Toledo, also saw the president at the presidential mansion. The regiment marched there on the morning of June 11th, having arrived from Johnson's Island the previous day. "Looker On" described the event for the hometown newspaper.

As it entered the Presidential grounds, the Band played "Hail to the Chief," until it arrived in front of the White House, where, by a series of well-executed movements, the whole body was brought directly fronting the colonnade of the portico, where the President greeted them with a short and fitting speech, thanking them in the name of the Government. They marched directly to the front, and appear in the best of spirits.

A second newspaper provided the president's remarks:

Soldiers, I understand you have just come from Ohio—come to help us in this the nation's day of trials, and also of its hopes. I thank you for your promptness in responding to the call for troops. Your services were never more needed than now—I know not where you are going. You may stay here and take the place of others who will be sent to the front; or you may go there yourselves. Wherever you go I know you will do your best. Again, I thank you. Good-bye.

Sergeant R. L. Evans of Company C, 159th Ohio, saw the president just five days later, at Havre de Grace, Maryland, as Lincoln traveled north on the railroad to Philadelphia.

Company C were drawn up in line and fired a salute of 21 guns, in honor to their Commander-in-Chief. We then called lustily for a speech, but were only gratified by his appearing on the platform of the car and returning our salute with a grateful bow.

At least one other regiment, the 166th Ohio, also saw Lincoln, probably at the White House. This unit had served in the Virginia forts, where it had suffered 39 deaths through disease. It is not recorded whether the president knew this when he spoke to the men on August 22nd.

Soldiers: I suppose you are going home to see your families and friends. For the services you have done in this great struggle in which we are all engaged, I present you sincere thanks for myself and the country.

I almost always feel inclined, when I happen to say anything to soldiers, to impress upon them, in a few brief remarks, the importance of success in this contest. It is not merely for today, but for all time to come, that we should perpetuate for our children's children that great and free government which we have enjoyed all our lives. I beg you to remember this, not merely for my sake, but for yours. I happen, temporarily, to occupy the White House. I am a living witness that any one of your children may look to come here as my father's child has. It is in order that each one of you may have, through this free government which we have enjoyed, an open field and fair chance for your industry, enterprise, and intelligence; that you may all have equal privileges in the race of life, with all its desirable human aspirations. It is for this the struggle should be maintained, that we may not lose our birthright—not only for one, but for two or three years. This nation is worth fighting for, to secure such an inestimable jewel.

After all the Ohio hundred-days regiments had returned home, the president publicly extended the troops his thanks. Here and there, today, the certificates bearing his name still survive among their papers.

THE UNITED STATE VOLUNTEER SERVICE
The President's Thanks and Certificate of Honorable Service

Whereas the President of the United States has made the following Executive Order, returning Thanks to the OHIO VOLUNTEERS FOR ONE HUNDRED DAYS, to wit:

Executive Mansion
Washington City, September 10, 1864

The term of One Hundred Days, for which the NATIONAL GUARD OF OHIO volunteered, having expired, the President directs an Official Acknowledgment to be made of their PATRIOTIC AND VALUABLE SERVICES during the recent campaigns. The term of service of their enlistment was short, but distinguished by memorable events. In the Valley of the Shenandoah, on the Peninsula, in the Operations on the James River, around Petersburg and Richmond, in the battle of Monocacy, and in the Entrenchments of Washington, and in other important service, the NATIONAL GUARD OF OHIO performed with alacrity the duty of Patriotic Volunteers, for which they are entitled to, and are hereby tendered through the Governor of their State, the NATIONAL THANKS.

The Secretary of War is directed to transmit a copy of this Order to the Governor of Ohio, and to cause a CERTIFICATE OF THEIR HONORABLE SERVICE to be delivered to the Officers and Soldiers of the OHIO NATIONAL GUARD who recently served in the Military Force of the United States as Volunteers for One Hundred Days.

ABRAHAM LINCOLN

Appendix B: Family and Friends

Besides being soldiers themselves, the hundred-days men were also relatives and friends of men serving in the three-year regiments. The Scioto Gazette newspaper in Chillicothe printed several letters from John M. Wisehart, a 52-year-old orderly sergeant in the 149th O.V.I. He sent his last one on July 24th from Camp Parole near Annapolis, Maryland:

I received a letter last week that brought me sad news. My son William, of Co. K, 63rd Regiment, O.V.I., was mortally wounded on the 19th of last month at Kenesaw Mountain.[2] He departed this life on the 24th of June at Resaca. His nurse wrote me that Willie, in his last moments, directed him to write to his father and mother that he died a soldier, and was not afraid to die. Mr. Editor, I loved that boy, and he is gone. He was a noble boy, a good soldier, and one consolation is, he died defending the right. Though the bereavement is a sad one, it was the will of Providence, and I submit.

Sergeant Wisehart's terrible loss wasn't unique. Private James E. Borton of the 130th Ohio had a brother, Simeon, killed in action at Chester Station, Virginia, on May 10, 1864, while serving in the 67th Ohio. James wrote home from Johnson's Island after learning of his death.

Dear Mother, Brothers, and Sisters:
I embrace the present opportunity of writing a few lines in answer to the one which came duly at hand today. Confirming the sad and mournful news of our once beloved Simeon's death. I saw his name in the Toledo *Blade* of the eighteenth. I couldn't read any further. I handed the paper to the owner and walked away. I knew it was him. I knew nothing of the circumstances of his death until today. Something seemed to tell me he was dead. That there was no mistake in the report.
Some of the boys would tell me not to mind it for it might be a mistake. I tried to think so but I couldn't. It seemed as true to me as if I had saw him fall almost. . . . Ah, many a bitter tear will sparkle in my eyes as I think of Simeon and how he died in a strange land with no kind mother to listen to his parting words. It seems hard to endure.

First Sergeant Noah N. Leohner[3] of Company H, 164th Ohio, wrote to the Summit County Beacon *from Fort Strong, Virginia, on June 7th, 1864:*

We received the *Beacon* dated May 26th, and it brought us sad news indeed of the gallant fighting 29th Ohio. I noticed an account of the dying words of a friend of mine, Sergt. Christian F. Remley, of Co. G.[4] His death reminds me of a

196

conversation between him and myself while he was at home last winter on veteran furlough.

He told me that the 29th would get into another fight and there would be at least seven killed and fifty wounded, and one of those killed would be C. F. Remley. Little did I think at the same time this would be his fate, and marked the words the brave hero said.

Correspondence flowed in both directions, of course, but few letters written to the soldiers now survive. Dr. John C. Williamson, surgeon of the 152nd Ohio, received this letter, dated June 21, 1864, from a friend in Versailles, Ohio.

Dr. Sir

At the request of Bro. Hughes & in accordance with my own feelings I send you a line. I miss you very much and the room looks lonely when we sleep, and in the family we wonder what the Dr. can be doing and where he is and how he fares. The town of Versailles looks forsaken, and indeed [in] the whole country wherever we go we meet the same things. I read the papers daily & try to look into the future to see the end, hoping and praying for success.

Your friends here inquire for you and long for your return. . . . We all presume as we sit and talk together in your old house that you have your hands full. . . . The weather is very dry, there has been no rain for several weeks. The oats & flax are suffering very much so also the corn & grass. But the most noticeable feature of our country is the great anxiety of the *People*. Every day anxious friends ask the question so hard to answer. How soon do you think this war will be over and how long will it last? I do not suffer myself to doubt the final result. Believing our cause to be just I do not think it can fail, but the cost in life and treasure is very great. This last call we feel more than all the rest.

I should like right well to drop in upon you & see how you are getting along. I must close as the train will be along in a short time. General health prevails at present in and around the village. We all join in sending you our kindest regards, and wish your safe return home again. A line from you would be very acceptable.

Yours Fraternally,
A. Harmount

Among the rare intact sets of family correspondence are the warm letters between Lieutenant Isaac Hambleton, Company C, 154th Ohio, and his wife, Jane, on the family farm in Madison County. The following is dated June 5th, 1864.

My Dear Husband and well tried Friend,

I sit down to pen you a few lines though I know not where you are. Some times we hear you one place and some times another. Wally and I walked up to Town last Evening expecting to get a letter but were disappointed. Mrs. Hancock told me you were at New Gap but that letters were still sent to New Creek Station. So I thought I would write to you and send you some Papers anyhow.

Yesterday Edmund said at the Table he would not be surprised if you would reenlist. Oh Isaac I cannot think of it, it seems to me my happy Days would all be over. I hope you will not, unless indeed you are sure it is your highest Duty and your desire is more to go than to stay. I do not wish to stand between any person and their Duty. Much as the heart may suffer, if it is right we must submit. But I pray you may feel otherwise.[5]

Your affectionate Wife
Jane B. Hambleton

Jane wrote the following on August 7th, after she had heard news of the 154th Ohio's fight at New Creek, West Virginia. (See "Back to the Valley" for Isaac's account of the battle.)

Dear Husband

What is it I have heard, your troubles have come at last and with them more anxiety at home. Early Saturday morning G. W. Lewis called to Wally and told him they had had a battle at New Creek. He said there were ten or a dozen killed and about fifty wounded. We could hear no particulars, perhaps you can imagine my feelings. I will not try to tell them.

I waited till after dinner, then Wally and I went to town to see if we could hear anything more. I got your letter. While I was reading it in the office a man came in, telling a Dispatch had been sent to London and word came back that our Boys were all right except Watson was missing. Oh, that it may be no worse. I wonder if this trouble will make any difference with your coming Home. I am afraid it will. Oh, what a sad time, our country is covered with Woe. . . .

Your Wife, Jane B. Hambleton

The troubles around New Creek and nearby Cumberland did keep Isaac's regiment on duty beyond the hundred days. Jane wrote to him again on August 17th, her anxiety evident in her somewhat jumbled words.

My Dear Husband,

We have been looking and looking for you so long and you do not come. Why is it you are still expecting to come that you don't write or what is the matter. Do write if you can and relieve our anxiety a little. . . .

The 133rd Regiment have got home and a great many of them are sick. Mother and I went to Scotts yesterday hoping you would come while we were gone. We stopped to see Jim G. He is very poorly, hardly able to be up. Wilson Goodson is very sick. Richard Vanhorn we hear is sick too. Killberry could not get home, they are afraid he will not live. One of the Gillen boys died.[6] Isaac, I have not patience to write much. I want to see you or hear from you. We are getting along as well as we can but we need you at home very much. Perhaps you cannot get paper or stamps. You can take this half sheet and I will send you a stamp. Oh, Isaac when will we meet again? If it were in our power, I do not think it would be long. Perhaps it won't, I hope not anyhow. Good-bye Dearest. May God in his mercy guide you and keep you from all evil.

Your anxious Wife, Jane B. Hambleton

Second Lieutenant Isaac H. Hambleton, described in his papers as 39, five feet ten, with gray eyes, light complexion and hair, occupation farmer, mustered out with his company at Camp Dennison, Ohio, on September 1, 1864.

Appendix C:
Enlistment and Discharge

*The hundred-days men began and ended their service as state troops. The follow-
ing are the enlistment and discharge papers of Edward McKee, Company A,
27th O.N.G. (149th O.V.I.). A former "Squirrel Hunter" and veteran of the
fight at Monocacy, McKee later helped form a militia company, the Campbell
Light Guards.[7] He entered old age as a respected banker and Sunday-school
teacher.*

In the Name and by the Authority of the State of Ohio.
David Tod, Governor and Commander-in-Chief of said State.
To Edward R. McKee, Greetings:
It appearing to me that on the Eleventh day of July, 1863, you were duly
elected First Lieutenant of Co. "A," 27th Battalion of Infantry O.V.M. (Ross Co.)
Now Know You, That by the power vested in me by the Constitution and Laws
of said State, and reposing special trust and confidence in your patriotism, valor,
fidelity and ability, I do by these presents COMMISSION you as First Lieutenant
as aforesaid, for the term of FIVE YEARS, unless sooner discharged, upon condition that you uniform within the time limited by law, and take the oath, or affir-
mation, endorsed hereon, within ten days from the receipt hereof, sending a certificate thereof to General Head Quarters; and I do hereby authorize and require
you to discharge, all and singular, the duties and services appertaining to your said
office, agreeably to law and general regulations, and to obey such orders and instructions as you shall, from time to time, receive from your superior officers.
> GIVEN under my hand, at Columbus, Ohio, this Twenty-
> Sixth day of July in the year of our Lord one thousand
> eight hundred and sixty-three, and in the eighty-eighth
> year of the Independence of the United States.
>
> [signed]
> David Tod

* * *

TO WHOM IT MAY CONCERN.
KNOW YE, That Edward R. McKee a 1st Lieutenant of Captain Peabody (A)
Company, 27th Reg't., Battalion, "OHIO NATIONAL GUARD," aged 23 years,
and residing in Chillicothe Ross County, Ohio, having joined said organization on
the 11th day of July A.D. 1863, to serve for the term of FIVE YEARS, and having served with his company, honestly and faithfully to the present date, is now
HONORABLY DISCHARGED from the military service of the State of Ohio, by

virtue of an act of the General Assembly, passed April 2d, A.D. 1866, entitled "an act to enroll the Militia of Ohio, to organize a volunteer militia, and to repeal certain acts therein named," the tenth section of which act requires the honorable discharge of all members of the "NATIONAL GUARD."

The said Edward R. McKee having been mustered into the U.S. Service in May, 1864, under the call for "one hundred days men," and honorably discharged therefrom, is exempt from militia duty excepting in case of war, insurrection, or invasion, or the reasonable apprehension thereof.

GIVEN, at Columbus, Ohio, from the office of the Adjutant General of Ohio, this first day of May, A.D. 1866.

By Order of Governor JACOB D. COX:

[signed]
B. R. Cowen
Adjutant General of Ohio

Appendix D:
Roster of Hundred-Days Regiments

Ohio:
  130th–172nd Regiments[8]
                                                                    35,982

Illinois:
  132nd–143rd Regiments[9]
  145th Regiment
  Alton Battalion
                                                                    11,328

Indiana:
  132nd–139th Regiments
                                                                     7,415

Iowa:
  44th–47th Regiments
  48th Battalion
                                                                     3,901

Wisconsin:
  39th–41st Regiments[10]
                                                                     2,134

Subtotal, western states:
                                                                    60,760

Delaware:
  9th Regiment
                                                                       635

Kansas:
  17th Regiment[11]
                                                                       455

Maryland:
  11th–12th Regiments[12]
                                                                     1,327

Massachusetts:[13]
  5th Regiment
  6th Regiment
  8th Regiment

42nd Regiment
60th Regiment

5,562

New Jersey:
37th Regiment

781

Pennsylvania:
192nd–197th Regiments
1st Battalion
1st Battalion (artillery)
Unattached companies[14]

7,675

New York:[15]
28th
54th
56th
58th[16]
77th
84th
93rd
98th
99th
102nd
1st Battalion Light Artillery

3,766

Subtotal, other states:

20,201

Total:

80,961[17]

Notes and Sources

Introduction

1. "Glory to God in the highest, Ohio has saved the Union," Lincoln had telegraphed to Brough on October 14th after his 100,000-vote victory. Eugene H. Roseboom and Francis P. Weisenburger, *A History of Ohio* (Columbus, 1988), p. 194. Some sources say "nation" rather than "Union." See Richard H. Abbott, *Ohio's War Governors* (Columbus, 1962), p. 40.

2. A Republican state legislator and military engineer-in-chief with the rank of colonel on Governor William Dennison's staff when the war began, Cowen enlisted as a private in the 15th Ohio. He was soon commissioned a first lieutenant, then appointed an additional paymaster. He was about to go to New Orleans as chief paymaster, Department of the Gulf, when offered the adjutant-general's post. Whitelaw Reid, *Ohio in the War: Her Statesmen, Generals and Soldiers*, vol. 1 (Cincinnati, 1868), p. 964.

3. Cowen, "The Hundred-Days Men of 1864," *G.A.R. War Papers: Papers Read Before Fred C. Jones Post, No. 401, Department of Ohio, G.A.R* (Cincinnati, 1891), p. 219.

While serving in the Army of the Potomac in 1861, Cowen had proposed essentially the same idea to President Lincoln and Secretary of War Stanton. "They were both apparently favorable to the suggestion, but seemed to have on hand about all [the troops] they could manage at the time. . . ." Ibid., p. 216.

The Ohio law establishing the state National Guard also funded it by providing, in Cowen's words, that "all men of military age [20 to 45], who owed military service, should either fish or cut bait; either join a company of the National Guard or pay four dollars a year for the benefit of those who did join. From this source in 1864 was collected $520,000, a sum sufficient to meet all legal demands upon the fund and to leave a handsome balance. . . ." Ibid., p. 218.

(Cowen also provided a second account of the Guard: "The One Hundred Days Men of Ohio," *Sketches of War History, 1861–1865: Papers Prepared for the Commandery of the State of Ohio, Military Order of the Loyal Legion of the United States* [Cincinnati, 1903]. With two exceptions, this volume cites the former, more comprehensive history.)

4. "Governor Brough did a noble part in that matter, and it is but just to his honored memory that the highest meed of praise be awarded to him. But the idea was first 'suggested' by Governor Morton. . . . Doubtless all of [the governors] had thought about some such movement, but if there is any special credit due for first suggesting it, Governor Morton is clearly entitled to it." *Report of the Adjutant General of the State of Indiana*, vol. 1 (Indianapolis, 1869), p. 39.

Morton had earlier campaigned for Brough in Ohio, as had Governor Richard Yates of Illinois.

5. Cowen, "The Hundred-Days Men of 1864," pp. 219–20.

6. Cowen, "The One Hundred Days Men of Ohio," p. 367.

7. Invited Michigan Governor Austin Blair could not attend. Although he telegraphed his willingness to participate, Michigan ultimately raised no hundred-days regiments.

8. *The War of the Rebellion: A Compilation of the Official Records of the Union and Confederate Armies* (Washington, 1884), ser. 3, vol. 4, p. 239.

9. Cowen, "The Hundred-Days Men of 1864," pp. 220–21.

10. Terrell, *Report of the Adjutant General of the State of Indiana,* vol. 1, pp. 38–39.

11. "However hard this order may fall upon some of our citizens," it also editorialized, "it is the consciousness of all intelligent persons that the military operations of the months May, June and July will have a most important bearing upon, and probably a decisive influence, in shaping the future of the Republic." Madison County *Union,* April 28, 1864.

12. Few regiments this late in the war enlisted the 1,000 men common earlier. In Federal service they became Ohio Volunteer Infantry (O.V.I.) rather than Ohio National Guard (O.N.G.) regiments, a distinction often overlooked by newspapers and the Guards themselves.

13. Indiana raised eight regiments; Illinois 13 and one battalion; Iowa four and a battalion; Wisconsin two and a battalion.

14. Delaware, Kansas and New Jersey each raised one regiment; Maryland two; Massachusetts five plus several independent companies; Pennsylvania six and a battalion, plus cavalry and artillery; New York 10 small National Guard regiments and a light artillery battalion.

The first of these regiments mustered in mid-June, the last in early September. Several were militia regiments with prior service; three later reorganized for one-year service. Ironically, a Pennsylvania regiment served in Ohio, and one from Massachusetts in Indiana. The Delaware, Kansas and Maryland regiments all served within their states, as did all but two of those from New York; only the 11th Maryland, 37th New Jersey and 84th New York National Guard saw fighting.

The 164th Ohio met two of these regiments at Fort Smith, Virginia, in the fortifications surrounding Washington. The 6th Massachusetts on July 24th was filled with "genuine Yankees and full of gab," while on August 10th "the 84th NY (100 days) passed through our camp en route for 'up the river. . . .'" Charles L. Morehouse, "Diary—1864."

15. Five also skirmished with rebel cavalryman Nathan Bedford Forrest in Memphis in August. These were the 39th, 40th and 41st Wisconsin, the 137th Illinois and a detachment of the 46th Iowa.

16. The problems of recruiting so late in the war were evident in, but hardly unique to, the 37th New Jersey. "The *personnel* of the regiment was not altogether encouraging. The medical examination was by no means searching, and as a result there were many with only one eye; several with less fingers than the regulations allowed; a few, long since past the age at which military service terminates; and scores of mere boys from 15 years of age upwards." John Y. Foster, *New Jersey and the Rebellion* (Newark, 1868), p. 671.

17. George Perkins, *A Summer in Maryland and Virginia* (Chillicothe, 1911, p. 14.

18. *Scioto Gazette,* May 3, 1864.

The *Gazette* and other papers later published on their front pages the lyrics to a song by Rev. B. R. Hanby, about a fictional hundred-days man named Timothy Huff.

> *O, Governor Brough! It's terrible tough!*
> *I declare you've treated us downright rough;*
> *'Tis a very unfortunate call!*
> *Why, hadn't the Gover'ment soldiers enough,*
> *That you make a demand upon Timothy Huff?*
> *It's agoin' to ruin us all.*

But in the end, "old hero" Brough convinces the reluctant soldier, who exclaims:

> *Call out your men till you're sure you've enough.*
> *Come on! you're welcome to Timothy Huff!*
> *Hurrah! hurrah! hurrah!*

19. "If any man in my regiment—for I have not been laying down any law for you that I am not going to enforce in my own command—fails, on the 2nd of May, next Monday, to report for duty, I intend to send a guard after him, with guns, and bayonets on them. . . ." Cincinnati *Daily Gazette,* April 27, 1864.

A veteran of First Bull Run and Perryville, Harris had commanded the 2nd Ohio before he was forced to resign by illness, and had later helped Cowen draft the bill that created the Ohio National Guard. His 7th regiment and the reluctant 10th O.N.G. both mustered and took the field. The 7th became the 137th Ohio, and included such colorfully named companies as the Guthrie Grays, Mahkatewah Guards, and Winfield Rifles.

The 10th O.N.G. became the 165th Ohio, and for a time guarded rebel prisoners at Johnson's Island in Lake Erie.

20. Cleveland *Plain Dealer,* May 2, 1864.

21. "TRIUMPHANT NEWS!!!" an *Ohio State Journal* headline proclaimed on May 16th during Grant's Spotsylvania campaign in Virginia. "THE REBEL ARMY ROUTED!! RICHMOND TO BE ABANDONED! HOW ARE YOU, JEFF. DAVIS?"

22. Cowen, "The Hundred-Days Men of 1864," p. 221.

23. The troops didn't hesitate to express their opinions, either. When newspapers reported that the 130th Ohio had volunteered for the front, for instance, its men quickly set the record straight. "We have not made any request or petition as to where we should go, and there has been no volunteering by us to go to the front (nor rear either, as yet)," wrote Chaplain J. W. Alderman. Toledo *Blade,* June 29, 1864.

"The impression seems to prevail that the 130th O.N.G. volunteered to go to the front and fight . . . ," an anonymous guard later wrote from near Bermuda Hundred, Virginia. "This is a mistake. The 130th Regiment never volunteered to go to the front, and the assertion that we did is a falsehood. We never expected to come to the front, and certainly did not wish to be brought here. . . .

"We are willing to do anything our Governor asks us to do, even to go to the front; but not under our present organization, for the reason that our companies are all from one township—all brothers and neighbors; and to annihilate one of these companies is to destroy the whole township." *Ohio State Journal,* July 7, 1864.

First Sergeant George F. Beardsley, Company B, 142nd Ohio, serving in the same brigade, attacked this "unmanly article" and declared, "We did not expect to remain in the field our hundred days with nothing to do, while our brothers were manfully fighting the great battle of freedom. . . ." He added that the 142nd felt that "neither Gov. Brough nor Father Abram [sic] will assign us to positions that we have not as yet been educated to fill." Ibid., July 21, 1864.

Quartermaster's Sergeant Henry L. Curtis, of the same regiment, wrote to the Mount Vernon *Republican* that while the 142nd hadn't *requested* duty at the front, "no injustice has been done us, and we have been ordered to do no more than we came out to do. . . ." Reprinted in the *Ohio State Journal,* August 9, 1864.

24. Three weeks later, from Virginia, he would gloomily write of the war: "I would have it stop now. There is no use of men killing one another any longer. I am of the opinion it must be settled some other way. The country we are fighting for is not worth the sacrifice of the men that are being cut off. I would let the South have it and be glad to leave it." British-born Private Timothy Rigby, Company I, 143rd Ohio, in John Brownhill Linn, "Civil War Diaries of Two Brothers: John Brownhill Linn and Thomas Buchanan Linn: Two Volumes in One; Followed by Three More Manuscripts from the 143rd Regiment O.N.G."

25. The 145th Ohio, on duty at Fort Whipple outside Washington, actually voted on whether to go to the front. "The Colonel called a meeting of the field and line officers, and they concluded to leave the question to the enlisted men to decide. It was then stated to the men that several regiments of the Ohio National Guard had volunteered and that the Government had received information that other regiments were desirous of going to the front, and that an opportunity would be given all to volunteer.

"Nine companies of our regiment voted on this question and but forty men were found willing to volunteer. The men felt that they were filling the contract they made with the Government, which was to do post and garrison duty, and to guard lines of communication, and prisoners, and no other duty could be justly asked of them." Letter signed "O.N.G.," Sandusky *Commercial Register,* July 1, 1864. The 145th remained at Fort Whipple.

26. "Don't it seem like it . . . when the rebels haint more than 30 or 40 rods from me now and within 7 miles in front of us there is from 30 to 60 thousand of them?" one of them wrote home from Point of Rocks, near Richmond, Virginia. "Borton Family: Personal Correspondence with Typewritten Transcripts." Letter by J. E. Borton, 130th Ohio, June 16, 1864. (Borton appears again later in this volume.)

27. "We of the old army feel indignant when we see so much in the papers about these tender plants, and so much said against putting them in the sun," a member of the 73rd Ohio wrote from Sherman's army that summer. "Send them all to the front, if necessary, and let them for a little time share our fortune, and let us hear less about their patriotic sacrifices until they can show some honorable scars, received in the *front lines of our army.*" Letter signed T. W. H., Cincinnati *Commercial,* July 14, 1864.

28. Cowen, "The One Hundred Days Men of Ohio," p. 361.

1. The Boys

1. Company I, 141st Ohio, for example, included William Frame, 48, and sons William P., 17, and James W., 15, of Adams County, all privates.

After muster began, Brough ordered that any Guard not yet 18 years of age would be discharged "on application to the proper officer, except the consent of parent or guardian is given as required in the case of minors in the regular service." Sandusky *Register,* May 10, 1864.

2. The change in their social status could sometimes bemuse the soldiers themselves, however. A member of the 150th Ohio who signed himself "Reliance" wrote to a Cleveland newspaper from his new and more humble post in Washington, D.C.:

"A few weeks ago I visited Washington in the character of a first class tourist. I put up at Willard's, paid three dollars a day for my board, was introduced to three or four Brigadiers, sauntered leisurely through the numerous fortifications, hobnobbed with the officers in command thereof, looked patronizingly upon the common soldiers under them—occasionally even returned a salute—and, in short, 'put on airs' equal to the Prince of Wales. How little I thought at that time that, in less than two months thereafter, I should return to Washington in the bewitching (!) toggery of one of those same soldiers! But such is the sad fact. I occasionally try to convince myself that I am dreaming; but alas! I cannot do so, as my huge, misshapen shoes, unsightly blouse, closely cropped head, and empty stomach are altogether too convincing of the opposite fact." Cleveland *Plain Dealer,* May 18, 1864.

3. Private Cecil C. Abbott, May 15, 1864. "Letters of Cecil C. Abbott, Co. B, 166th O.V.I., to His Parents in Wakeman, Ohio."

4. The name was coined by Cowen's predecessor, Charles W. Hill, adjutant-general under Brough's predecessor, Governor David Tod. Both had been instrumental in organizing the Ohio militia in the 1862–63 legislative session. When the Brough administration took office, the state Standing Committees on Military Affairs asked Hill to meet with them and Cowen, and to review the reorganization bill. "He gave it thorough attention, proposing a large number of amendments, including a change of name of the volunteer militia from 'Ohio State Guard' to 'National Guard.' Most of the amendments were adopted *verbatim* by the Legislature." Reid, *Ohio in the War,* vol. 1, p. 815.

An Ohio newspaper later editorialized that it was due chiefly to the "foresight and labors" of Tod and Hill "that Ohio had a National Guard to tender to the Government in the present crisis; and it is no disparagement to the just claims of anyone to say that [Hill] is the one most entitled to the thanks of the State and of the nation for this timely aid." Toledo *Blade,* May 24, 1864.

At the time of the hundred-days muster, Hill was appointed colonel of the 128th Ohio, a long-service regiment then guarding rebel prisoners at Johnson's Island. He was later breveted brigadier-general and major-general for war service. Reid, *Ohio in the War,* vol. 1, p. 815.

5. In the law establishing the National Guard, "the elective system for the commissioned officers, being provided for in the [state] Constitution, was necessarily retained, but it was possible to mitigate the embarrassments arising therefrom by urging the election, so far as practicable, of honorably discharged officers and soldiers, of whom there were many at that time in the state. It was found that this element of experience was a powerful aid to the work of preparing the Guard for active field service, as the presence of such men also contributed greatly to the efficiency of the service in the field." Cowen, "The Hundred-Days Men of 1864," pp. 218–19.

6. Cowen apparently refers to Herman M. Chapman, quartermaster of the 150th Regiment, who was Cleveland's mayor the following year, 1865. The regiment's lieutenant-colonel, John N. Frazee, was the city marshal at the time of the call-up.

7. The Spencer Rifles, Company A, 159th Ohio, boasted an impressive range of occupations. "We have 4 Attorneys, 1 Merchant, 1 Banker, 22 Clerks, 1 Photographer, 2 Machinists, 3 Grocers, 5 Carpenters, 2 Teachers, 18 Farmers, 4 Laborers, 2 Jewellers, 1 Tinner, 3 Boilermakers, 1 Moulder, 1 Tailor, 1 Carriagemaker, 2 R. R. firemen, 1 Chandler, 1 Music teacher, 2 Shoemakers, 1 Cooper, 1 Trunkmaker, 1 Bricklayer, 1 Cabinetmaker, 2 Engineers, 1 Saddler, 1 Wagonmaker, 1 Castmaker, 1 Cigarmaker, 1 Painter and 1 Butcher." Letter from "Co. A," Zanesville *Courier,* June 20, 1864.

8. At Columbus and Lake Erie, respectively. For the 130th Ohio at Toledo, "The information this morning that they had not been assigned to duty at Johnson's Island rather increased their enthusiasm, as many supposed it would be very monotonous watching a few hundred rebels pent up within the narrow confines of the island. . . ." Toledo *Blade,* May 12, 1864.

The 130th Ohio did serve briefly on the island, however, before leaving for Washington, D.C., and hard service at the front outside Petersburg, Virginia.

9. Company B, 40th Battalion, O.N.G. The dismissal order prohibited any member of the company from enlisting in another. "This order was read to every Ohio regiment in the field, and was keenly felt by the members of the disgraced company, many of whom afterward applied for the removal of the disability thus created," Cowen added. Cowen, "The Hundred-Days Men of 1864," p. 226.

Individual soldiers in various regiments also refused to be sworn into U.S. service; others disappeared during or after muster. A correspondent in the 139th Ohio, mainly Cincinnati men from the 9th O.N.G., reported that his regiment mustered 688 men, "although one company (Capt. Ellich's) deserted in squads, also a few from different companies." "Doc," Cincinnati *Times,* June 7, 1864.

(Ellich's name doesn't appear in *Official Roster of the Soldiers of the State of Ohio in the War of the Rebellion, 1861–1866,* hereafter *Official Roster,* although Company K shows neither a captain nor any second lieutenants, and just 48 men under a first lieutenant.)

(*Official Roster* was authorized by the General Assembly and compiled by a special commission, and is the central source for regimental and company data in this volume. It contains many inaccuracies, however, and in their accounts soldiers occasionally provide different spellings for companions' names. Such discrepancies are noted, except when a man is spelling his own name.)

One National Guard regiment from New York, the 11th, also refused to report for hundred-days service in July, on the grounds that it wasn't subject to duty outside of the state. Its colonel was court-martialed for disobedience, but the conviction was later reversed. The controversy delayed or canceled marching orders for other NGSNY regiments.

10. "Efforts have been made to poison the minds of these gallant men, by seeking to make them believe that they were called unconstitutionally and illegally into the service which they have so well performed," Brough would declare during a speech at Circleville, welcoming home the hundred-days men. "If the call was not constitutional and legal, the services of the men have been magnificent and glorious. If it was not constitutional to save the country, they have violated the constitution for the good of our country." Summit County *Beacon,* September 22, 1864.

11. The "gallant Twenty-Ninthers," according to a newspaper, were the cream of Cleveland's young men, "admirably officered, and uniformed and equipped in the most thorough and perfect manner. . . . We make bold to say that no finer regiment than the

29th will be sent into the field under the late call. . . ." Cleveland *Plain Dealer,* May 10, 1864.

Dover refers not to the present-day town of that name, which lies some 100 miles to the south, but to a township just west of the city around what is today called Westlake.

12. Gleason delivered these remarks in 1899.

13. Because of his father's poor health, "Mark" Hanna had earlier sent a substitute to take his place in the army. But he also joined a militia company called the Perry Light Infantry, which later became Company C. He performed the duties of a higher rank, although commissioned a second lieutenant. "I never supposed I was entitled to stand with the men who were veterans of four years' terrible war," the senator told the Grand Army of the Republic on attending his first camp-fire in 1901. "I am but a four months man." Herbert Croly, *Marcus Alonzo Hanna: His Life and Work* (Hamden, 1965), pp. 44–45.

14. Colorado. "Silver State" is a present-day nickname for Nevada.

15. Insects.

16. Nash did become Ohio's governor, 1900–1904.

17. The call-up hit Oberlin especially hard, as a newspaper editorial later noted: "Every new call for soldiers has made a new inroad upon the number of students, but the call for the hundred days' service has been felt most severely of all. Taking as it did the best half of all the classes, it interfered with the enthusiasm and working spirit of the College, and made the summer term just past the smallest of any for many years." Cleveland *Herald,* August 27, 1864.

18. Company K was not the only academic company. Company D of the 44th Iowa, the "University Company," included hundred-days men from the State University of Iowa, Cornell College at Mt. Vernon, and Western College. Wisconsin's adjutant-general reported "at least two companies of the 41st [Wisconsin] being made up almost wholly from the state university, Beloit and Appleton colleges"; two other schools were also represented in the state's force.

19. Lieutenant-Colonel Frazee commanded the regiment after Hayward's promotion.

20. One of the fortifications protecting Washington, D.C.

21. "Our patriotic friend C. M. Nichols . . . has gone to war with the hundred days National Guards," *The Herald* in Washington (Court House), Ohio, reported May 12th, 1864. "He wields the pen right vigorously and we believe there is a plenty of the true yankee grit in him to use the *'shooting stick'* equally well."

22. At Murfreesboro, Tennessee, December 31, 1862–January 2, 1863. Today generally referred to as the battle of Stones River, although the singular or possessive use was common at the time.

23. Edward M. Doty, who owned a hardware business and was active in civic organizations.

24. "The efforts made by the higher powers to prevent the wide gulf between officers and privates in the hundred days' service being bridged over is something amusing to the latter," a soldier-correspondent in the 138th Ohio would report puckishly from Virginia in July. "Some time ago we had an order read on dress parade, detailing the enormities committed by a surgeon of the 5th New York Cavalry, who had not only eaten with two enlisted men, knowing them to be such, but had actually drank with them, possessing the same knowledge. The whole line listened in still expectancy for

the sentence which should be commensurate with such outrageous offenses, and how we were disappointed to find that the said surgeon had only been dismissed in disgrace from the service, instead of being shot to death by musketry. Notwithstanding this affecting example of perverted taste and their results, some of the officers, not having their fear of losing caste before their eyes, would not take warning. Whereupon our corps commander, growing desperate, issued a general order stating that officers were presumed to know the regulations of the service, and as orders to them had been vain, hereafter any private gaming or associating with an officer would be punished. . . . It was found that privates didn't scare any worse than officers; and so things jog along in the old fashion, gentlemen meeting together in social intercourse without much reference to shoulder straps." Letter signed "H. P.," dated July 31. Cincinnati *Gazette,* August 3, 1864.

25. The following entries are excerpts. Morehouse, like many soldiers, wrote in a small, durable, black-leather diary. Some of these diaries survive in surprisingly good condition today.

26. The identity of "George" is unclear in the diary, but is evidently a friend or relative.

27. The 49th Regiment was consolidated with the 54th Battalion O.N.G. to create the 164th O.V.I. Morehouse became a private and acting corporal in Company A.

28. Formerly the 8th Ohio National Guard, mainly from Cincinnati.

29. Several letters signed only "G. L. L." appeared in the Cincinnati *Times* during the hundred days. In Company F, only Laboytreaux possessed these initials. The *Times* had a second correspondent in the 138th, a soldier who signed himself "Crescent," whose letters show only that he served in Company D. The *Times* usually labeled G. L. L.'s letters "from the Eighth O.N.G." and Crescent's "from the 138th O.N.G." Both refer to the 138th O.V.I., the regiment's correct designation while on Federal service. Excerpt from Cincinnati *Times,* July 11, 1864.

30. Laboytreaux was 44 years old at muster. His friends Privates Balser P. Dom (spelled "Domm" in *Official Roster,* and to whom he refers elsewhere as a postmaster) and William A. Craig, mentioned in other letters, were 49 and 53, respectively. The roster also lists William Craig, no middle initial, age 24.

31. Samuel S. Fisher, a Cincinnati attorney.

32. Laboytreaux dryly acknowledged his military limitations, however, in describing his unexpected encounter on camp guard with a forgiving colonel named Lambert. "O Lord, how I jumped! And in response to his handsome salute, terribly bewildered, I gathered up my gun and I 'trailed' it and 'shouldered' it, and 'supported' it, and—well, I believe I went through the whole manual before I could bring it to a 'present'—that feat being finally accomplished, the Colonel smiling pleasantly said, 'that's it, sir,' and passed on." Cincinnati *Times,* July 22, 1864.

33. CHAPTER SOURCES:

a. Cowen. "The Hundred-Days Men of 1864," pp. 221–32.

b. Gleason. William J. Gleason, *Historical Sketch of the 150th Regiment Ohio Volunteer Infantry* (Rocky River, 1899), pp. 6, 18–19.

c. Burrell. James C. Cannon, *Memorial, 150th Ohio, Company K* (Lakewood, 1907), p. 14.

d. Nichols. Clifton M. Nichols, *A Summer Campaign in the Shenandoah Valley, in 1864* (Springfield, 1899), pp. 39, 50–53, 128.

e. Morehouse. Morehouse, "Diary—1864."

f. Laboytreaux. Cincinnati *Times,* July 11, 1864.

2. Muster

1. Ohio National Guard regiments were sworn into U.S. service at three main camps: Camp Chase at Columbus, Camp Dennison outside Cincinnati, and Camp Cleveland near Cleveland. Some regiments first passed through smaller camps nearer to their home counties.

2. The 172nd Ohio, the last of the state's hundred-days regiments, primarily guarded government stores in the Ohio River town of Gallipolis. Two of its companies, however, briefly reinforced the 141st Ohio in West Virginia.

3. An Akron newspaper commented on this extraordinary late cold snap in its weekly edition. "We are having a very backward Spring, indeed, the weather for a few weeks past more resembling that usually prevailing in November, than the ordinary April and May weather. . . . On both Monday and Tuesday, there was mingled with the prevailing cold rains an occasional flurry of snow, which with the moist conditions of the streets, gave matters and things generally—especially soldiers—rather a 'bluish' tinge. Brighter skies, however, may be expected soon." Summit County *Beacon,* May 5, 1864.

At the end of the following week a Cleveland newspaper observed, "The fickleness of the weather, together with the impatience with which news from our gallant armies is awaited, has quite prostrated the business of the city for the past week. Adding the draft, and the departure of the National Guard to these, and we know of no week for a long while past which has been more depressing than the present." Cleveland *Plain Dealer,* May 13, 1864.

4. Camp Tod lay north of downtown, between it and what is now the Ohio State University campus.

5. West Virginia.

6. Accepting a lower rank rather than returning home was not unusual. Major James B. Templeton of the 39th O.N.G. (consolidated into the 157th O.V.I.), "disdaining the idea of returning home, on account of position, desired he would go with the regiment in any capacity, and finally received the appointment of First Lieutenant in Capt. Smith's Company." Steubenville *Herald,* June 9, 1864.

7. This does not agree with Cowen's account, and records conflict as to which was the first regiment to leave the state. Cowen, "The Hundred-Days Men of 1864," p. 228.

8. Near Cincinnati. Enjoying more seasonable weather later in the month, Sergeant Thomas Green, Company I, 156th Ohio, wrote to his wife that "this is a beautiful place right on the Little Miami [River]. Beautiful hills all around."

Green had earlier written home about deciding whether to be sworn into Federal service. "We have not been mustered in yet [May 16th]. But I think we will be tomorrow. I think the Boys will all take the oath. It is the best we can do. If we refuse to be sworn they will put us in the guard house for a while then send us to Columbus to do state duty for four years & and not get to come home for that time."

Largely untrue (although anyone refusing to take the oath might well have been briefly arrested), this camp tale could have been mere rumor; or, more deviously, it conceivably could have been disinformation meant to dampen dissent. Thomas Green, "Letters, to Sarah J. Green, Montezuma, O., from her husband, Sgt. Thomas Green, Co. I, 156th O.V.I," May 24th and 16th, respectively.

9. Major-General Lew Wallace.

10. Then the correct spelling for Pittsburgh. The Ohio hundred-days men were nearly universal in their praise of the Ladies' Aid Society of Pittsburg and the handsome hospitality they extended to troops.

11. Ohio.

12. The unfortunate 8th New York "Heavies," with 12 large companies, had 33 men killed, wounded and missing in its first action, Spotsylvania. At Cold Harbor, it lost 80 men killed (including Colonel Peter A. Porter), 339 wounded and 86 missing. In subsequent actions June 15–23 around Petersburg, it lost 42 killed (including Colonel Willard A. Bates), 261 wounded and 5 missing. William F. Fox, *Regimental Losses in the American Civil War, 1861–1865* (reprint, Dayton, 1985), p. 188.

Colonel Harris's 137th Ohio escorted the bodies of both fallen colonels through Baltimore, Porter's on June 8th and Bates's the first of July. Cincinnati *Commercial,* June 13 and July 7, 1864.

13. Brigadier-General John Hunt Morgan, Confederate cavalryman, had led a raid into Indiana and Ohio in 1863. The nickname "Squirrel Hunters" had originated a year earlier, attached to a motley army of volunteers who rushed to defend Cincinnati during the Confederate invasion of Kentucky in 1862.

14. On May 10. The men had reported to nearby Camp Lowe on May 2, only to be furloughed until departure.

15. By the end of May, Camp Chase was once again a camp for Confederate prisoners. "Only a few days ago, the whole common on the west of the camp was covered with white tents, the temporary habitations of nearly 15,000 men; now not a tent is to be seen." Letter signed "M," Guernsey *Times,* June 2, 1864.

The 88th Ohio, a long-service regiment that had guarded the camp since the previous fall, expected to be sent to the front with the hundred-days regiment. It remained at Camp Chase, however, aided for a time by the 162nd Ohio.

16. Maryland.

17. "He had forgotten the number of his original [O.N.G.] Regiment, and in addition to this, it had been consolidated, which had changed its number—but the great difficulty was, they did not believe his story. He was taken from the guard house at Cincinnati, sent twice to Louisville, three times to Cairo [Illinois], once to Memphis, and twice to this city. On Saturday [a major] sent him to Adjt. Gen. Cowen, who speedily straightened matters up, and sent him to his place at Camp Dennison. He estimates that in his travels he has commanded the service of a company of men, varying at different times from one to ten. He has seen the elephant." *Ohio State Journal,* July 6, 1864.

18. "This call will settle the question of this war," Brough told the Guardsmen, in a speech published around the state. "It will seal the fate of this country. The hundred days to come will settle the contest for good or for evil." He promised that the government would send them back home after the 100 days, but in the optimism of the period added a caveat. "Should there be a prospect of taking Richmond by two or three days' fighting after the expiration of 99 days of your service, I should expect you to remain there and take it. [Cries of 'We will!'] . . . I want Ohio to be the first to report

her men in the field. That she may be the first to say, 'We are coming father Abraham, three hundred thousand more.'" Cincinnati *Daily Gazette,* May 6, 1864.

19. A Springfield druggist "who has no 'doses' now, except for secessionists," according to Nichols, Bushnell was later elected governor of Ohio. He held office 1896–1900, during the Spanish-American War. Nichols served in Bushnell's Company E in the new regiment.

20. CHAPTER SOURCES:

a. Cowen. "The One Hundred-Days Men of 1864," pp. 226–29.

b. Sherman. Sylvester M. Sherman, *History of the 133d Regiment, O.V.I.* (Columbus, 1896), pp. 14–24.

c. Perkins. *A Summer in Maryland and Virginia, or Campaigning with the 149th Ohio Volunteer Infantry,* pp. 14–16.

d. Stipp. Joseph A. Stipp, *The History and Service of the 154th Ohio Volunteer Infantry* (Toledo, 1896), pp. 5–8.

e. Vail. Henry H. Vail, *What I Saw of the Civil War* (Woodstock, 1915), pp. 15–19.

f. Nichols. *A Summer Campaign,* pp. 11–20, 22–24.

g. Eames. William Mark Eames, "Papers, 1862–1864," Box 1, folder 4, letter dated May 16, 1864.

3. New Creek

1. "The town of New Creek is at the east end of the valley, and had long been used as a base of supplies where large quantities of government property had been stored," Private Joseph Stipp of the 154th Ohio later noted. "New Creek was formerly known as Paddytown, the name being changed in June 1861." Stipp, *History,* pp. 33, 46.

Some maps show New Creek and Paddytown as adjacent, distinct villages. The name of this combined location has since changed again, to Keyser, West Virginia. A smaller community also named New Creek now stands some seven miles to the southwest.

2. Samuel McCoy Bell, 159th Ohio, "One Hundred Days' Service: The Civil War Diary of Samuel McCoy Bell," May 13, 1864.

3. The 146th Ohio, which would later skirmish with guerrillas along West Virginia's rivers, had an early taste of southern sentiment within the state. Private William C. Reeder, Co. B, later recorded:

"We found Charleston had been a pretty place, but having been the scene of a battle had been somewhat damaged. . . . We got permission one night to go to the town. There were several hundred rebel prisoners to be sent to Camp Chase, Columbus, and Companies A and H of our regiment were to go as guards. After traversing a part of the town, we took courage and forded the almost bottomless street and reached the top of the river-bank at the bottom of which was a steamer containing the prisoners. The latter were full of malice and did not scruple to jeer at and curse us, and the predominant feeling of the citizens was sympathy for the prisoners. This was not shown by the men, but the women who crowded the balconies on the river side, took frequent opportunities to wave handkerchiefs, and as the boat left for its course down the river, a cheer went up." William C. Reeder, "Papers."

4. Franz Sigel, veteran of the Prussian army. Sigel played a key role in enlisting German-American soldiers to the Union cause. Their informal motto was "I fights mit Sigel." Sigel was not near Richmond but instead met defeat on May 15th at New Market, in the Shenandoah Valley.

5. Major General John C. Fremont, called "The Pathfinder" for his exploration of the West.

6. Maryland.

7. Nichols also reported this reaction to the arrest of Samuel Medary, publisher of the Columbus *Crisis,* which was vehemently and perhaps treasonously critical of the war: "The 133d Ohio, made up mainly of Franklin County men, gathered at once, on the receipt of the news, and held an indignant meeting! Because of the 'arbitrary arrest' of their 'esteemed fellow citizen?' Scarcely; but because he had not been arrested long ago. Of the hundreds of National Guards from Franklin County now in Camp New Creek, scarcely one is a Copperhead." *A Summer Campaign,* p. 43.

8. The Ohio regiments kept tabs on one another. "Two regiments of One Hundred Days men, the 152d and 154th, came in today, and camped on the ground just west of us along the creek, being over a week behind us," Sergeant Sherman of the 133rd recorded. Sherman, *History,* p. 46.

9. Lieutenant-Colonel Doty reported tongue-in-cheek from New Creek, "On my way to camp I had time, in Columbus, to offer Gov. Brough, on behalf of the 152d, an invitation to spend a night with us in camp, and agreed to give him exclusive use of *one dog tent,* the common soldier getting only one half tent each." Springfield *Republic,* June 3, 1864.

10. Nathan Wilkinson.

11. Private David W. Segrove, Company E.

12. Lieutenant-Colonel J. F. Hoy, 6th West Virginia. Nichols earlier in this dispatch had identified him as "an old Cincinnatian, who has been ordered to drill the National Guards in this camp and prepare them for active service in case their cooperation in the field should be required by our veteran regiments."

13. Company K.

14. "On May 29th the 154th O.V.I. went down to Greenland Gap and relieved the 2d Maryland, which came into New Creek to take the cars," Sergeant Sherman of the 133rd Ohio recorded. "The 152nd O.V.I. was also sent east, and felt very hard that our regiment should be left to do guard while they went to the front. Some of them began burning the boards they had floored their tents with, so that we could not have the use of them. But our commander soon convinced them that they were sent to protect Uncle Sam's property, instead of to destroy it." Sherman, *History,* pp. 48–49.

15. Cavalry raiders John H. McNeill, W. H. Harness, John Mosby, John Imboden, William "Grumble" Jones and Thomas Rosser. Of these, Mosby was most feared.

"We hold ourselves in readiness to give Mosby, or any other man a warm reception, that may venture to approach these defenses in an unfriendly spirit," a soldier-correspondent in the 145th Ohio wrote from Fort Whipple outside Washington. "Occasionally we hear some startling story of Mosby's doings, gotten up for the occasion, but the story is forgotten to be succeeded by one still more exaggerated; either that Mosby has made a raid on our picket lines, or that he has burned some Union man's property, or run off someone's stock, etc." Letter signed "100 Days," Sandusky *Register,* June 23, 1864.

16. Company E.

17. Colonel Jacob Higgins, 22nd Pennsylvania Cavalry, Commanding at Green Spring.

18. Second Lieutenant Isaac Hambleton, of Company C, wrote to his wife on June 12th, "The boys got back Tuesday tired enough, not so keen to go scouting as they were." Isaac Hambleton, "Hambleton Family Papers."

General Kelley officially reported "a severe engagement with McNeill and Harness, near Moorefield. . . . Our loss four killed and nine wounded, but drove the enemy to the mountains."

19. London, Ohio, seat of Madison County, site of the Hambleton farm.

20. In dispatches General Kelley mentions a West Virginia unit he first calls the Swamp Dragoons (i.e., mounted infantry), then later "a scout of State troops, or, as the rebels call them, 'Swamp Dragons. . . .'" Hambleton, too, uses both Dragoons and Dragons (misspelling the latter "Draggons," corrected in the text). This might be the same unit referred to elsewhere as "Swamper's Home Guards." *Official Records,* ser. 1, vol. 37, pt. 1, pp. 601, 687; ibid., ser. 1, vol. 25, pt. 1, p. 83.

21. CHAPTER SOURCES:

a. Nichols. *A Summer Campaign,* pp. 27–33, 35–36, 44–45, 54.

b. Stipp. *History,* pp. 12–18.

c. Hambleton. "Hambleton Family Papers."

4. Washington

1. Here Grant made his famous report that he would "fight it out on this line if it takes all summer." *Official Records,* ser. 1, vol. 36, pt. 2, p. 672.

2. "[S]hould Lincoln be elected," rebel former U.S. congressman J. L. M. Curry had proclaimed during an April speech at Talladega, Alabama, "our fond hopes will be dashed to the ground, our independence but a thing dreamed of, for we have exhausted our resources, and could not possibly hope to be able to continue the war four years longer." Chattanooga *Gazette,* reprinted in Gallipolis *Journal,* July 14, 1864.

3. See various accounts of meeting the president in Appendix A.

4. "H. W.," 164th Ohio. Summit County *Beacon,* May 26, 1864.

5. One of the ring of forts protecting Washington, D.C.

6. West Virginia.

7. Private Hezekiah Price of Company C described the view in a letter to his young daughter. "Our quarters are in a grove in the rear of the house. We can see the great bridge across the Potomac River. It is one mile long and is built for a railroad track on one side and the other is for wagons. We can see the steamboats and sail boats going up and down the river. There is a place in the bridge that they draw apart and let the boats go through and then they close it up and the cars run over it." Letter to Lizzie Price, May 28, 1864. Hezekiah Price, "Papers 1863–1865."

8. The former home of Robert E. Lee is now the grounds of Arlington National Cemetery.

9. The Battle of the Wilderness.

10. Company F (Akron Guards), 164th Ohio, also relieved veteran troops, at Fort Corcoran on Arlington Heights across the Potomac River from the capital. "H. W." explained the veterans' reaction to his hometown newspaper.

"The troops just gone to the front, whose quarters are now in possession and use of the one hundred men, have been right here for three years and more. They are much perplexed at the approach of new men to take their places. To leave their old tents and lodgings on these beautiful hills, and go to the wilderness and swamps of Southern Virginia, makes them sad as when the Jews sat down by the river of Babylon, Jerusalem behind them." Summit County *Beacon,* May 26th, 1864.

11. Private Charles L. Morehouse, substitute, 164th Ohio. Morehouse, "Diary—1864."

12. "Doc," 139th Ohio, Cincinnati *Times,* June 7, 1864.

13. "Two of Co. C's and three of A's boys wandered into 'Barnum's' and slightly surprised the Baltimoreans by executing several difficult pieces on the piano; the idea of private soldiers 'shaking up' a piano in that style took the natives down 'a few.'" Letter by "R. O. L.," Cleveland *Herald,* May 19, 1864. From other letters it is clear that R. O. L. served in Company A. He likely was Corporal Lemuel O. Rawson, the only man in the company with these three initials.

14. The 150th would earn no friends in the 143rd, a hundred-days regiment from rural eastern Ohio. Writing from Wilson's Landing on the James River, Virginia, in late June, Commissary Sergeant George L. Brooks of the 143rd explained his disgust with the proud city boys:

"The 150th O.N.G. from Cleveland, Ohio, who had been garrisoning Fort Bunker Hill—and some of the forts near them—were ordered to the 'White House' [landing] in the Pamunkey River—to help guard that position. They had been constantly boasting of their superiority over all other Ohio regiments and tried to make it appear that none were so brave as they—but when this marching order came they immediately set themselves to work to get it countermanded & succeeded in doing so by representing that they had *400* men on the sick list and that the rest were clerks etc. and could not stand *much service,* but thought the 143rd ought to be sent—as they were all mechanics, farmers, etc.—and could better stand the service. So we were sent in their place and they are still staying at Bunker Hill—where there is no danger of hurting their precious bodies or getting in the way of Rebel Bullets." George L. Brooks, in Linn, "Civil War Diaries of Two Brothers."

A newspaper correspondent noted that the 150th men at forts Lincoln and Bunker Hill "showed manliness under their order to go to the front which had just been received. Yet we fancied there was a sudden increase of admiration for the charming view that lay spread at their feet." When the order was canceled, he noted, "the 'boys' tonight will feel happy that—*on account of their friends at home*—they are not to be disturbed in their present sightly post." Cleveland *Herald,* June 9, 1864.

An officer in Company E at Fort Thayer apparently agreed, writing that the countermanded orders "gave great satisfaction to the boys, as they think they have got a fine location here." Letter signed "Iron Clad," Cleveland *Plain Dealer,* June 13.

Five privates in Company C of the 150th Ohio requested and received an extremely rare transfer into Company A of the 143rd. These were Linton Chamberlain; Arthur DeLair; Herman G. Norton; Ira D. Thorpe; and Henry R. Wolcott (or Wolcutt). "All honor to their noble action," concluded Sergeant Brooks.

15. Zouaves were infantrymen whose colorful uniforms and tactics were modeled on those of French colonial soldiers.

16. Ohio congressman, former major general of volunteers, and future president of the United States.

17. Anson H. Robbins.

18. Elihu C. Barnard.

19. Major-General Silas Casey, veteran of the Mexican and Indian wars.

20. Edward A. Ells.

21. George W. Keyes.

22. Pennsylvania, during the train trip from Camp Cleveland.

23. CHAPTER SOURCES:

a. Chadwick. Wallace W. Chadwick, "Into the Breach: Civil War Letters of Wallace W. Chadwick" (Columbus, 1943), pp. 161–63.

b. Gleason. *Historical Sketch,* pp. 7–8.

c. Cannon. Cannon, *Record of Service of Company K, 150TH O.V.I., 1864* (Lakewood?, 1903), pp. 9–13.

d. Holtz. Jacob Souder Holtz Collection, Box 1, folder 2-2.

e. Lemmon. "169TH OVI Reunion Scrapbook 1887–1909."

5. Maryland

1. Samuel McClain, "Papers, 1864," MS-640, folder 7, letter dated June 3, 1864, Center for Archival Collections, Bowling Green State University.

2. A soldier-correspondent in the 137th Ohio who signed his reports "Sandy" described the defenses around Fort McHenry, where that regiment was headquartered for most of the hundred days.

"Fort McHenry is situated on a peninsula, between the harbor and the Patapsco River. About half a mile from the point of the peninsula a brick wall runs across it. Inside of this is called 'the fort,' but the fort proper is situated near the center of the enclosure, and does not occupy a tenth part of it. The peninsula at the wall is about a quarter of a mile wide, and is not much wider half a mile further up—being, for that distance, mostly a common, with but one or two houses. This common is subject to a direct fire from the guns of the fort. and to a cross-fire from gunboats either in the harbor or in the Patapsco, and is also in range of the guns of Fort Marshall; and, in order to approach the peninsula at all, Federal Hill must be taken."

Sandy in the same dispatch notes that "quite a number of our officers have been shortening their '100 days' by having their wives with them." Cincinnati *Commercial,* July 15, 1864.

3. Colonel John G. Lowe, commanding the regiment.

4. Major-General Benjamin "Spoons" Butler, an inept political general and sometimes military governor, now commanding the Army of the James.

5. The 42nd Massachusetts, a hundred-days regiment, later saw punishment delivered to a bounty-jumper outside Washington.

"September 16th—All troops in the command were paraded to witness an execution of a private, Fourth Maryland Volunteers, shot for desertion, at eleven A.M., in the open field northwest of Sickel Barracks Hospital. The negroes in and around Alexandria made a gala occasion of the affair, with tents pitched near the spot for sales of cake, pies, lemonade, etc.

"So far as appearances went, the man to be shot, a thick-set fellow, with heavy, black whiskers, was more indifferent to his fate than the soldiers formed to occupy three sides of a square, obliged to be unwilling witnesses. On the open side were gathered a curious crowd of colored people. The condemned man was marched upon the ground, a band playing a dirge. He was followed by a faithful Newfoundland dog, who had to be taken away when his master took position in front of his coffin, face to the firing party.

"In a speech he confessed to being a professional bounty-jumper, worth at that moment near $20,000, the proceeds of his work in jumping 16 bounties. When the detail of soldiers fired upon him, he fell lengthwise upon his coffin. The troops were then filed past him, and had just commenced the movement when signs of life were shown, necessitating a second file of men to be ordered up and put another volley into him." Charles P. Bosson, *History of the Forty-Second Regiment Infantry, Massachusetts Volunteers, 1862, 1863, 1864* (Boston, 1886), p. 451.

6. In early July, as part of General Jubal Early's invasion of Maryland, Confederate cavalry under Brigadier-General Bradley T. Johnson failed in a bold plan to liberate rebel prisoners held at Point Lookout, near the city. Early's campaign is addressed at length in the Monocacy chapter.

7. The 8th Massachusetts hundred-days regiment also served in Baltimore, reporting at the end of July. Private William Eaton of Company E (Richardson Light Guard) later recalled the hostile rebel feeling that infused the city.

"Soon after the regiment went into camp at Manakin's woods, the Richardson Light Guard was furloughed to attend a gala day at Druid Hill Park, Baltimore's popular resort. Immense crowds were in attendance, and as the soldiers mingled with the people it was soon evident that the soldier element was not popular, for on all sides the crowd would gather and flaunt in their faces some Confederate emblem or the verses of 'My Maryland.' When Jackson crossed the Potomac his troops sang it with enthusiastic demonstrations, tossing their caps high in the air. No song during the civil war had such a hold on the South as 'My Maryland;' it was sung in their camps, on the march, in the theaters and houses throughout the entire South:

> *The despot's heel is on thy shore,*
> > *Maryland!*
> *His torch is at thy temple door,*
> > *Maryland!*
> *Avenge the patriotic gore*
> *That wept o'er gallant Baltimore*
> *And be the battle queen of yore,*
> > *Maryland! My Maryland!*

"The crowds were warned by the soldiers that if the song was kept up there would be trouble, and as soon after the warning was given, 'My Maryland' was coming from the throats of thousands, a riot was soon in progress and bloody forms were seen in every direction, but the soldiers quickly succeeded in getting the upper hands of the wild rebel element." William Eaton, *History of the Richardson Light Guard, of Wakefield, Mass., 1851–1901* (Wakefield, 1901), pp. 95–96.

8. The Cincinnati *Times,* which reprinted the letter, spelled the name Kiensted.

9. Although some troops did react badly to working with African-American troops, Kiersted's positive reaction was not unique. The nearer their regiments moved to the front, the more the Ohioans' respect grew. "A great many colored troops are encamped here," Corporal Benjamin Linville of the 134th wrote in his diary on July 4th, north of the James. "They bear the appearance of good soldiers." Benjamin A. Linville, "Diary, May–Sep. 1864."

Other troops agreed. "A negro regiment was here, but have left since we arrived,"

138th Ohio's "Crescent" wrote from Spring Hill, Virginia. "We had actually seen negro troops and troops, too, who have seen hard service and done glorious execution. It was marvelous to see what a change a few hours intercourse with these colored troops had wrought upon our men. They learned to respect them as they never had before, and all their prejudice against negro soldiers vanished in thin air in a wonderfully short time." Cincinnati *Times,* June 27, 1864.

10. 1st Sergeant John C. Donovant [*Official Roster* spelling], Private Henry Wilson.

11. Probably Captain Nathaniel S. Hubbell.

12. Private Bartholomew Fanning.

13. Private Moses Phillips, 52.

14. "After having belonged to the 71st and 13th Battalions, 50th and 169th Regts. and 82nd Batt., we have finally settled down on the tail end of the 139th regt. where it is to be hoped we will remain. The most of our regt. is from Cincinnati and is commanded by Col. Jones of that city. He seems to be a fine man. The Cincinnati men seem to be very quiet orderly fellows. . . ." Letter from Camp Chase, May 22, 1864. William Miller, "Miller Family Papers," Box 2, folder 48.

15. The attitude was fairly common among the regiments. A soldier in the 131st Ohio who signed his letters "Sidney" reported this from Baltimore:

"For several days the entire force at Federal Hill has been confined to the Fort. . . . The reason seems to be that in the vicinity of the city there are a number of regiments of hundred day men who believe in 'living off the country,' and who have been carrying that policy into execution in 'My Maryland.' For the purpose of correcting this, General Wallace issued a general order prohibiting the granting of passes to all troops 'in the vicinity' of Baltimore. Inasmuch as we were really *in* the city and not 'in the vicinity' . . . we thought this did not apply to the 'One Hundred and Thirty-firsters.'" Dayton *Journal,* August 4, 1864.

16. Captain Wilson S. Miller felt compelled to offer his brother a peek at the real war in a letter dated August 2nd. "[W]e have been closing in gradually on Atlanta until we are within a mile and a half of the doomed city," he wrote. "Our division has had no hard fighting, but have done considerable skirmishing. A few days ago our Regt. charged on a line of rifle pits and drove the rebs out, and occupied them ourselves. The main works of the enemy are about half a mile from ours. . . ." Miller, "Miller Family Papers," Box 2, folder 60.

17. The *Official Records* and the Steubenville *Herald* use "Daton"; the *Official Roster* has "Dayton."

18. Brigadier-General Erastus B. Tyler, commanding the First Separate Brigade, VIII Corps.

19. George W. McCook, commanding the regiment, was one of Ohio's famous "Fighting McCooks" and Edwin Stanton's law partner. He took leave of the regiment during the hundred days when his brother Brigadier-General Dan McCook died of wounds received at Kenesaw Mountain, Georgia.

20. Jefferson County, Ohio, home of much of the regiment.

21. These thirteen Pennsylvania militia regiments could not be absorbed into the Union army early in the war, and initially were trained and equipped at state expense. Eventually designated the 30th through 42nd Pennsylvania Volunteers, their enlistments expired in May 1864. Men who reenlisted formed the 190th and 191st Pennsylvania and fought on as the Veteran Reserve Brigade.

22. William Dennison was Ohio governor 1860–62, David Tod 1862–64. Ser-

geant Albert H. Black of Company C reported that "we came upon our worthy Ex-Governor, Tod, standing upon the sidewalk, and each company, as they came opposite, saluted him with three hearty cheers." Steubenville *Herald,* June 15, 1864.

The 133rd Ohio had seen Dennison and other Republican delegates pass through New Creek aboard a B&O train on June 2nd. "The governor had a pleasant smile, a kind word, and a hearty shake of the hand for us all, and the same can be said for the rest of the party." Letter signed "Hayden Guards," *Ohio State Journal,* June 7, 1864.

23. This was the primary responsibility of the hundred-days regiments of the National Guard of the State of New York, most of which did not leave that state. Guards at the Elmira camp thwarted an escape attempt by the rebel captives in late August.

"They had managed to dig a breach under ground a distance of some forty feet past the enclosure of the grounds, and under the hospital building. The rebels, when discovered, were briskly engaged at work in the trench, and were aiming for the sutler's tent. The ditch was only about two and a half feet high, and about three feet under ground, and only two men could get in at a time. They had no tools to work with, and how they managed to get so far in hard gravelly soil is a mystery." Rochester *Express,* quoted in Sandusky *Register,* September 2, 1864.

24. Henry Vail of the 131st Ohio also attended the convention. "I was fortunate in being present when Abraham Lincoln was nominated for a second term of office. . . . I had no difficulty in entering the convention. It was understood that the nominations would be made on that day [June 8th]. While on the lower floor of the theater, I heard the resolution read by Mr. Raymond [Henry J. Raymond, of New York, who asked for Lincoln's nomination by a call of the states], and the nomination of Abraham Lincoln. I then went up into the gallery where I could look down on the scene. I was there when the ballot was taken.

"At the announcement of the result, a cloud of hats came up, and the cheering was so loud and long that for some time I could not hear the music of the large brass band that I could see playing in the gallery facing the stage. When the cheers subsided a little, the audience heard the notes of the *Star Spangled Banner,* and another cheer burst forth. There was no enthusiasm over the nomination of Andrew Johnson as vice president." Vail, *What I Saw,* pp. 23–24.

25. The island was a man-made extension of a sandbar that was naturally submerged by high tide. It was now surrounded by a levee six to ten feet high, prompting a newspaper correspondent to observe that "the island, with its dikes and moats, is a miniature of the Kingdom of Holland." Steubenville *Herald,* August 24, 1864.

26. Private Henry H. McElhinny of Co. A described Fort Delaware: "The interior of the Fort is an open square, in which are two yellow washed buildings, one used as a Post Office and office of [the] Provost Marshal, the other as a barracks for soldiers escorting prisoners to the island. The remainder of the vacant space—except what is occupied for streets—is surrounded by a low fence and covered with grass. The main entrance to the Fort is called the 'Sally Port,' the entrance to which can be raised or let down at pleasure. It is opened at reveille and closed at retreat. It answers as a door, closing the entrance when raised, and as a bridge to enter the Fort when let down. . . . The columbiads of the Fort present their round black mouths to the [prisoners'] 'Bull pen,' and hold the rod over them *in terrorem.*" Ibid., July 6, 1864.

27. Brigadier-General Albin Francisco Schoepf, a Hungarian-born immigrant. "A graduate of the Vienna military academy and a Prussian officer, he went to Hungary to fight under Kossuth in 1848 and was exiled to Turkey, where he fought with and in-

structed the Ottoman Army." Mark M. Boatner, *The Civil War Dictionary* (New York, 1991), p. 726.

The general's children enjoyed riding about the post in a carriage driven by a stout Dutchman and pulled by a pair of trained goats. When this unlikely assemblage somehow all fell off a bridge into the moat, Captain Thomas A. Gamble, of Company E, leaped to the rescue.

"The General sent for Capt. Gamble, expressed to him his profound gratitude for saving his children from drowning, and '*last but not least,*' gave him a furlough and $50 to go to Philadelphia and buy himself a brand new suit of military clothes." Steubenville *Herald,* August 24, 1864.

28. Sergeant Vail of the 131st Ohio also visited Fort Delaware, when he helped a friend escort a prisoner there. "Fort Delaware was built in the middle of the Delaware River on made land. It was made of stone and was much like Fort Sumter. I slept in a casemate, prepared for a cannon; but the room was perfectly empty. The next morning I took my breakfast with the soldiers that guarded the fort. Around the fort was a large level field, built up upon a shallow in the river and this swarmed with thousands of Confederate prisoners. I was allowed to go among them and talk with them. Many of them had trinkets that they had made from the bones that came in their meat. These they offered for sale. I bought a bone ring as a keepsake. I left before noon and went back to Baltimore." Vail, *What I Saw,* pp. 31–32.

29. Private William Negus of Company F also reported an escape attempt: "On a dark night lately, a few of them tried to swim the Delaware and thus escape. One was drowned, a boat picked up another, a third returned after contending for two hours with the watery element, and the fourth was arrested in Delaware City next morning. These rebs are, most of them, a dirty, ragged and lousy set. Among 10,000 of those that are here, it would puzzle any man to find two who are uniformed precisely alike." Steubenville *Herald,* July 13, 1864.

30. On the Baltimore & Ohio Railroad, between Baltimore and Washington.

31. "The river is very wide here," wrote a member of the regiment, "and the view is perfectly delightful to us land lubbers from the Buckeye State." Letter signed "Limeric," Steubenville *Herald,* June 15, 1864.

32. The fortress overlooked Hampton Roads, midway between the mouths of the James and York rivers at Chesapeake Bay. Sergeant Vail of the 131st Ohio, a peripatetic sort, also visited here. "I went down by steamer and at once finished my errand. I then wandered over the fort, which was then a very busy place. It was at the time that Grant moved his army south of the James River. From the walls of the fort I saw hundreds of vessels, filled with soldiers, cannons, horses, and all manner of warlike supplies, moving past the fort. It was a continuous procession. At that time no one at the fort knew where this army was going." Vail, *What I Saw,* pp. 32–33.

33. The 157th Ohio, raised along the Ohio River, didn't escort rebels to the prison camp in Lake Erie. Some of its members instead went to sea, guarding 600 prisoners bound from Fort Delaware for Hilton Head, S.C. Their ship, the steam transport *Crescent,* grounded off Cape Roman on the night of August 23rd. One prisoner jumped overboard and escaped, and the 157th braced for an attack to free the others. No attack materialized, and the vessel was soon refloated. *Crescent's* captain and mate were later convicted of neglect of duty.

"When the vessel grounded, the guard were all (without hint or order from authority) engaged in looking carefully to their arms, and could be heard the quiet expression of determination, *'Boys, we'll never go ashore, and under no circumstances shall all our prisoners.'* " New York *Times,* reprinted in *Ohio State Journal,* Columbus, September 1, 1864.

34. *Official Records,* ser. 2, vol. 7, p. 452.

35. Eames, "Papers, 1862–1864," folder 4, letter dated July 15, 1864.

Colonel William Hoffman, 3rd U.S. Infantry, Commissary-General of Prisoners, added a withering endorsement to the board's finding: "There are many ways of punishing a prisoner for disobedience of a sentinel's order when not attended with a demonstration of violence without going to the extremity of shooting him down; and in the case reported there seems to have been nothing to call for such severe measures. If the sentinel was governed by his orders, as from the proceedings it may be presumed he was, he is excusable, and the responsibility rests upon the commanding officer." *Official Records,* ser. 2, vol. 7, p. 454.

36. CHAPTER SOURCES:

a. Perkins. *A Summer in Maryland and Virginia,* pp. 16–17, 63–65.

b. Vail. *What I Saw,* pp. 21–23, 25–26, 33–34, 37.

c. Kiersted. Cincinnati *Times,* June 9, 1864.

d. Miller. "Miller Family Papers," Box 2, folder 54.

e. Daton. Steubenville *Herald,* June 22, 1864.

f. Sharon. Ibid.

g. Douglass. *Official Records,* series 2, vol. 7, p. 453.

6. The Shenandoah

1. West Virginia.

2. The supply train included "some 200 wagons," according to a letter from the 160th Ohio signed "Salemite," Zanesville *Courier,* June 14, 1864. The newspaper had earlier published another account of escorting this train:

"We arrived at Harper's Ferry on the 15th inst., went into camp at that place and remained there two days, at the end of that time, received orders to return to Martinsburg for the purpose of guarding a supply train up to General Sigel's distance 40 miles up the valley of the Shenandoah. This proved somewhat disastrous to the regiment. The men were compelled to march day and night, which you know would be hard for new recruits. It produced about 200 sick and sore footed men, quite a number of which are now under the care of the Surgeon, but all will be right in a few days I think. These men were all sent back to this place." Private D. N. Burton, Company C, letter from Martinsburg, May 28, 1864. Zanesville *Courier,* June 4, 1864.

3. The train was now in Virginia.

4. Major-General David Hunter. A friend of President Lincoln's, veteran of the frontier, the Mexican War and Kansas, he had graduated from West Point more than 40 years earlier (1822).

5. "One man, a young man by the name of Jackson, from Perry county, was shot by three balls, and was thought to be mortally wounded for a time, but he is rapidly recovering, and was yesterday in camp, walking about on his crutches, receiving the congratulations of his friends. Mr. Kelly of the Q.M. Department while assisting Jackson from the field was taken prisoner by the rebs. He was directed to go to a certain point, assured he would be shot if he undertook to get away. He started in the

direction indicated, but waiting his chance, eluded his captors, and with his friend Jackson, found our boys, who gladly welcomed them both for a passage to Martinsburg and our camp." "Salemite," Zanesville *Courier,* June 14, 1864.

The bugler was likely William Jackson, Company G, the only musician among three Jacksons in the regiment. Mr. Kelly was likely Commissary Sergeant Nathan S. Kelly, who died at Baltimore on August 17, 1864.

6. "Salemite" and the regimental history in *Ohio in the War* (vo. 2, p. 690) place rebel casualties at 14 killed and an unknown number of wounded.

7. Also a hundred-days regiment.

8. Virginia, not to be confused with the Maryland town near Monocacy Junction.

9. "The 152d has just started for the front with a train of 199 wagons, each drawn by four or six horses or mules, and stretching along the Winchester Pike for three miles," reported Corporal Nichols of the Springfield *News,* who did not accompany the train. Nichols, *A Summer Campaign,* p. 68.

10. Captain John H. McNeill, whose McNeill Rangers particularly worried the hundred-days men. After his mortal wounding and capture, he died in Federal hands on November 10, 1864. His son Jesse then led the Rangers in their most celebrated exploit, the capture of generals B. F. Kelley and George Crook at Cumberland on February 21, 1865.

11. Colonel Milton Wells, 3rd Brigade; Brigadier-General Jeremiah C. Sullivan, 1st Division, West Virginia.

12. Hunter ordered the burning of VMI, an act for which he was reviled throughout the South. In a series of long reports written during the trek, another member of the 152nd, who signed the letters "E. M. D.," wrote: "All its glory was shorn by the ravages of war; and in the place of noble libraries, apparatus and buildings, there only remained the charred and cracked timbers and walls." The writer almost certainly was Lieutenant-Colonel Doty, although the newspaper had previously published letters under this full name. Springfield *Republic,* July 27, 1864.

13. E. M. D. reported: "In the cemetery in Lexington, [[Jackson's] soldier-grave was the point of greatest interest to our soldiers, who had just captured the town, and the rebel flag, which a devoted wife had erected over his tomb, was soon made to strike its defiant rebellious position to the boys who took it." Ibid.

14. People in Springfield also worried over the regiment's whereabouts. Corporal Nichols reported from Martinsburg, "We have various rumors, one to the effect that the men are on their way to Ohio, via Beverly and Grafton, guarding prisoners; another that they have gone to suppress a new Butternut rebellion in the Buckeye state; another that they are lying at Strasburg, waiting for an outgoing wagon train, and another that they are lying at Winchester. We think they are not lying anywhere, but that the persons who circulate these rumors are doing the lying." Nichols, *A Summer Campaign,* p. 75.

15. Actually, West Virginia. The train at this point left the Shenandoah Valley.

16. Both in West Virginia.

17. E. M. D. reported: "The contrabands, in eager crowds, now began to flock in—strong young men and women, gray-haired old men and women; every conceivable style of bundle—old clothes and traps, bread, meat, etc. The only greater variety was to be found in the wagons, where they stowed away their surplus articles. . . . They

follow us of their own accord, with a distinct idea that they are leaving slavery and going to freedom, that this is the time of their deliverance, and they hail it with joy." Springfield *Republic,* July 27, 1864.

18. Nichols soon reported from Martinsburg that the quartermaster there had received a telegram from Colonel Putman: "Beverly, Va., June 27, 1864.—My command is here and all safe, except Daniel Thomas, killed." Nichols later reported that "Daniel Thomas, Company H (Darke County), was shot through the head and killed almost instantly." Nichols, *A Summer Campaign,* p. 86.

19. CHAPTER SOURCES:
  a. Siegfried. Zanesville *Courier,* August 23, 1864.
  b. Cochran. Nichols, *A Summer Campaign,* pp. 148–59.

7. Cynthiana

1. Surgeon Willis Danforth of the 134th Illinois later recorded the harshness of war in Kentucky. "The rebels were organizing for a raid upon Paducah. Guerrillas made frequent attacks upon our troops, and in one of their encounters, we captured one of their captains who had received a severe wound in the head, shattering the bones of the left side of his face. He was under my care, and had so far recovered as to be able to be up and dressed, when . . . [Brigadier-General Eleazer A. Paine] ordered me and the 134th Regiment to report there to duty. He also ordered Captain [Jim] Kesterson, the guerrilla, to be sent there.

"Arriving at his headquarters, he at once reappointed me his medical director, ordered the guerrilla captain to be brought before him and sentenced him to be shot at six A.M. the next day. (I attended the execution [on July 27].) He then put P. B. Jacobs, a rebel sympathizer, on a United States horse, requiring him to visit every rebel commander in the district and read them his proclamation as follows:

" 'I have this day shot Captain Kesterson, taken prisoner in guerrilla warfare, and shall shoot in like manner all prisoners so taken, and if I am credibly informed of retaliation being practiced on Union men living in my district, I will walk out five of the most prominent citizens of Paducah and shoot them dead for every Union life so taken. Gen. E. A. Paine, Brig.-General.'

"We held Jacobs' father and two brothers as hostages for his return within ten days. Jacobs returned on time with the signatures of rebel commanders on the back of the proclamation. While this was going on, Gen. Paine exiled 50 of the most prominent rebel families to Canada. I saw them go under command of . . . a company of colored soldiers (former slaves of these masters). They were sent to Detroit and landed at Windsor, and remained there until the rebellion closed."

In a letter to Grant, Paine's predecessor, Brigadier-General Henry Prince, bitterly denounced these and other incidents as a "policy calculated . . . to spread ruin and devastation, and having no good in it." Paine was relieved. Willis Danforth, "How I Came to Be in the Army, and General E. A. Paine's Plan of Federal Salvation" (Milwaukee, 1891), pp. 330–31.

2. He had also provided an offhand reassurance: "If you hear any tale of our leaving you need not believe it, when they took two companies and detail about two hundred men every night for picket guard and camp duty. You need not expect us to leave when they need so many men as that. The secesh [secessionists] is trying to dig out. They are digging from under their barracks. They have four feet of dirt and four

feet of thin sand stone to dig through. Then they [find] a kind of dry sand and loam. The officer of the night went in last evening and caught twenty of the rebs with their digging suit on. He put them in a cell for safe keeping until the war is closed. . . ." Letter dated June 6, 1864. Mortimer C. Thompson, "Two Letters to his Father, Grovenor J. Thompson, Niles, Trumbell County, Ohio from Johnson's Island, June 6 and 9, 1864."

3. Stephen G. Burbridge, commanding the district of Kentucky.

4. Samuel P. Heintzelman.

5. In a letter to the hometown newspaper, a 168th soldier who signed himself only as "L. C." reported that "At Covington [June 9th], some of the companies stacked arms, and refused to go into the presence of the enemy with antiquated muskets, some of them older than themselves; but persuasion and threats induced them to take arms and proceed." *The Herald,* Washington (Court House), July 7, 1864.

6. A single-page history of the 168th states: "At six o'clock on the morning of the 11th, a large force of cavalry flanked the pickets on the Davis Pike and moved against the town. The regiment formed rapidly, but being subjected to an enfilading fire on both flanks, it seized the nearest buildings, and for two hours the fight continued. The Rebels set fire to the building adjoining; the ammunition was almost exhausted, and the men were suffering intensely from heat and smoke. Colonel [Conrad] Garis stepped out to offer terms of surrender, when several shots were fired at him, wounding him in the arm and shoulder. The regiment lost eight men killed, 17 wounded, and 280 captured, together with the quartermaster stores and camp equipage. The prisoners were robbed of their money, watches, hats, boots, and other articles of clothing." Reid, *Ohio in the War,* vol. 2, p. 698.

Soldier-correspondent "L. C." reported that "We fought them as best we could for about an hour and twenty minutes." Captain Ephraim Henkle, Company F, told a Cincinnati newspaper correspondent that his men had been "well posted" in the Cynthiana depot during the fighting. "They could not have burned us out, but did compel Garis to surrender by burning the dwellings. After he had surrendered, we kept up firing. When they sent in a flag of truce, we surrendered. . . . They stripped all our men of everything valuable, of their money and equipments, even to canteens." Cincinnati *Daily Gazette,* June 14, 1864.

7. Corporal Spencer G. Frary of Company K, later wrote: "Cynthiana, being about a mile distant from where we were, could not be seen on account of hills and woods intervening. We could not tell who held the city. Gen'l Hobson commanding our forces came to me and asked if we had a brave and trusty man in our company who could cross the river and ascertain the strength of Morgan's forces, saying it would be a dangerous undertaking. After calling for a volunteer, [Private] E. Smith Woodworth stepped out, saying he would make the perilous attempt—which he did with success and credit to himself, although he came very near being captured. . . . Before Woodworth's return, we were attacked by 1500 of Morgan's cavalry. . . ." Spencer George Frary, "An Account of the encounter of the 171st Ohio Infantry with Confederate Forces under command of Gen. Morgan and their return to Johnson's Island, 1863–1864," p. 3.

8. "Near Cynthiana, Ky., June 11, 1864.

"I, Brig. Gen. E. H. Hobson, commanding forces U.S. Army, and the following officers, John S. Butler, captain and assistant adjutant-general; George G. Lott, captain and aide-de-camp; Joel F. Asper, colonel, One hundred and seventy-first Ohio National

Guard; Herman R. Harmon, lieutenant-colonel, One hundred and seventy-first Ohio National Guard; M. A. Fowler, major, One hundred and seventy-first Ohio National Guard; Lieut. J. W. Arnett, Fifty-second Kentucky, and W. Lee Osborn, first lieutenant and aide-de-camp, this day captured by Brig. Gen. John H. Morgan, C.S. Army, do hereby give our parole of honor to place ourselves in immediate communication with the military authorities of the United States for the purpose of obtaining an exchange for officers of equal rank with ourselves, and should we fail to accomplish said exchange we give our word of honor that we will report direct to Brig. Gen. John H. Morgan in the shortest time practicable, and by the most direct route, under charge of three officers and one private selected to escort us.

[signed by above]

"Witness:"
B. H. Allen,
"Inspector-General, Morgan's Cavalry."
Official Records, ser. 1, vol. 39, pt. 1, pp. 36–37.

9. Kentucky.

10. A prisoner-of-war camp in Lake Erie. A newspaper on the mainland at nearby Sandusky editorialized that the 171st was "composed of most excellent material, in command of Col. Asper, formerly of the 7th O.V.I., in which he served with credit and honor." Upon the regiment's later release from service, the paper added, "Few of the 100-days men have had a more varied experience than the 171st, and few if any have suffered as much." Sandusky *Register,* June 14 and August 22, 1864.

11. Colonel L. H. Giltner.

12. Lieutenant-Colonel R. M. Martin.

13. Garis was popular enough that his officers had presented him with a saddle and equipment at Camp Dennison. Although severely injured, he was mistakenly reported mortally wounded back in Ohio. Sergeant Thomas Green of the 156th O.V.I., himself recovering from an illness, wrote mournfully to his wife, "Sarah, you know that Regiment that was on drill the day you was at Camp [Dennison]? Well they was in that fite at Cinthiana with Morgan and their was a good many of them kild and the rest taken prisoners and their Colonel was kild poor fellow. I saw him every day I was at Camp but now he is dead. . . ." Green, "Letters."

14. Among the dead was Private Mort Thompson. Corporal Frary recalled another of the casualties, Private Henry A. Millikan: "I went to see my dear friend Millikan as he lay bleeding from a ghastly wound through the lungs. He sent a message by me to his wife. He lived nearly an hour after he was shot by a Rebel bullet." Frary, "Account," p. 4.

15. "Lexington, June 14, 1864. (Received 15th.)

"The general commanding [Burbridge] considers no officers and men prisoners of war except such as Morgan retained and took off with him, and directs that you and your staff report here for duty as soon as practicable, and that the three rebel officers be held as prisoners."

"Lexington, June 15, 1864. (Received 16th.)

"The general commanding directs that yourself and staff and Lieut. J. W. Arnett, Fifty-second Kentucky, come here via Louisville, and bring with you the rebel officers and privates as prisoners of war. The Ohio 100-days' officers had better go to Cincinnati."

Official Records, ser. 1, vol. 39, pt. 1, p. 62.

16. Columbus.

17. Probably Brigadier-General Robert B. Vance, in Tennessee.

18. "After the fight [at Keller's Bridge], General Morgan stated that this attack upon him delayed his movements and prevented his reaching Covington and Cincinnati," Hobson's A.A.G., Captain Butler, wrote shortly afterward. Cincinnati *Commercial,* June 14, 1864.

Burbridge fought Morgan on June 12th, the following day.

19. Burdened by red tape and legal uncertainties, the 171st was quartered temporarily at Camp Dennison. A newspaper called their quarters filthy, hot, and unhealthy after three men died of disease within two weeks. "Some effort should be made by the citizens of Cincinnati to have those worthy boys transferred to some more desirable location. We are indebted much to that gallant band." Cincinnati *Commercial,* June 27, 1864.

The regiment eventually moved back to its old post at Johnson's Island, but "no duty was required of the paroled officers and men until an order from the War Department declared the parole invalid, when the regiment was re-armed and placed on duty. About the same time an order announced the arrangement between General Hobson and General Morgan binding, and the Rebel officers, who were held until that time as prisoners of war, were released. The regiment remained on Johnson's Island during the remainder of its term, and was mustered out on the 20th of August, 1864." Reid, *Ohio in the War,* vol. 2, p. 702.

Rebel Surgeon Richard R. Goode, however, might have wished later that he had remained in Federal hands. The Confederate Army charged him in November with stealing $72,000 from a Mount Sterling bank during the Morgan raid. Others were charged with stealing $10,000 from a bank at Lexington.

20. There were "about 1200" Federal prisoners, including the 171st, 168th and "part of the 12th Ohio Cavalry captured two days before at Mount Sterling." Frary, "Account," p. 6.

21. First Lt. William H. Earl nonetheless returned with his regiment.

22. The enlisted men signed nothing, but officers signed the following, witnessed by Captain Allen:

"Near Claysville, Ky., June 12, 1864.

"We the undersigned officers of the Army of the United States, having been captured by Brig. Gen. John H. Morgan, of the C.S. Army, do hereby give our parole of honor not to engage in military service against the Confederate States until duly exchanged for officers of equal rank." *Official Records,* ser. 1, vol. 39, pt. 1, p. 62.

23. CHAPTER SOURCES:

a. Thompson. Thompson, "Two Letters to his Father."

b. Hobson. *Official Records,* ser. 1, vol. 39, pt. 1, pp. 33–36.

c. Asper. Ibid., pp. 55–61.

d. Swindler. Ibid., pp. 63–64.

8. Petersburg

1. Bermuda Hundred was the first incorporated Virginia town in 1614. An anonymous newspaper correspondent reported the scene there on the morning of May 6th, 1864:

"The work of landing the troops, stores, horses, and artillery, went on last night with uncommon dispatch, considering that the necessary wharves had first to be constructed. The shallow water near the banks of the James River at this point does not admit of the very close approach of the transports, and pontoon bridges and other temporary landing places had to be made. Everybody having anything at all to do with the debarkation exhibited great energy and heartiness in the work, and this morning there were plenty of evidences that very few persons connected with the expedition had passed the night in sleep. On the river banks, and in the fields some distance inland, huge piles of ordnance, commissary and quartermaster stores—all the bulky and vast material needed for the effective working of a grand army—reared themselves as monuments to the industry of the chiefs of the Engineers, and Quartermaster's Departments." Sandusky *Register,* May 16, 1864.

2. These were the first and second brigades, Third Division, X Corps, Army of the James. The division formed on June 19, 1864, after some Ohio units had already served in other divisions. The first brigade comprised the 133rd, 143rd, 148th and 163th Ohio, and at various times artillery and engineer detachments from other states, plus two companies of U.S. Colored Cavalry. This brigade served at Fort Powhatan, Wilson's Wharf, and Bermuda Landing.

The second brigade comprised the 130th, 132nd, 134th, 138th (detached to the Eastern Shore on July 14th), and 142nd Ohio. This brigade served on the left in the entrenchments in front of Bermuda Hundred. *Official Records,* ser. 1, vol. 40, pt. 1, pp. 212–13, 234–35, 264–65.

Two other Ohio regiments—the 153rd and 155th—also served in the Army of the James. The 37th New Jersey hundred-days regiment, too, served in the trenches outside Petersburg; it relieved the 138th Ohio at Fort Ohio, Spring Hill, on July 14th.

3. The Toledo *Blade* defined the 130th Ohio's position outside Petersburg on June 21 as "near 'the front' as they can well get without actual collision with the enemy."

4. Possessions.

5. Not to be confused with the presidential home. White House landing was "a point about 22 miles from Richmond, and, before the war, a place of resort for 'F.F.V.'s' [First Families of Virginia]. Only the chimneys of the White House now remain to mark the place where General Washington first made the acquaintance of the beautiful and accomplished Miss Custis, his future wife, while his ever faithful servant stood without holding his noble steed, wondering why his master stayed so long. This was the base of supplies for Gen. Grant's army." Captain F. S. Whitslar, Company D, 155th Ohio, Mahoning *Register,* July 14, 1864.

6. Brigadier-General John J. Abercrombie.

7. The 131st Ohio's "Sidney" traveled up the James River in August. "As you pass up the river," he recorded, "you are scarcely done looking at one interesting object than another presents itself for consideration. There is Chickahominy, Fort Powhatan, Wilson's, Wilcox's, and Harrison's Landings, and Malvern Hill, all places now of historic interest." Dayton *Journal,* August 24, 1864.

8. The 134th Ohio had arrived here the previous day. "Our position is not a pleasant one as the rebels shells are bursting all around us. There are several forts about here. We are S.W. of Bermuda Hundred in a very beautiful country & close to the Appomattox River and near the Point of Rocks near where Pocahontas saved the life of Captain Smith. It is about 4 mi. N.E. of Petersburg. We arrived here at 3 1/2 P.M.

There are about 3000 men here. There is a Lookout [tower] here about 125 ft. in height which the rebs are trying their skill on. This is the extreme left of our army." Linville, "Diary, May–Sep. 1864."

9. Joseph Steely.

10. Private Hezekiah Price of the 138th Ohio described veteran troops surrounding the hundred-days men for his school-age daughter: "Well our Redg [regiment] does not know anything about the hardships that the auld Veterans has to go through with. There is thousands of men now laying in the rifle pits on their backs, breasts or anyway to lay at all, and [they] have to crawl 1/2 mile to get their water and food. They dare not raise their heads above the bank of dirt that is in front of them without being hit by the sharpshooter's ball. Our Redg would not stand it one day and they would be so anxious to see the Rebs that they would half of them get shot. I have saw as much of the front as I want to see. So I will let them go to the front that wants to go and I will work in the fort in hot sun in preference to laying in rifle pits for a mark." Letter to Lizzie Price, July 10, 1864. Price, "Papers, 1863–1865."

11. An Ohio newspaper printed this description of the area:

"Petersburg was a handsome and flourishing post town and port of entry in Dinwiddie county, Va., on the right or south bank of the Appomattox river, at the crossing of the Great Southern Railroad, twenty-two miles south of Richmond, and ten miles from James River at City Point. It was the third town of Virginia in respect of population, and possessed extensive facilities for business. Vessels of four hundred tons can ascend the river to the landing, six miles below. The south side railroad has its terminus at this place, and the Appomattox Railroad connected it with City Point at the mouth of the river. The large vessels engaged in the trade at Petersburg discharge their cargoes at City Point. . . ." Erie County *News,* July 28, 1864.

12. General P. G. T. Beauregard, commanding Petersburg's small, beleaguered force of defenders.

13. Actually, William F. "Baldy" Smith of the XVIII Corps.

14. The 134th Ohio near Bermuda Hundred also heard the firing on June 15th. "A squad of us went to the river at night. We could distinctly hear the firing of artillery, plainly see the flashes from the guns on both sides & hear the rumbling of cars on the Petersburg R. R. by which the enemy were reinforced largely. Altogether made an awfully grand entertainment to those who were only witnesses but perhaps at a vast expense to some of those who were engaged." Linville, "Diary."

With the Army of the Potomac crossing the river to join Butler's Army of the James, Beauregard's 2,200 rebels on the evening of the 15th faced perhaps 38,000 Federals. Beauregard later wrote that Petersburg was then "clearly at the mercy of the Federal commander, who had all but captured it, and only failed of final success because he could not realize the fact of the unparalleled disparity between the two contending forces." P. G. T. Beauregard, "Four Days of Battle at Petersburg," *Battles and Leaders of the Civil War* (New York, 1887), vol. 4, p. 541.

The Confederates held out June 15–18, until reinforced by the Army of Northern Virginia. With General Lee's arrival, all prospect of a quick victory at Petersburg vanished.

15. *Front,* wrote "Crescent" of the 138th Ohio, "is a convertible term and susceptible of many modifications, just as 'out West' or 'down East.' . . . [T]here are degrees of 'the front,' which become more nearly and still nearer and nearer yet, and again

nearer and nearest till you are face to face with Rebel bayonets. If you go to any of the army corps about Petersburg, no matter how close up the reserve may be, they will talk of going up to 'the front.'" Cincinnati *Times,* July 21, 1864.

16. Brigadier-General John W. Turner.

17. Sherman notes: "When the order was given to fall back, the regiment halted at the first convenient place to see that all were present. These companies being absent, the Colonel asked someone to volunteer to carry an order to their captains to rejoin the regiment. Private Joseph Gregg at once offered to perform the duty, and started to carry the order.

"On arriving at the breastworks which the regiment had just left, the messenger, seeing a lot of soldiers behind them, ran up and said, 'The Colonel directs that you join the regiment immediately.'

"The reply was, 'That is a Yankee, catch him.'

"Gregg turned and ran for dear life and liberty. Some six or eight rebels ran to catch him; but he was too swift to be picked up, and with these men behind him, the rebels could not fire on him for fear of killing their own men. They yelled to their men to fall to the ground and give them a chance to shoot. This the pursuers soon did, and more than a hundred shots were aimed at Gregg. Three balls cut his hat, some five others cut his clothing, but not a drop of blood flowed." Sherman, *History,* pp. 76–77. Gregg received the Medal of Honor for this exploit in 1899.

18. A soldier-correspondent in the 133rd who signed himself A. B. B. (four men with the first and last initials A. B. are on the regimental roster) sent this account of the retreat to a Columbus newspaper:

"At about 5 P.M. a general withdrawal of our forces commenced, and after moving back about half a mile, the right, containing seven companies of the 133d, was halted behind a line of slight breastworks. Here our men, not being generally aware of their being now in the advance, and not having had any dinner, commenced to prepare refreshments; and some had already made their coffee, when suddenly a loud rebel yell was heard, and the 'greybacks' were seen coming on about 200 yards off.

"Taken completely by surprise—without knowing what was, or ought, to be done, and influenced by the bad conduct of a New Hampshire regiment, which broke first, a considerable portion of our left gave way in confusion and fell back a short distance. Here, by the exertions of their officers, and as if they had come to their senses, they rallied with a tremendous shout, and cheeringly came back to the trenches, which they held for two hours, firing about 25 rounds each. The right of our regiment, under the immediate eye of Col. Innis, did not give way at all, but remained, firing all the time, the Colonel himself being entirely cool and self-possessed throughout. . . .

"The three detached companies of the 133d were on the extreme left and were the last troops withdrawn. If they had been left five minutes longer they would probably have been captured as their position was occupied by the rebels in a very short time after they left. Our boys felt somewhat chagrined at their sudden surprise and confusion, but it was the general impression . . . that if the rebels had advanced upon them after they rallied, they would have held them like veterans and to the last extremity." *Ohio State Journal,* June 24, 1864.

19. Gustavus Swan Innis's son Henry was a private in Company H. The elder Mrs. Innis, Sarah, wrote to her colonel husband from Columbus after the battle:

"I was feeling very anxious about you, you may be sure. I did not know what dreadful news might be brought by the next mail—perhaps husband and son wounded or dead on the field of battle. It seems hard when we think of strangers being mangled and slain so far from home and friends, but to contemplate our own near and dear friends suffering such pain and hardship—the thought is positively terrible. I have been repeatedly assured by those who I thought ought to know something about the rules of war that your regt. would not be sent into battle, but it seems they knew no more about it than I did. But I am thankful that although you were called on to fight you acquitted yourself with honor and came out with credit and so little loss . . . Now if the *Col.* will see to it that my husband is well taken care of and [gets] his proper share of rest I will be much obliged to him." Innis letters, The Charles T. R. Bohannon Collection, 1 box, U.S. Army Military History Institute, Carlisle Barracks, letter dated June 26, 1864.

20. The Confederates had silently withdrawn to a shorter, more defensible line during the night of June 17th–18th. "The firing lasted, on the 17th, until a little after 11 o'clock P.M.," General Beauregard wrote. "Just before that time I had ordered all the camp-fires to be brightly lighted, with sentinels well thrown forward and as near as possible to the enemy's. Then, at 12:30 A.M., on the 18th, began the retrograde movement, which, notwithstanding the exhaustion of our troops and their sore disappointment at receiving no further reinforcements, was safely and silently executed, with uncommonly good order and precision, though the greatest caution had to be used in order to retire unnoticed from so close a contact with so strong an adversary." *Battles and Leaders,* vol. 4, p. 543.

On the afternoon of the 18th, as Union forces pressed their attack, the 1st Maine Heavy Artillery, withdrawn from the Washington defenses for Grant's campaign, suffered the heaviest single loss of any Federal regiment during the war—632 out of 900 men killed or wounded.

After the attacks of June 18th failed, Grant ordered the Army of the Potomac under cover, thus beginning the siege of Petersburg. The armies remained in essentially the same positions until the war ended.

21. Present-day Hopewell, Virginia.

22. Gilbert Laboytreaux, also in Company F, 138th Ohio, described the experience:

"My own ears have heard it—that unearthly, indescribable, never-to-be-forgotten whizzing of the 'shell.' I am ready now to acknowledge the wonderful power of music.

"You dodge, you blink, you squat, you shrink, you jump, you 'flank it' and wink, and you look very much like a toad working his way out from under a harrow. . . .

"At this moment, 2 o'clock P.M., June 28th, heavy blows are being given, either for our weal or our woe. Petersburg seems to be the center of attraction just now. The 'war dogs are howling' up there at a furious rate." Cincinnati *Times,* July 2, 1864.

Yet another correspondent in the 138th, who signed himself "Bond," offered a more sanguine view. Although "I believe we are as near the front as any of the 100 day men," he reported, ". . . we have never been in danger, and do not appear to have any chance to try our mettle. The Rebels most perversely and persistently ignore our existence, and while shells are thrown in every other direction, and even directly over our heads, we are not favored by a single notice." "Bond," Cincinnati *Times,* July 8, 1864.

23. "I cannot think that the salvation of Grant's army depends on our reaching his lines," Chadwick wrote from Fort Tillinghast on June 4th, "but it may be that he has more important posts to be guarded in the front than these, and we will go where they send us." Chadwick, "Into the Breach," p. 166.

24. Apparently Samuel S. Fisher, commanding the regiment.

25. Southern sympathizers in the North.

26. In its post at Fort Ohio, Spring Hill, on the Appomattox River (three miles from the James), the 138th was only five miles from Petersburg, "Crescent" reported. "We can see the spires of the churches from our fort. . . . [W]e can hear the cars on the Petersburg and Richmond Railway going and coming at all hours of the day and night, and we can see from some of our signal stations whether they are loaded with soldiers or not, and of course whither bound to Richmond, or coming to Petersburg." Cincinnati *Times,* July 5, 1864.

At Bermuda Hundred, on the James River, a correspondent in the 142nd Ohio wrote that "the boys have been lulled to sleep by a very strange music . . . ; we are within nine miles of Petersburg where Gen. Grant has been grinding his organ for some time; yet we are not a mile from the Rebs. From a point near our headquarters, on a clear day, we can see the smoke arising from the city of Richmond, the chief city of Rebeldom." "E. L. W.," Cincinnati *Times,* July 8, 1864. Although other E. W.'s served in the regiment, this was likely Private Elias L. Waltz, Company F.

27. Brigadier-General Godfrey Weitzel, chief engineer, Army of the James.

28. After the war, as the *General Grant,* the gunboat again served as a New York City steam ferry.

29. Armstrong's regiment, the 134th Ohio, reported just 316 men fit for duty on July 18th, out of 853 originally enrolled. *Roster of the 134th Regiment, O.V.I.*

His entire message to Lincoln:

"Head Quarters 2nd Brigade 3rd Div. 10 AC

"Near Bermuda Hundred, Va., July 19 1864

"To His Excellency the President of the United States

"Sir: I send by the hands of a friend a statement herewith, which is meant as an appeal to you the highest authority in the law in behalf of my brigade of Ohio Hundred (100) days men.

"For obvious reasons, this appeal is made directly to your Excellency—though I am aware it is unmilitary—but the excuse must be the urgent nature of the case, which will allow me to claim in behalf of this command the special notice of the Executive, more as a citizen than as a soldier—because of the following reasons.

"This is the only Brigade of this class of troops so near the front. The unusual nature of our fatigue duties has borne so heavily upon our unseasoned men—together with the climate, that, unless we are relieved, I have reason to fear our numbers will be so reduced by disease and death as not even to leave skeleton Regiments to take home the middle of August—Not counting casualties and deaths by disease—I have the honor to submit the enclosed copy of yesterday's report of the strength of the 130th 132nd 134th & 142nd Regs. O.V.I. of this Brigade—with the further remark that the daily list is increasing 40 to 50 men per diem, without adequate hospital accommodations.

"I am very Respectfully

"Your Obedient Servant

"J. B. Armstrong Col.

134th Reg O.V.I. com'g Brig."

James B. Armstrong, "Copy of a letter, July 19, 1864, from Col. J. B. Armstrong, Cmdr. 134th Regt., O.V.I., to President Lincoln," VFM 101, Ohio Historical Society.

30. Corporal Benjamin Linville, serving in Co. F of Armstrong's regiment (134th

Ohio), here records a single day at the front outside Petersburg. The entry is dated Tuesday, June 21st.

"Ate our breakfast, got our rations & 20 rounds more of cartridges making in all 60 rounds, also our blankets & started at 4 1/2 [A.M.]. Marched to Gen. Terry's Headquarters there met with the 130th, 132nd, 142nd, who went with us to the James River. About 10 mi. from camp crossed on a pontoon & halted at 9 A.M. Threw off all our traps & were set immediately to digging at the fortifications on a bank close to the river. Were relieved in an hour. Then had 2 hrs. in which to eat our dinners & went to work again.

"At 2 P.M. took our guns and marched out about 1/2 mi. to work on another fort. Here before going to work loaded our guns, as the rebs were but a short distance to protect the workmen. We worked all night (with reliefs). We are 1 1/2 mi. S.E. of Malvern Hill, 17 mi. from Richmond by land & 50 or 60 by water. This is a good situation for a fort being well elevated. The wheat is ripe. This place has only been occupied by our troops a couple of days." Linville, "Diary, May–Sep. 1864."

31. Sergeant George Bailey of 132nd Ohio recorded their passing:

"The talk among the boys is what a gay time they are going to have when they get home. All seem to think they will get home—but some will never see their friends again. Another man of Co. F [died] today. They pass away. Some half a dozen have died already. When they started out they intended to return. But fate ordered it otherwise & they sleep the sleep that knows no waking on the sacred soil of Virginia." George F. Bailey, "Journal (1864) Kept While Serving with Company G," July 22, 1864.

32. "There was considerable talk of the regt. being ordered to Washington & it was the impression among most of the men that [the] Col. was opposed to going as he would then lose his chances for Brigadier," Linville recorded on June 25th, after the 134th had shifted its camp north of the James. "Some of the companies refused to pitch their tents at first, but that talk finally played out."

The corporal, like so many others, was later stricken with fever. He entered the army hospital at Point of Rocks on July 16th, and remained there until returning to Ohio with his regiment. Linville, "Diary."

33. "I wouldn't be surprised to hear of you being on the way to Richmond," Susan Harrod had written presciently in early May. "It appears that your company, most of them, was anxious to see the Elephant. I am afraid you will have an opportunity to see it before you get home. I don't like the idea of you forming a part of the army of the Potomac. If you should be put in the rear when the front is broken, then who is in the front then?" "Harrod, Sue: Letters to husband John Harrod, May–August 1864," The John Harrod Papers, U.S. Army Military History Institute, Carlisle Barracks.

34. The uniformed woman was Sarah Jane Perkins. After imprisoning her first at Point Lookout, authorities later moved her to a prison at Fitchburg, Massachusetts, which was better equipped for women. Several people recorded impressions of this unique prisoner.

"Six hundred prisoners came in today, with them a lady, who is an artillery sergeant," North Carolina sharpshooter Lewis Leon wrote in his diary at Point Lookout on June 8. "Being questioned by the provost marshal, she said she could straddle a horse, jump a fence, and kill a Yankee as well as any Rebel." Harry Simonhoff, *Jewish Participants in the Civil War*, p. 221. (Also see A. M. Keiley, *In Vinculis; Or, The Prisoner of War*, pp. 81–82, and *Official Records*, ser. 2, vol. 7, p. 450.)

Women also served in the Federal army. See *An Uncommon Soldier: The Civil War letters of Sarah Rosetta Wakeman, Alias Pvt. Lyons Wakeman, 153rd Regiment, New York State Volunteers, 1862–1864* (Pasadena, 1994), edited by Lauren Cook Burgess, who graciously identified Sarah Jane Perkins and traced her movements.

35. U.S. Colored Troops.

36. Major-General George Meade commanded the Army of the Potomac under Grant. The pontoon bridge—a "triumph of military engineering," according to Boatner—included 100 pontoons and three schooners. Boatner, *The Civil War Dictionary,* p. 646.

37. "The James River opposite Fort Powhatan is about three-fourths of a mile wide and 114 feet deep," Sergeant Sherman recorded. "The tide rises from three to four feet, and when it goes out leaves the marshes above the fort uncovered for a space of several acres." Sherman, *History,* p. 115.

38. Both were cavalrymen. According to Sergeant Sherman, "The rebels stripped their bodies of clothing, mutilated them shamefully and left them in the public road. This action of the rebs called for revenge." Ibid., p. 98.

39. This expedition, according to Sherman, was partly to revenge the mutilation of the cavalrymen. Ibid.

40. Jefferson H. Darrah.

41. The soldier chased by rebels after the June 16th fight (see note 17). *Official Roster* lists Joseph O. Gregg as a private in Company F.

42. After the war, Westervelt became a clergyman.

43. An ingenious but failed attempt on July 30, 1864, to break the rebel defenses through an underground bomb. An 8,000-pound charge planted by miners from the 48th Pennsylvania exploded with devastating effect. The following infantry attack, however, hamstrung by appalling generalship, led to defeat and Union losses of nearly 4,000 men.

44. CHAPTER SOURCES:

a. Sherman. *History,* pp. 57–73, 76–79, 81.

b. Chadwick. "Into the Breach," pp. 168–71.

c. Todd. *Roster of the 147th Regiment, Ohio Volunteer Infantry* (West Milton, 1899), pp. 2–4.

d. Harrod. John Harrod, "Letters to Wife, Sue, May–Jun 1864; Jul–Aug 1864," The John Harrod Papers, 1 box, U.S. Army Military History Institue, Carlisle Barracks.

e. Sherman. *History,* pp. 80–84, 107–8, 113–15, 137–38.

f. Ender. Ibid., pp. 95–98.

g. Westervelt. Ibid., pp. 99–104.

9. Fourth of July

1. "Some fine flags were hung out," a local newspaper added, "and a few rounds of cannon fired, but taken as a whole, the day was quiet as any other. Our people have daily evidence of the stern realities of this war. Particularly is this the case just now. With a Hospital crowded full of sick and wounded soldiers, and the roll of the muffled drum daily sounding in their ears, as some brave hero is taken to his final resting place, they do not feel that the time of rejoicing has yet arrived." Gallipolis *Journal,* July 7, 1864.

2. A soldier-correspondent of Company H, who signed himself "G," offered this picture of the nautical splendor: "The boats of every description upon the river are dressed out in the gayest colors today. The famous *Atlanta* [a Confederate ironclad ram captured and recommissioned by the U.S. Navy in 1863], which lies opposite the Fort, today sports the *old American flag* and to amend for her former bad conduct has added 30 or 40 flags of all colors and shapes.

"One of the prettiest sights that the majority of us have ever had a chance to see was a large ocean steamer that passed down the river this afternoon from Bermuda Hundred. Every available rope and part of rope seemed to hold a flag. It was impossible to count them as she passed; but there must have been nearly a hundred and no two alike." *Ohio State Journal,* July 12, 1864.

3. Von Shilling commanded a detachment of the 3rd Pennsylvania Heavy Artillery at the fort.

4. The gunners celebrated the holiday with two gallons of whiskey. One got so "hilarious" that he struck and injured another with a bucket. "This was probably some of the fighting whiskey that General Grant was said to drink," Sergeant Sherman later observed. Sherman, *History,* p. 127.

5. Georgia, northwest of Atlanta, which itself would not fall until September 1st.

6. Brigadier-General John Imboden, who had once commanded the First Partisan Rangers. Rebel forces led by Imboden and "Grumble" Jones had raided West Virginia in April 1863.

7. Benjamin Franklin Kelley was a memorable figure, a New Hampshire-born Virginia militia officer who had raised a Union regiment of loyal West Virginians in Ohio rather than secede. Stipp later recalled him: "A man of medium height, compactly and proportionately well built; a large and well poised head, with dark hair that fell in waving ringlets about his neck; a handsome face that beamed with intelligence, kindness and cordiality—unostentatious, yet stern and dignified in his military bearing; courteous, affable and approachable at all times.

"He had come to see us in an *Iron Clad* car. This railroad battery was constructed in rather an ingenious manner. It consisted of a platform car with a protection of railroad or T iron placed on its sides and ends at an angle of about 45 degrees. The sides were pierced with port holes for the use of infantrymen, the ends for artillery. Inside of this car were two 12-pound brass pieces. This car was propelled by a locomotive, and was used for patrolling the Baltimore & Ohio railroad." Stipp, *History,* p. 55.

8. West Virginia, the latter town not to be confused with the besieged city in Virginia.

9. Hoy in fact sent three, bearing duplicate messages.

10. Colonel James Mulligan of the 23rd Illinois.

11. The order to retreat failed to reach three companies of the 135th Ohio guarding a blockhouse on the Baltimore & Ohio at North Mountain. "There, after fighting five hours against a body of 3,000 rebels, with five pieces of artillery, they surrendered and were taken to Andersonville prison, where 55 died, being about one-half of the whole number captured." Cowen, "The Hundred-Days Men of 1864," p. 233.

The 135th's seven battle deaths and 66 deaths by disease (mostly at Andersonville) constituted the highest aggregate losses by far of any Ohio hundred-days regiment.

A detachment from another Ohio regiment, the 153rd, was ambushed by Confederate cavalry on July 3rd while scouting along the north fork of Big Cacapon. One man was killed and about 34 captured. Another company of this regiment fared better in a fight along the railway near Green Spring the next day. Lieutenant-Colonel Doty of the 152nd reported from Cumberland:

"The bridge near Patterson's Creek was a small one, and was held by Capt. McKinney's company [E] from a blockhouse erected to command the bridge. This company was attacked on the afternoon of July 4th by a strong force of rebels, who brought a piece of ordnance to bear upon the blockhouse, and knocked one upper corner off. The boys were below, and getting rifle range on the rebels the next time they tried their gun, and down came the gunners. The rebels then tried to run in and fire the bridge; but our noble men made them fly like grasshoppers, actually mowing them down. About this time one of our ironclad mounted cars came up from below the bridge, and the rebels, getting the idea that a communication with Martinsburg was opening on their rear, fled in dismay, and have not since made any demonstrations. This company lost only one man. Their praise is in everyone's mouth here." Springfield *Republic,* July 11, 1864.

The 153rd troops captured the previous day clearly heard the fighting as they trudged past nearby, headed toward southern prisons. See Thomas W. Rathbone, "Brief Diary of Imprisonment," July 4, 1864.

12. Mulligan and his 23rd Illinois were fighting Bradley Johnson's cavalry, which they managed to check after receiving reinforcements from Sigel. For more on Mulligan's pivotal role on July 3rd, see Frank E. Vandiver, *Jubal's Raid: General Early's Famous Attack on Washington in 1864* (Lincoln, 1992), pp. 78–79.

13. This is a decidedly Union perspective on the Battle of Antietam (or Sharpsburg, as the Confederates knew it), which McClellan could have won but did not. At best this battle on September 17, 1862—the bloodiest single day in American history—was a draw, which represented victory for heavily outnumbered General Lee.

14. CHAPTER SOURCES:
   a. Sherman. *History,* pp. 126–27, 133–35.
   b. Laboytreaux. Cincinnati *Times,* July 12, 1864.
   c. Reid. Cleveland *Plain Dealer,* July 7, 1864.
   d. Bailey. Bailey, "Journal (1864)."
   e. Stipp. *History,* pp. 20–27.
   f. Siegfried. Zanesville *Courier,* August 23–24, 1864.
   g. Bell. Bell, "One Hundred Days' Service."

10. Monocacy

1. Companies B, G, and I. Shanks had a brother and cousin serving in the latter company.

2. First Lieutenant George Weddell, Co. I, Shanks's cousin.

3. Written on the march, McClain's hurried letter understandably contains some inaccuracies. His company arrived at Frederick, Maryland, not near Harper's Ferry, as he believed. He apparently began writing the first entry dated July 8th on the 7th, then resumed it on the 8th.

4. Frederick, sometimes then called Frederick City.

5. "All Maryland from the Monocacy River to the Chesapeake Bay, and beyond to the sea, with Delaware, made a comprehensive charge, to keep which the small total of troops left me by General Grant was many times divided and widely distributed," Wallace later recorded in his autobiography. "And what might be taken had to be without exposure of the localities the commands were holding. In fine, the operation was

like gleaning in a lean field a second and third time." *Lew Wallace: An Autobiography* (New York, 1906), p. 705.

6. "There, within the space of two miles, converge the pikes to Washington and Baltimore, and the Baltimore and Ohio railroad; there also is the iron bridge over the Monocacy, upon which depends railroad communication to Harper's Ferry," Wallace later recorded in his official report. "Moreover, as a defensive position for an army seeking to cover the cities above named against a force marching from the direction I was threatened, the point is very strong; The river covers its entire front. In a low stage of water the fords are few, and particularly difficult for artillery, and the commanding heights are all on the eastern bank, while the ground on the opposite side is level and almost without obstructions." *Official Records*, ser. 1, vol. 37, pt. 1, p. 193.

7. About 2,500 men, composed of the Third Regiment, Potomac (Maryland) Home Brigade, Colonel Charles Gilpin; 11th Maryland (a hundred-days regiment), Colonel William T. Landstreet; seven companies of the 149th and three companies of the 144th Ohio, consolidated temporarily under the 149th's Colonel Allison L. Brown; Captain Frederic W. Alexander's Baltimore battery; and 100 volunteers from the 159th Ohio, serving as mounted infantry under Captain E. H. Lieb, Fifth United States Cavalry, and Captain N. S. Allen.

Wallace also had Lieutenant-Colonel David Clendenin's squadron of 250 men, Eight Illinois Cavalry, and four companies (some 200 men) of the First Regiment, Potomac (Maryland) Home Brigade.

8. The first brigade included the 106th New York, 151st New York, 14th New Jersey, 10th Vermont and 87th Pennsylvania; the second brigade included the 138th Pennsylvania, 9th New York, 126th Ohio, and 110th Ohio. The rest of the division was expected, but never appeared on the field.

9. Wallace later wrote, "When I ran over all the consequences of the capture of that city, they grouped themselves into a kind of horrible schedule.

"Thus, at the navy yard there were ships making and repairing, which, with the yard itself, would be given over to flames.

"In the treasury department there were millions of bonds printed, and other millions signed ready for issuance—how many millions I did not know.

"There were storehouses in the city filled with property of all kinds, medical, ordnance, commissary, quartermaster, the accumulation of years, without which the war must halt, if not stop for good and all.

"Then I thought of the city, the library, the beautiful capital, all under menace— of prestige lost, of the faith that had so sublimely sustained the loyal people through years crowded with sacrifices unexampled in history now struck dead—of Louis Napoleon and Gladstone hastening to recognize the Confederacy as a nation.

"Certainly these were calamities, every one of them in the category of what would happen if Washington fell; yet, strange to say, not one or all of them projected itself in the swarming of my thoughts with such instantaneous hardening of purpose as an apparition of President Lincoln, cloaked and hooded, stealing like a malefactor from the back door of the White House just as some gray-garbed Confederate brigadier burst in the front door." Wallace, *Autobiography*, p. 726.

10. Wallace first met Brown and the two Maryland colonels on the morning of July 8. "Brown and Gilpin won my confidence at sight," he wrote, while one glance at Landstreet "satisfied me of his rawness as a soldier."

The general learned from Brown that although he commanded hundred-days men, "the wise governor of his state had selected for the companies all the veteran officers he could secure. He made no doubt of a good report of them should it come to a fight. . . . Upon the strength of his eulogy, and the impression he himself made upon me, I started him immediately for the stone bridge over the Monocacy on the Baltimore pike. . . ." Ibid., pp. 720–21.

11. In burning the wooden bridge, Wallace stranded skirmishers—including both regulars and hundred-days men—on the opposite bank. This caused him considerable anguish until late in the afternoon, when he saw 200 or 300 men suddenly rise up and rush under rebel fire across the open girders of the nearby railroad bridge. He sent an aide to find out who had led this remarkable retreat.

"Colonel Catlin brought me the name of the leader—Lieutenant George E. Davis, of the Tenth Vermont Infantry.

"'Lieutenant?' I said. 'Only a lieutenant! There were captains over there. Where are they?'

"I had this answer:

"'The first companies were hundred-day men of Colonel Brown's, green in service, officers and privates. When Lieutenant Davis arrived, Brown's captains voluntarily offered to put themselves under his orders.'" Ibid., p. 795.

Young Lieutenant Davis declined to leave his regiment while under fire to meet his commanding general. For his actions at the bridge, he later received the Medal of Honor.

12. When Brigadier-General John McCausland's dismounted cavalry rashly charged the Federal position, Ricketts's men rose from hiding and decimated them. "My God!" gasped one of Wallace's aides. "They are all killed!"

Years later, Wallace met General (then U.S. Senator) John Brown Gordon in a White House reception room. He asked the former rebel about the rash attack. Their exchange, which Wallace later recorded, revealed an unintentional influence of the hundred-days men:

"In course of the conversation I remarked: 'The strangest thing of the whole battle was the conduct of the officer who made the first attack upon General Ricketts. Did he imagine he could stampede veterans of the old Sixth Army Corps by a rush without fire?'

"'Ah, that's the very point,' Gordon replied. 'We did not know of the presence on the field of any portion of the Sixth Corps. They told us in Frederick you had only hundred-day men, a class of soldiers we had often met and cleaned out without firing a shot—exactly as General McCausland attempted.'" Ibid., pp. 770–71.

13. Wallace expected the three last regiments from Ricketts's division to join him on the field.

14. At one o'clock, Wallace wrote, "Off Crum's ford, about a mile above us, the enemy were assembled as if to attack; but the bluff was steep, and could be easily held by the two or three companies who had the locality in charge. Colonel A. L. Brown . . . had his hands more than full, having the stone bridge and another ford beyond it to keep with but seven companies of his own regiment and Captain Lieb's mounted infantry.

"The colonel had his command posted on the crest of a ridge on the Frederick side of the river. Attacked by a largely superior force, Brown had succeeded in repelling several charges supported by artillery, and was in good spirit. His hundred-day men were behaving splendidly." Ibid., p. 775.

15. Wallace later reconstructed his orders to Tyler this way: "Let your men cut

their way out, all who can—not a difficult thing to regiments like Gilpin's and Brown's, since the pursuers will be in disorder and few in numbers when they reach the pike. Should there be any who cannot cut their way out, order them to disperse, every man for himself, with New Market or Monrovia for rendezvous. It will be desperate work. What do you say?"

After Tyler assented to his dramatic orders, Wallace turned to Landstreet. "That gentleman came to attention and saluted. He was not wanting in the technique of military manners. Still, it was very needful for me to be careful with him.

" 'You will take your regiments, marching rapidly, to the Baltimore pike,' I said. 'There turn to the right in the direction of Baltimore, and, when two miles out, halt, deploy, with your colors in the center of the road, and face to the rear. Our men will come to you in numbers, disorganized, of course. Stop all of them who have guns and cartridges—stop all officers and make them help you rally the fugitives. Tyler, here, will have ultimately to abandon the bridge. When that takes place, cover his retreat as best you can, moving along the pike and halting when required to stay the pursuit.' I wound the instructions up by what I thought an appeal to his pride. 'In short, colonel, I mean your regiment to become our rear-guard, an important and, under the circumstances, a most honorable duty.'

"He saluted again, and, answering with confidence, left me, and shortly after was seen in the saddle leading his regiment from the height." Ibid., pp. 787–88.

The 11th's performance hardly proved stellar, however. Sergeant William James of Company G later recounted serious straggling, but insisted that "the charge that we ran from the field made by persons who were 50 miles off is absurd." James himself didn't manage to rejoin the regiment until Baltimore. "Upon my arrival at home I shaved, took a bath and put on clean clothes, and after a few hours rest was all most myself again. In the afternoon I ascertained that the regiment were encamped at Greenwood out Gay Street, and joined them that evening, where I was gladly welcomed back by my comrades who had feared that I had been gobbled up by the rebels." William H. James, "A Baltimore Volunteer of 1864" (Baltimore, 1941), pp. 29, 31–32.

16. Regimental historian Perkins later recorded, "When Col. Brown and his brave little army overtook General Wallace, the latter was much affected. He embraced him, the tears starting from his eyes, and said, 'Colonel, I never expected to see you again.'" Perkins, *A Summer in Maryland and Virginia,* p. 21.

Brown later wrote to an uncle, "I ran many narrow escapes. Was struck once, but it didn't amount to much, as it was a spent ball." *Scioto Gazette,* July 19, 1864.

17. Tyler later wrote, "No officer did his duty better than Colonel Brown, and no troops could have done more than did the men under his command in that unequal combat. It seldom falls to the lot of veterans to be more severely tried than were the Ohio National Guard at the stone bridge, and none ever carried out trying and hazardous orders better or with more determined spirit than did the 149th, and the men associated with it." Reid, *Ohio in the War,* vol. 2, p. 680.

18. Ricketts's missing regiments, which had halted short of the battlefield. Ricketts later dismissed the officer commanding them.

19. The size of Early's Army of the Valley has never been precisely fixed. In his memoirs, Early put the figure at "10,000 muskets," included dismounted cavalry, while Major Henry Kyd Douglas, one of his staff officers, put it at "12,000 effectives." Early's figure, at least, does not include mounted cavalry (2,000 by his recollection, 4,000 by other sources) or artillery. Union estimates were much higher than the Con-

federates', but the rebel numbers are likely near the mark. Hard fighting and marching steadily whittled the rebel army; when it reached Washington, Early had, by his estimate, "about 8,000 muskets."

20. Union losses at Monocacy Junction are somewhat difficult to determine. Wallace probably lost about 1,300 men, roughly half of whom were wounded or killed and the remainder captured.

A U.S. Army surgeon inside the Confederate lines at Frederick during the battle reported 121 Union dead buried on or near the battlefield by July 11th, and 204 Union wounded in nearby hospitals the following day (*Official Record,* ser. 1, vol. 37, pt. 1, p. 203). Some early Union casualties were also evacuated by rail, while others undoubtedly accompanied the retreating regiments.

On the Southern side, General Early later wrote that his army suffered "about 700" casualties, but General Gordon, whose division bore the brunt of the fighting, alone reported 698.

21. No monument bearing these precise words today stands on the battlefield.

22. After the war, Brown was twice elected to the state senate.

23. Thomas B. Jenkins, Co. E, Charles W. McGinnis, Co. C.

24. A hundred men from the 159th Ohio.

25. Post-war rosters of the 144th and 149th regiments identify eight killed or mortally wounded, six wounded, and about 80 captured.

26. There is confusion about the correct spelling of the major's name. Brown and *Official Roster* spell it "Rozelle." Sergeant Sherman and the local *Scioto Gazette* newspaper, however, drop the final "e" (including in an account in Sherman's regimental history that he attributes directly to the major). Various Ross County histories use the first spelling for the major, but the second for Ebenezer Rozell Sr., a veteran of the War of 1812 and presumably the major's father.

27. Surgeon Brown, apparently no relation to his colonel, wasn't the only Federal surgeon who remained behind with the wounded. Freed when Union troops recaptured Frederick, he returned home with his regiment.

28. This detachment of the 159th Ohio, assembled at Camp Bradford on the night of July 4th, included 40 men from Company B and twenty each from companies E, G, and K.

29. Private Charley H. Wine, Co. E, 159th Ohio, described the retreat in a letter to his mother. The captain he refers to likely wasn't Lieb, but Captain H. S. Allen of the 159th, who served under Lieb.

"The Johnnies formed their skirmishers in line and we did the same. Our company was ordered to advance and form our line of skirmishers, which we occupied until 4 o'clock in the afternoon, when we were ordered away from our posts by the Captain. When we came up on the road we found ourselves surrounded on all sides by the Johnnies; we were cut off from the rest of the command and we knew not what to do, so the Captain said, 'Boys, let's get out of here,' and we made a charge up the pike, and went through the Johnnies and their fire, all right and safe, without harm. We retreated down the pike on the way to Baltimore. We were ordered to cover the retreat, so we had to go back and give the Johnnies another volley. By that time the whole of our men were safely in front of us, and we brought up the rear of the column." Zanesville *Courier,* July 22, 1864.

30. The company lost four men captured, two of whom later died.

31. A few men from the 137th Ohio at Fort McHenry apparently approached the early fighting. "Some of our boys were out near enough to hear the roar of battle at Frederick and Monocacy. First a detachment from Company D went out to Frederick guarding an ammunition train, and afterward Company F went out on the same duty. The latter company went on the 7th and returned the evening of the 8th." "Sandy," Cincinnati *Commercial,* July 15, 1864.

32. Apparently referring to the 149th Ohio, a far harsher assessment than those of Colonel Brown and the commanding generals.

33. John McKee, company commander.

34. Private William Barton.

35. Barton, a piper, was a close friend and tent-mate. *Official Roster* spells his full first name "Findlay." McClain gives it various spellings, but usually shortens it familiarly as he does here.

36. Private Frank died in the rebel prison camp at Danville, Va., on October 2.

37. Private McCracken survived imprisonment and returned home in March, 1865.

38. CHAPTER SOURCES:

a. Shanks. Tommy Shanks, "Weddell Family Papers."

b. McClain. Samuel McClain, "Papers, 1864," folder 14.

c. Wallace. *Official Records,* ser. 1, vol. 37, pt. 1, pp. 196–200.

d. Brown. Ibid., pp. 216–19.

e. Lieb. Ibid., pp. 221–23.

f. Earl. *Scioto Gazette,* July 19, 1864.

g. Vail. *What I Saw,* pp. 28–29.

h. McClain. "Papers, 1864," folder 14.

i. Browning. Perkins, *A Summer in Maryland and Virginia,* pp. 51–53.

11. Fort Stevens

1. "All the hills around Washington are bristling with large numbers of defiant looking cannon," Corporal William Miller of the 139th Ohio wrote May 29th aboard a steamer on the Potomac. Miller, "Miller Family Papers," Box 2, folder 51.

2. Wallace, *Autobiography,* p. 701.

3. Edgar S. Dudley, "A Reminiscence of Washington and Early's Attack in 1864" (Cincinnati, 1883), p. 115.

4. From Piney Point on the Potomac, the 139th's Corporal Miller saw them rushing for the capital. "Last Monday [July 11th] steamers loaded with troops were passing up the river all day. We had heard that Harper's Ferry had been taken by the rebels, but did not know that any large force was invading Maryland. We could not imagine where all those could be going. Did not know whether Grant had taken Richmond and was sending troops to some other point, or had been defeated and was retreating to Washington. Some of the boys said the war was over and that the soldiers were going home. We had no way of finding out and could do nothing but watch them. Fully twenty thousand must have passed here that day. Next day we heard that Baltimore was threatened by the rebs." Letter to Wilson Miller, July 18, 1864. Miller, "Miller Family Papers," Box 2, folder 58.

5. Allured Bayard Nettleton, a major at the time of the battle.

6. Major-General Robert E. Rodes. An engineer and V.M.I. graduate, he had survived some of the bloodiest fighting of the war. He would die at Winchester, Virginia, on September 19, 1864.

7. In his memoirs, Early said he rode ahead of his infantry and shortly before noon caught sight of Fort Stevens, which was "but feebly manned." He ordered Rodes's division to move on the works as quickly as possible.

Before the division could be brought up, however, "we saw a cloud of dust in the rear of the works towards Washington, and soon a column of the enemy filed into them on the right and left and skirmishers were thrown out in front, while an artillery fire was opened on us from a number of batteries. This defeated our hopes of getting possession of the works by surprise. . . ." Jubal Anderson Early, *Narrative of the War Between the States* (Philadelphia, 1912), pp. 389–90.

The dust marked the timely arrival of reinforcements from Grant's hardened VI Corps.

8. Lieutenant-Colonel Frazee's report after the battle states, "The troops garrisoning the fort were composed of Company K, 150th Regiment Ohio National Guard, 78 men, Capt. A. A. Safford; 13th Michigan Battery, 79 men, Capt. Charles Dupont; 52 convalescents, commanded by Lieutenant [Henry L.] Turner, of Company K., 150th Regiment Ohio National Guard." *Official Records,* ser. 1, vol. 37, pt. 1, p. 247.

9. General Horatio Wright, VI Corps, and William Emory, XIX Corps.

10. William H. Ryder.

11. George W. Fackler.

12. Usually, mounted sentries posted ahead of pickets. These men, however, appear to have been on foot.

13. Privates John A. Bedient, Buel Chidester, and Edgar L. Beech.

14. Private Bedient seemed to be everywhere during the fighting. "He was so exhausted," Cannon recorded, "that he was taken with the fever that night and was sent to the hospital next morning." Cannon, *Record of Service,* p. 16.

15. Hinman, William E. Leach, and Chalmers Hammond. According to regimental historian Cannon, their post was located "on a road which branched off from Seventh Street northeasterly." Ibid., p. 14.

16. In a handwritten account, on stationery of the Pittsburg *Dispatch,* where he was editor, Hudson misidentifies the location throughout as "Fort Sumner." He apparently composed this undated account many years after the event, when memory had perhaps dimmed.

17. According to company historian James C. Cannon (and *Official Roster*), Leach actually died on July 13th at nearby Fort Slocum, despite being "kindly nursed" by Private Alfred A. Wildman. Cannon, *Record of Service,* p. 15.

18. Even Fort Lincoln, which "did not fire a shot," was almost overrun with brass. "I never saw so many officers together in my life as there were here. Stars and eagles were at a discount. Maj.-Gens. [Christopher] Auger, [Quincy] Gillmore and [Alexander] McCook; Admiral [Louis] Goldsborough; Brigadiers without number and Colonels by the dozens. A private was a rarity." "R. O. L.," Cleveland *Herald,* July 19, 1864. (Spellings of names corrected.)

19. Peter Henry Kaiser, "Papers," folder 1. Letter dated July 9, 1927.

20. The 150th held a reunion at Beach Park, Cleveland, on July 12, 1919, 55 years after the attack on Fort Stevens. George B. Christian, formerly a private in Company F and now regimental secretary, entered the account into a reunion ledger kept

for many years; it is unclear whether this was his recollection or that of a comrade. "Ohio Volunteer Infantry, 150th Regiment, Reunion Records, Roster & Minutes, vol. 1894–1927."

Frazee's obituary in an unidentified newspaper in 1917 (filed with the regimental records) claims a rebel fusillade began as soon as Lincoln stepped down. It quotes the president saying to Frazee, "If someone had to die, it might as well have been I as you." Ibid., vol. 2, folder 2.

21. Bedient later recalled, "On reaching the fort at 9 A.M. the men were at the guns. Lincoln was standing on the parapet. As I entered the fort he pointed to the line of men a mile and a half away on the ridge, and said, 'Who are those men?' I said, 'Rebels' and ordered him off." Ibid.

His wasn't the only blunt warning to the president. Massachusetts Captain (and later Supreme Court Justice) Oliver Wendell Holmes, noticing only a tall civilian drawing fire, yelled, "Get down, you fool." Vandiver, *Jubal's Raid,* p. 168.

22. "President Lincoln was in the fort with Secretary Stanton and others, and exposed himself in quite a hazardous position in his anxiety to see what was going on in the field," Cannon recorded. "His tall form was plainly seen by the enemy's sharpshooters, and a bullet struck the gun by which he was standing, and glancing off wounded Surgeon C. C. V. Crawford in the leg. The President then prudently withdrew to a safe position." Cannon, *Record of Service,* p. 16.

23. Indeed, Lincoln displayed considerable compassion for the casualties at Fort Stevens. A wounded VI Corps veteran, Merrick C. Smith of the 122nd New York, recalled the president asking if he was badly hurt, then turning to Wright and asking why the wounded weren't being moved quickly to safety.

"The President, standing erect, and pointing over in the direction where the Tenth Massachusetts was, said: 'Send for the commander of that regiment, and I want a sufficient detail to attend to this matter, if it takes the whole regiment.' Mr. Lincoln then took me by the hand, and placing his other hand on my shoulder, with his arm partly about my neck, and looking me in the face, said: 'God bless you!' Then addressing an officer near him, whom I took to be a surgeon, Mr. Lincoln said: 'Take good care of this boy!'" "Ohio Volunteer Infantry, 150th Regiment, Reunion Records, Roster & Minutes," folder 1, ledger p. 48.

24. "For over sixty years I have been accustomed to say that during all the time I was in Uncle Sam's uniform I did not once fire my gun at the enemy," former Company K private Charles F. Hall wrote in 1926. "This is quite true and yet I may have been of some service for I was one of those detailed for artillery work. All of one morning we were firing cannon and some of the results of our fire we were able to note." Kaiser, "Papers," folder 1.

25. The Confederates actually burned Postmaster General Blair's house in Silver Spring.

26. Brigadier-General Frank Wheaton, temporarily commanding the Second Division, VI Corps. See Vandiver, *Jubal's Raid,* pp. 167–68.

27. Later that night, Early quipped to Major Henry Kyd Douglas, "Major, we haven't taken Washington, but we've scared Abe Lincoln like hell!" To which Douglas replied, "Yes, General, but this afternoon when that Yankee line moved out against us, I think some other people were scared blue as hell's brimstone!"

In his memoirs, Douglas could offer no reason for the late Union attack, "unless it was to see if we were still there." Henry Kyd Douglas, *I Rode with Stonewall,* p. 284.

28. "The enemy were very bold to advance in plain sight of our flag and almost to the mouth of our big guns," wrote Private Charles E. Bingham of Company A at Fort Lincoln. "There was evidence, not far from Silver Spring, of severe fighting on both sides. The fences were full of balls from both armies. For a day or two after the fights, many rebel dead were hanging on the fences where they had been shot in trying to get over them." Cleveland *Herald,* July 25, 1864. (Signed "C. E. B.," initials unique to Bingham within the company.)

29. Colonel Dan Bidwell, commanding the 3rd Brigade, 2nd Division, VI Corps.

30. "H. B. D.," a Clevelander who had arrived in Washington on Saturday evening, July 9th, provided this account of the fort:

"Slocum was defended by Co. G and the 14th Michigan Battery, Stevens by Co. K and the 13th Michigan Battery. Both forts were well mounted with heavy 4 1/2 inch rifle and siege guns, and Slocum with a 24 pounder in addition. On Monday at noon, our pickets were driven in, and the rebels had so far advanced that their situation and design could be easily seen and understood by the officers on the parapet, with the aid of their field glasses.

"About 2 o'clock Slocum received orders to open fire. In an instant a shell went whizzing through the air and burst directly over the heads of our Southern friends about two miles distant.

"Capt. John Nevins being obliged to take charge of his company [G], yours truly was invited to take his glass and report the result. Great economy! how they scattered. Solid shot and shell were poured in upon them rapidly for an hour.

"Stevens was also blazing out streams of fire from its embrasures, and occasional shots were sent from other guns of shorter range and less caliber from Fort Massachusetts." Cleveland *Herald,* July 18, 1864.

31. R. O. L. would write from nearby Bladensburg, Maryland, on July 23rd, "The storm has passed; the raider has skedaddled, and 'all is quiet on the Potomac' again— so quiet that five of us on picket duty have little else to do than sit and watch the trains on the B&O R. R., which bring the 100 days men from New York and Pennsylvania, and wave our handkerchiefs at the ladies; also keep a sharp look-out for the officer of the day, that he don't catch us with our equipments off."

Later that same day, R. O. L.'s squad of pickets would shoot and kill a Union deserter who tried to run from them. Cleveland *Herald,* July 27, 1864.

32. CHAPTER SOURCES:

a. Laird. Cannon, *Memorial,* pp. 8–9.

b. Cannon. *Record of Service,* pp. 13–14.

c. Hudson. Kaiser, "Papers," folder 4.

d. Laird. Cannon, *Memorial,* pp. 9–10.

e. Hinman. Cannon, *Record of Service,* p. 33.

f. Browning. Perkins, *A Summer in Maryland and Virginia,* pp. 53–54.

g. Cannon. *Record of Service,* pp. 16–17.

h. Laird. Cannon, *Memorial,* pp. 10–11.

12. Back to the Valley

1. Virginia.

2. Haystacks had obstructed Gordon's division's line of battle as it charged Ricketts's division.

3. Brigadier-General George Crook, who would win his greatest fame fighting Indian tribes after the war.

4. Acting on Early's orders, General McCausland burned Chambersburg, Pennsylvania, on July 30, 1864, after the town refused to pay a large ransom. The raid was a reprisal for Hunter's destruction in the Shenandoah.

5. Today called Charles Town, West Virginia (not to be confused with Charleston, the capital).

6. Brigadier-General William W. Averell. Twice relieved for lack of aggressiveness during the war, he would afterward become a wealthy industrialist.

7. The Chesapeake & Ohio Canal.

8. Privates Watson Taylor and Arthur Coffield. In an article he wrote for a Maryland newspaper (picked up by a competing hometown paper under his byline), Nichols reported: "Coffield said to his commander, Capt. Cross, 'I am bound to give them one more shot.' He did so, and had not moved twenty paces to the rear before he received a mortal wound in the bowels and fell, saying to his comrades, 'I am going now boys. Good bye.'" Cumberland *Union,* reprinted in Springfield *Republic,* August 12, 1864.

9. A frequent correspondent from the 153rd's Company E, who signed his letters "Lengthy," offered an account of Coffield's passing similar to Nichols's. He also reported: "Taylor, of New Carlisle, was shot at the cars. Both lived several hours. . . . He was cheerful, and said he would die." Springfield *Republic,* August 19, 1864.

10. Corporal Cochran of the 152nd (as "Valedo") filed a newspaper report on the rebel movements in front of Cumberland:

"On Monday afternoon [August 1] it was definitely ascertained that the enemy was 3,000 strong, and was advancing upon us under Johnson and McCausland. All the forces at the place were at once placed in position, and about 4 o'clock the ball opened. It was almost entirely an artillery duel, the infantry being held in reserve and to support the batteries.

"The firing lasted until 7 o'clock, when the decreasing sound of the enemy's guns indicated to the troops and the citizens of Cumberland (many of whom occupied the adjacent hills, anxiously watching the progress of the fight) that the foe had been worsted and was now retreating. The retreat turned into a rout. . . .

"On Tuesday afternoon the excitement of the preceding day was renewed. The 152nd whilst at the depot about to take the train for South Branch to reinforce Colonel Stough (news of his surrender not having reached here) was ordered back. This regiment, with the 156th [another hundred-days regiment], was immediately posted in the fort, to the northeast of the city, guarding the road on which the enemy was reported to be approaching 5,000 strong. A flag of truce had been sent in, demanding a surrender, which General Kelley, after the results of the fight on Monday, very naturally declined to make. . . . But the enemy came not. He had tried us to his satisfaction, and passing around us, felt our neighbors at New Creek, where his reception was equally warm." Springfield *Republic,* August 15, 1864.

11. West Virginia.

12. Major-General Robert Ransom. A former Indian fighter and West Point cavalry instructor, he had led a division at Fredericksburg. His brother Matt was a Confederate brigadier-general.

13. "General Sheridan, in one of his reports, says: 'McNeill is the most daring and dangerous of all the bushwhackers in this section of the country.'" Stipp, *History,* p. 50.

14. See Appendix B for some of Jane Hambleton's letters.

15. Captain Alexander Swanston, company commander.

16. Private Kepler survived and mustered out with the company.

17. First Sergeant James T. Arndt and Sergeant John A. Watson, who were recaptured and returned to the regiment on August 6th.

18. *Official Roster* shows one man mortally wounded and seven captured, not including Arndt and Watson. Two of the seven later died in captivity at the Confederate prison camp in Salisbury, N.C.

19. Privates William and Wilson Brown, Company I, ages 20 and 18, respectively.

20. Privates Isaac and Eli Vanhorn, ages 32 and 20, were both briefly missing after Monocacy.

21. Two of his children.

22. Although also a nickname for Confederates, in this case "graybacks" refers to lice.

23. Virginia.

24. Ghormley was captured.

25. Lewis Adie, Company D, of Leesburg, one of two Confederates killed at Berryville on August 13th, but apparently not an officer.

26 CHAPTER SOURCES:

a. Perkins. *A Summer in Maryland and Virginia,* pp. 18, 21, 24–27, 29–33, 36, 61–62, 64–66.

b. Nichols. *A Summer Campaign,* pp. 135–42.

c. Stipp. *History,* pp. 35–36, 40, 46–52.

d. Hambleton. "Hambleton Family Papers."

e. McClain. "Papers, 1864," folder 18.

f. Perkins. *A Summer in Maryland and Virginia,* pp. 33–37, 64.

13. Prisoners of War

1. Sergeant Rowland and a Private Josiah Hays both mustered out with the company.

2. *Official Roster* lists the names as Nicholds, McCrackin, Brodess, Howser, Crute, and Gharrett, with the others as given. Since spellings vary even within the account, for consistency the first are used throughout. Browning shared his recollections in 1911, nearly 50 years after these events.

3. The Company E roster shows Miller dying March 25, 1865, at Annapolis, Md., where he would have been under Union care.

4. Private Samuel O. Jones, Company C, is recorded as "no further record found" after his capture. Private Joseph Shepherd, Company D, was mustered out of the army on October 20.

5. This name doesn't appear on a roster of the 23rd Ohio.

6. Roper Hospital at the Work House prison, Charleston.

7. Lieutenant-Colonel Marcellus A. Leeds of the 153rd, captured the same day as Rathbone and his men.

8. S. A. Glenn, Elam Day, J. V. Baird and C. E. Harrison, all of the 89th Ohio, all captured a year earlier at Chickamauga, Tennessee. Coincidentally, Lieutenant-Colonel Leeds of Rathbone's regiment and Colonel A. L. Brown, 149th Ohio, had served as captains in the 89th.

9. All privates except Rozell.

10. Ghormley was mistaken. Private Zachariah D. Hickman appears in the company roster as captured at Monocacy, but he apparently escaped. He mustered out with Company B.

11. Sayre died a prisoner in Salisbury, N.C., on December 2, 1864. Fix died there on February 13, 1865. McCommon refers to Fix as "George."

12. Benner died November 1.

13. On October 23.

14. After a healthy record earlier in the war, Salisbury Prison had become horribly overcrowded. By October 1864, 10,000 prisoners languished in space previously occupied by 1,500. Nearly 3,500 died that winter.

15. Ghormley died December 24th.

16. A false report.

17. Sergeant Theodorus H. C. Frisbie, 39, Company K.

18. The second of the Brown boys, William, would die December 7th. Isaac Vanhorn, the private who had lost a child shortly before his capture, would survive.

19. Wheeler was not from either the 144th or 149th Ohio.

20. McClain here misstates the day for the next five days.

21. Private Walter Wood, 18, Company B, 144th Ohio.

22. CHAPTER SOURCES:

a. Browning. Perkins, *A Summer in Maryland and Virginia,* pp. 54–60.

b. Rathbone. Thomas W. Rathbone, "Brief Diary of Imprisonment."

c. Ghormley. *Scioto Gazette,* September 6, 1864.

d. Rozell. Perkins, *A Summer in Maryland and Virginia,* pp. 47–48.

e. McCommon. Ibid., pp. 39–45.

f. McClain. "Papers, 1864," folder 19.

14. The Other Enemy

1. Frederick H. Dyer, *A Compendium of the War of the Rebellion* (reprint, Dayton, 1994), shows 41 enlisted men dead by disease, all buried at Arlington, Virginia (vol. 1, p. 1553). *Official Roster* shows three additional deaths, two in Ohio and a third at an unidentified location with burial in Ohio.

2. Clipping, unknown newspaper, "169TH OVI Reunion Scrapbook 1887–1909."

3. Colonel Nathaniel E. Haynes. "He was one of God's noblemen, brave, generous to a fault, and I could not allow myself to think long of him because the tears might flow," his adjutant, John L. Greene, told a subsequent reunion. The regiment attributed Haynes's death in 1869, at age 37, to the strain of command during the hundred days. Ibid.

4. The Ohio regiments lost 868 men to disease and 66 to combat during the hundred days, a ratio of roughly 13:1. The Federal army as a whole lost 199,720 to disease and 110,070 in combat, less than 2:1. Of the hundred-days regiments, only the two that fought Morgan at Cynthiana lost more men in battle than to sickness. Many of the disease deaths in the three regiments sustaining the highest casualties (135th, 144th, and 149th Ohio) occurred in Southern prisons. (Figures from Dyer, *Compendium,* vol. 1, pp. 12, 18; vol. 2, pp. 1549–1553.)

5. This letter appeared in the Dayton *Journal,* August 11, 1864, signed simply

"Chaplain." The newspaper had described Twitchell on May 3, 1864, as "a live man, as well as an excellent preacher."

6. The 131st Ohio had just two deaths during the hundred days, a record equaled by only two other regiments and bettered by none.

7. Chaplain James Mitchell, *Ohio State Journal,* August 6, 1864.

8. Staff officer.

9. Captain Lilley was 33 years old. "I was informed concerning our lamented Captain Lilley, of company K, that extreme care for men, in connection with a broken constitution, caused by former exposures in the service, had much to do with his sickness working death," Chaplain Mitchell wrote. "Our grief in giving him up was mitigated in ascertaining that for many years he had been preparing for the 'Saint's Rest.' His quiet demeanor at once commended him to the stranger, a generous nature endeared him to his men. When lying upon his sick couch a serene countenance bespoke a heart at peace with God. From boyhood he had followed Christ in the way of regeneration. To a confidential friend he expressed regret that he had allowed the military life somewhat to divert attention from the soul's destiny—yet hope forward God was not obliterated. Peace to his memory, and tenderest regards of sympathy to all bereaved friends of this regiment." Mitchell, *Ohio State Journal,* August 6, 1864.

10. An Ohio newspaper printed a description from Fortress Monroe of some of the medical facilities there:

"Chesapeake Female College, founded in 1854, is a large brick building five stories high, with a piazza in front resting on large high pillars and fronting on the bay, with a cupola sixty feet high, pleasantly situated with grounds tastefully laid out in walks running to the water's edge.

"This building now is known as Chesapeake Hospital, with quite a number of buildings and tents adjoining for hospitals and hospital purposes. There are said to be some eight hundred officers in these buildings from Butler's army, wounded by rebel bullets and shots. . . . A short distance from this place is what is called the McClellan Hospital for Soldiers. These buildings were erected during McClellan's Campaign up the Chickahominy and they now contain some three thousand of our intelligent and brave boys, confined there most of them by wounds received in the neighborhood of Petersburg." Dispatch signed "H.," Sandusky *Register,* July 20, 1864.

11. Henry L. Whitehead, Company D.

12. William Ewing.

13. "The sunshine of their presence, like the shadow of St. Peter upon the sick, exerts a cheering and wholesome influence," reported Chaplain Mitchell. *Ohio State Journal,* August 6, 1864.

14. Gilbert Laboytreaux of Company F, 138th Ohio, also at Fort Powhatan, described the experience:

"At White House I was ordered to be taken down to the boat on a stretcher. How much rather I would have gone down on a 'bender;' but there was no choice, I had to obey orders, and [the surgeons] had been so kind, and had treated my case so skillfully. I was all obedience, and would have rode down on a rail if they had ordered it.

"So upon the stretcher I stretched myself, whereupon two of my good friends . . . lay hold of the machine and off we went, and off I came very near going too, more than once. Being carried on a stretcher is like riding on a camel. There is a swinging, unsteady motion that one does not get the hang of immediately, nonetheless it was an act of kindness on their part, and willingly performed; many thanks to them. They carried me out of *Camp Dysentery* on their shoulders, and in my memory I will carry them." Cincinnati *Times,* June 25, 1864.

15. "Jake is sick with typhoid fever. You better come." The telegram was signed J. R. Drown, a friend from home and private in Company H.

16. Possibly John C. Lee, colonel of the regiment.

17. Letter from Holtz descendant Paul J. Buskirk to editor, July 28, 1998.

18. Sanitary Commission. "The health of our company has improved a great deal this last few days," Private Timothy Rigby, Co. I, 143rd Ohio, wrote from Wilson's Landing, Virginia, on July 16. "I think a great deal is owing to the vegetables that we have had sent here by the Sanitary Commission. We have had Potatoes, onions, Cabbage and dried Apples. I believe that if we can get such things every few days there would not be so much sickness. The Doctor has also ordered that every man has half a gill of whiskey every day. They say that we need it in this climate. I can assure you that we don't feel anything the worse for it." Rigby, in Linn, "Civil War Diaries of Two Brothers."

19. Colonel Fisher was a stranger to most of his men when they mustered. On the drowning death of Fisher and his young son ten years later, he was diplomatically eulogized for "the healthy discipline he enforced, and the consequent morale attained by the regiment." *In Memoriam: Samuel S. Fisher* (Cincinnati, 1874), p. 68.

20. Sgt. Peter Poole, although *Official Roster* lists "Pool."

21. Waiting at Cherry Stone, Virginia, to go home, Private Hezekiah Price described the sickness in Company C. "Poor Theodore Moore is nothing but a skeleton. He got weighed yesterday and 118 pounds is all he could make of himself." Letter to Rachel and Lizzie Price, August 24, 1864. Price, "Papers, 1863–1865."

22. Corporal John C. Myers of the 192nd Pennsylvania offered an equally moving tribute to a teenage hundred-days soldier who died of typhoid at Gallipolis, Ohio, on October 25.

"Death comes unbidden to our ranks, and sweeps away our brightest jewels. True it is, in the decease of our young friend Edward F. Taylor, that death loves a shining mark. This young man died on Monday evening at 9 o'clock, regretted and mourned by his entire regiment. He was too good, manly and brave: too gifted in mind and generous in thought to have an enemy. All loved him who came to know him." John C. Myers, *A Daily Journal of the 192d Reg't Penn'a Volunteers* (Philadelphia, 1864), p. 140.

23. The letter is unsigned, but *Official Roster* and other documents within the family collection show that its author was almost certainly Freeland Hood.

24. Private John C. Fillmore.

25. Charles F. Dutton, regimental assistant surgeon.

26. Privates James E. Todd, Thomas J. Frazer, and Henry S. Bennett.

27. Corporal Edward Ells.

28. George Morgan, R. Dwight Burrell, Lemon L. Hudson, Cyrus M. Johnson, Harlan P. Jackson, and Joel M. Partridge.

29. Visits by relatives of sick or dead soldiers were not unusual. The 37th New Jersey recalled a "very sad incident, that of Geo. Bronson, Co. A, of Jersey City, who died of Typhoid, and whose brother came south for his body—and with others tried to snatch his body at night, and was nearly successful, but which a violent storm made

impossible; he returned to his home, and died of the same disease in two weeks, the only sons of a widowed mother." *Souvenir of the First Annual Reunion, 37th Regiment New Jersey Volunteers* (New York, 1889), p. 18.

30. A Borton family history says Silas was one of three Borton brothers who served in the 67th O.V.I., the three-year regiment in which Simeon Borton was killed. Before its enlistment expired, the 67th had served outside Petersburg near the 130th. There James had seen Samuel, his other brother in the veteran regiment.

The family history, however, puts Silas in "Company J," a designation that did not exist in the Union army. He is clearly at home at the time of this letter.

31. CHAPTER SOURCES:

a. Twitchell. Dayton *Journal*, August 11, 1864.

b. Sherman. *History*, pp. 130–33, 137.

c. Eames. Eames, "Papers, 1862–1864," Box 1, folder 4, letter dated May 31, 1864.

d. Holtz. Jacob Souder Holtz Collection, folder 4-1.

e. Egbert. Ibid., folder 4-1.

f. Chadwick. "Into the Breach," pp. 170–72, 179–80.

g. Laboytreaux. Cincinnati *Times*, August 22, 1864.

h. Nichols. *A Summer Campaign*, pp. 116–17.

i. Hood. "Hood Family Papers," one folder, undated and unsigned letter, Civil War Miscellaneous Collection, U.S. Army Military History Institute, Carlisle Barracks.

j. Cannon. *Record of Service*, pp. 17–18.

k. Borton. Borton, "Borton Family: Personal Correspondence."

15. Johnny Comes Marching Home

1. Brough died in office on August 29th, 1865, "literally worn out in the public service." His administration "was at once the most vigorous and the most unpopular, as well as perhaps the most able with which Ohio was honored throughout the war." Reid, *Ohio in the War*, vol. 1, pp. 236–37.

2. Corporal John C. Myers and the 192nd Pennsylvania (a hundred-days regiment) watched the 172nd Ohio muster out at Gallipolis, Ohio, on August 27th. He later reported the scene and Colonel John Ferguson's memorable speech to his men.

"Col. Ferguson, having nearly his entire regiment in town, ready for mustering out, brought his command upon the public square this afternoon, and, after giving the manual of arms, formed his regiment into numerous positions on the double-quick, all the movements showing considerable practice and knowledge on the part of the men who executed all the orders of their colonel promptly and handsomely. Col. Ferguson then delivered a farewell address to his regiment. He closed by saying that the term for which the men enlisted had expired, and that as soon as the man with the greenbacks made his appearance, the regiment would be mustered out of service.

"He also remarked that they were farmers, an honorable calling which they had still more ennobled as soldiers for the defense of their government, the Union, their homes and firesides, and their civil and religious freedom. They had shown the world that farmers could be soldiers, of this he had convincing and proud proof. The Colonel is a veteran, an old army officer, and every inch a soldier. It was a treat to behold the gray-headed warrior delivering his speech, which was eloquent and patriotic in its every utterance." Myers, *A Daily Journal*, pp. 62–63.

Ferguson's 172nd Ohio was headquartered in Gallipolis during the hundred days. "During his administration, Col. Ferguson has conducted the affairs of the Post in a manner highly gratifying to all concerned. By his gentlemanly deportment, he had made hosts of friends, and none of his predecessors have succeeded in discharging the duties of the office with more firmness and ability. The Colonel will bear with him, we are sure, the good wishes and respect, of our citizens." Gallipolis *Journal*, August 25, 1864.

3. Lincoln presented a similar, joint certificate to the hundred-days men from Indiana, Illinois, Iowa, and Wisconsin, detailing their combined contribution "in the recent campaign of General Sherman. . . . It was their good fortune to render efficient service in the brilliant operations in the Southwest, and to contribute to the victories of the national arms over the rebel forces in Georgia under command of Johnson and Hood."

4. A detachment from the company had escorted rebel prisoners to Camp Chase in Columbus about two weeks earlier.

5. Jane Hambleton wrote back that she was "glad you are willing to do as you are ordered. I would not have you do anything that's wrong or dishonorable for anything, but I could not blame you much if you did come home." Isaac's estimate proved exact, and he mustered out with the regiment on September 1st. Hambleton, "Hambleton Family Papers."

6. Private, Company E.

7. Hot, dry summer weather had disappeared somewhat violently a week earlier. At Point Lookout, Maryland, the morning of August 6th, Sergeant W. P. Worth of Company E, 139th Ohio, reported that "One of the grandest yet most fearful spectacles we ever beheld was presented to our view. It was what was called by sea-faring men a water-spout."

This "immense spiral column of cloud" tossed a vessel on the Potomac River onto its end beams, injuring some guards on deck, swept ashore to demolish two commissary depots, a hospital, and a sutler's store, then headed for a large pine grove. "Some of the 139th were on guard in this grove. I have no doubt if they had been in front of Richmond they would have made a stand and contested their ground, but they thought the whirlwind a stronger argument than powder and ball, and acted accordingly." Cincinnati *Times*, August 10, 1864.

8. Apparently Sergeant William W. Neal; the others were privates.

9. West Virginia.

10. Company E, Captain Bushnell, and Company K, Captain Welsh, arrived home in Springfield at 1 A.M. on Wednesday, September 7.

11. Excerpts from his diary.

12. Port.

13. Private Zaccheus Armstrong of Company A drowned in the bay.

14. Such delays were common, and infuriated the press nearly as much as they did the men. "We have been unable to fully investigate this matter, but we are satisfied that there is a *screw* loose," the *Ohio State Journal* declared on August 27th. "Gov. Brough became convinced yesterday that such was the fact, and immediately went to work to find who were the delinquent parties. A very short investigation convinced him that the fault was with the mustering out officer—the 145th Regiment having been mustered out of the service, and the mustering rolls were detained in the hands of the mustering out officer, instead of being handed over to . . . the paymaster.

"Such kind of blundering ought to make an end of the official existence of the blunderers," the 145th's hometown newspaper thundered. "The service of the National Guard has been of incalculable advantage to the National cause, and has brought more honor to Ohio than any one thing since the breaking out of the rebellion. Such being the case, delays and blunders in remitting them speedily to their homes when their service is ended are utterly inexcusable." Sandusky *Register,* August 29, 1864.

15. Sandusky, Dayton & Cleveland.

16. Charles P. Weatherby, 26, and Levi H. Loudon, 36. The distance is about 20 miles.

17. The 130th Ohio, a hundred-days regiment from Toledo, remained until September 7.

18. The 150th O.V.I.; even the guardsmen themselves sometimes misstated the official designation.

19. William Dennison, former Ohio governor who replaced Blair in the cabinet.

20. CHAPTER SOURCES:

a. Cowen. "The Hundred-Days Men of 1864," pp. 229–31, 234–35.

b. Laboytreaux. Cincinnati *Times,* August 29, 1864.

c. Hambleton. "Hambleton Family Papers."

d. Perkins. *A Summer in Maryland and Virginia,* pp. 37–39.

e. Nichols. *A Summer Campaign,* pp. 145–47.

f. Bailey. "Journal (1864)."

g. Sherman. *History,* pp. 143–51.

h. Wild. "Program, 61st Annual Reunion, 137th O.V.I."

Appendixes

1. Private Charles Morehouse, the substitute from Company A, recorded the meeting: "Agreeable to orders we packed up this A.M. and waited patiently until noon when we commenced leaving the 'sacred soil.' After some delay at Fort Corcoran we proceeded to cross the Potomac. Stopped at White House on the way down Pa. Avenue—where Uncle Abe addressed a few remarks to us. On reaching the depot we found that cars would not be ready until 6 A.M. tomorrow." Morehouse, "Diary—1864," August 18, 1864.

2. Georgia, during Sherman's Atlanta campaign. Although the battle was June 27th, several days of skirmishes preceded it.

3. The letter was signed "N. L." Leohner was the only man in the company with these initials.

4. Remley's last words were "among the many gallant, dying words given utterance" by men of the 29th at Mill Creek Gap, Georgia, on May 8th, 1864: "Tell my mother I died like a man, doing my duty in defense of my country." Letter to the *Beacon* by Major Myron T. Wright.

5. "You need not fret about that," Lieutenant Hambleton replied on June 12th. "I assure you I did feel it my duty to go this time. I feel it is my duty to stay with my family after my time is up if I am spared." He completed his service and returned home after mustering out with his regiment. Hambleton, "Hambleton Family Papers."

6. The 133rd was primarily from Franklin County, adjacent to Madison County where the Hambletons lived. The identity of Jim G. is unknown. Allowing for Jane's distress and the vagaries of spelling, *Official Roster* shows the others as Private William

J. Goodson of Company K, and Corporal Richard VanHorn, Corporal Armenas F. Kilbury, and Private John Gilliland of Company D. All but the latter are listed as mustering out with their companies. Gilliland, 18, died August 7th at Fortress Monroe, Virginia. Two other privates named Gilliland appear in the Company D roster. Harrison Gilliland, 21, is shown as "Absent, sick in hospital at Washington, D.C. No further record found." Hamilton Gilliland, 20, mustered out with his company on August 20th.

7. Several veterans of the 149th were original members of the Campbell Light Guards in 1873. Among them was regimental historian George Perkins, a sergeant in "Squad A."

8. The 158th Ohio was not completed. The 165th Ohio was a battalion of eight companies.

9. The next regiment, 144th Illinois, was organized for one year.

10. The 41st Wisconsin, although designated a regiment, was battalion strength with seven companies.

11. Although designated a regiment, the 17th Kansas comprised just four small companies and part of a fifth; not to be confused with the 17th Kansas militia regiment, which served briefly in October.

12. The 12th Maryland, although designated a regiment, was battalion strength with five companies.

13. The Massachusetts total includes several unattached companies. The 5th, 6th, 8th, and 42nd Massachusetts were militia regiments with prior service. They and the new 60th Massachusetts were officially known as Massachusetts Volunteer Militia (M.V.M.).

14. One infantry company; one infantry company, U.S. Colored Troops; Keystone Battery independent artillery; five cavalry companies.

15. Unlike their Ohio counterparts, the New Yorkers retained the identity and regimental numbers of the National Guard of the State of New York (NGSNY) during Federal duty. Confusingly, regular New York infantry often bore the same numbers at the same time; for example, the 102nd Regiment, NGSNY, and the 102nd New York (Van Buren Light Infantry) served simultaneously. In addition to the official hundred-days units, the 69th Regiment, NGSNY, called up for 60 days in late June to man harbor defenses in New York, voluntarily extended to a hundred days.

16. Including companies A and B, 50th, attached as Companies L and M.

17. APPENDIX A SOURCES:

a. McKee. Perkins, *A Summer in Maryland and Virginia,* pp. 49–50.

b. "H. W." Summit County *Beacon,* June 9, 1864.

c. "Looker On." Toledo *Blade,* June 14, 1864.

d. Evans. Zanesville *Courier,* June 25, 1864.

e. Lincoln. "Abraham Lincoln to the 166th Ohio, August 22, 1864" (Chicago, 1943).

f. President's Thanks. *Official Records,* ser. 3, vol. 4, pp. 707–8.

APPENDIX B SOURCES:

a. Wisehart. *Scioto Gazette,* August 2, 1864.

b. Borton. "Borton Family."

c. Leohner. Summit County *Beacon,* June 9, 1864.

d. Harmount. John C. Williamson, "Papers."

e. Hambleton. Hambleton, "Hambleton Family Papers."

APPENDIX C SOURCES:

a & b. Edward R. McKee, "Papers."

APPENDIX D SOURCES:

a. Ohio. Cowen, "The Hundred-Days Men of 1864," p. 228.

b. Illinois. *Report of the Adjutant General of the State of Illinois* (Springfield, 1866), vol. 1, p. 181.

c. Indiana. *Report of the Adjutant General of the State of Indiana,* vol. 1, p. 38.

d. Iowa. *Report of the Adjutant General of the State of Iowa* (Des Moines, 1864), p. vi.

e. Wisconsin. *Annual Report of the Adjutant General of the State of Wisconsin* (Madison, 1864), p. 401.

f. Delaware. Historical Society of Delaware figure.

g. Kansas. *Report of the Adjutant General of the State of Kansas, for the year 1864* (Leavenworth, 1865), p. 690.

h. Maryland. *History and Roster of Maryland Volunteers, War of 1861–5* (Baltimore, 1898), vol. 1, pp. 375–93, 421–30.

i. Massachusetts. *Annual Report of the Adjutant-General of the Commonwealth of Massachusetts* (Boston, 1864,) p. 17.

j. New Jersey. *Record of Officers and Men of New Jersey in the Civil War, 1861–1865,* vol. 2, p. 1095.

k. Pennsylvania. *Annual Report of the Adjutant General of the State of Pennsylvania* (Harrisburg, 1864), p. 6.

l. New York. *Annual Report of the Adjutant General of the State of New York* (Albany, 1865), vol. 1, p. 202.

Bibliography

Books and Articles

Anonymous and Institution Publications

Annual Report of the Adjutant-General of the Commonwealth of Massachusetts. Boston, 1864.

Annual Report of the Adjutant General of the State of New York. Albany, 1865.

Annual Report of the Adjutant General of the State of Pennsylvania. Harrisburg, 1864.

Annual Report of the Adjutant General of the State of Wisconsin. Madison, 1864.

Battles and Leaders of the Civil War, 4 vols. New York, 1887.

The Bermuda Hundred Campaign in Chesterfield County, Virginia. Chesterfield, 1993.

History and Roster of Maryland Volunteers, War of 1861–5. Baltimore, 1898.

In Memoriam: Samuel S. Fisher. Cincinnati, 1874.

Official Army Register of the Volunteer Force of the United States Army for the Years 1861, '62, '63, '64, '65. Washington, 1865.

Official Roster of the Soldiers of the State of Ohio in the War of the Rebellion, 1861–1866. Cincinnati, 1889.

Record of Officers and Men of New Jersey in the Civil War, 1861–1865, vol. 2. Trenton, 1876.

Report of the Adjutant General of the State of Illinois. Springfield, 1866.

Report of the Adjutant General of the State of Indiana. Indianapolis, 1869.

Report of the Adjutant General of the State of Iowa. Des Moines, 1864.

Report of the Adjutant General of the State of Kansas, for the year 1864. Leavenworth, 1865.

Roster of the 134th Regiment, O.V.I. PA Box 726, pamphlet 28, Ohio Historical Society.

Roster of the 147th Regiment, Ohio Volunteer Infantry. West Milton, 1899.

Souvenir of the First Annual Reunion, 37th Regiment New Jersey Volunteers. New York, 1889.

The War of the Rebellion: A Compilation of the Official Records of the Union and Confederate Armies. Washington, 1884.

Works by Named Authors

Abbott, Richard H. *Ohio's War Governors.* Columbus, 1962.

Boatner, Mark M. *The Civil War Dictionary.* New York, 1991.

Bosson, Charles P. *History of the Forty-Second Infantry, Massachusetts Volunteers, 1862, 1863, 1864.* Boston, 1886.

Bright, Simeon Miller. "The McNeill Rangers: A Study in Confederate Guerrilla Warfare." *West Virginia History,* vol. 12, issue 4, pp. 338–87. Charleston, July 1951.

Buel, Clarence C., and Robert U. Johnson, eds. *Battles and Leaders of the Civil War.* 4 vols. New York, 1888.

Cannon, James C. *Memorial, 150th Ohio, Company K.* 1907.

——. *Record of Service of Company K, 150TH O.V.I., 1864.* 1903.

Chadwick, Wallace W. "Into the Breach: Civil War Letters of Wallace W. Chadwick," Mabel Watkins Mayer, ed. *Ohio State Archaeological and Historical Quarterly,* vol. 52. Columbus, 1943.

Cooling, Benjamin Franklin, III, and Walton H. Owen, II. *Mr. Lincoln's Forts: A Guide to the Civil War Defenses of Washington.* Shippensburg, 1988.

Cowen, Benjamin R. "The Hundred-Days Men of 1864." *G.A.R. War Papers: Papers Read Before Fred C. Jones Post, No. 401, Department of Ohio, G.A.R.,* vol. 1. Cincinnati, 1891.

——. "The One Hundred Days Men of Ohio." In *Sketches of War History, 1861–1865; Papers Prepared for the Commandery of the State of Ohio, Military Order of the Loyal Legion of the United States.* Cincinnati, 1903.

Cox, Jabez T. "Civil War Diary of Jabez T. Cox." *Indiana Magazine of History,* vol. 28. Indianapolis, 1932.

Croly, Herbert. *Marcus Alonzo Hanna: His Life and Work.* Hamden, 1965.

Danforth, Willis. "How I Came to Be in the Army and General E. A. Paine's Plan of Federal Salvation." In *War Papers, Military Order of the Loyal Legion of the United States, Wisconsin Commandery,* vol. 1. Milwaukee, 1891.

Dornbusch, C. E. *Military Bibliography of the Civil War.* New York, 1967.

Douglas, Henry Kyd. *I Rode with Stonewall.* Chapel Hill, 1940.

Dudley, Edgar S. "A Reminiscence of Washington and Early's Attack in 1864." *Sketches of War History, 1861–1865,* Ohio Commandery, MOLLUS, vol. 1. Cincinnati, 1883.

Dyer, Frederick H. *A Compendium of the War of the Rebellion.* Dayton, 1994 [reprint].

Early, Jubal Anderson. *Narrative of the War between the States.* Philadelphia, 1912.

Eaton, William. *History of the Richardson Light Guard, of Wakefield, Mass., 1851–1901.* Wakefield, 1901.

Foster, John Y. *New Jersey and the Rebellion.* Newark, 1868.

Fox, William F. *Regimental Losses in the American Civil War, 1861–1865* (reprint). Dayton, 1985.

Fox, William L. "Corporal Harvey W. Wiley's Civil War Diary." *Indiana Magazine of History,* vol. 51. Indianapolis, 1955.

Gleason, William J. *Historical Sketch of the 150th Regiment Ohio Volunteer Infantry.* 1899.

Gordon, John B. *Reminiscences of the Civil War.* New York, 1903.

Harper, Robert S. *Ohio Handbook of the Civil War.* Columbus, 1961.

Horack, Frank E. "The Flag of the University Company." *Iowa Historical Record.* Iowa City, 1899.

James, William H. "A Baltimore Volunteer of 1864." *Maryland Historical Magazine,* vol. 36. Baltimore, 1941.

Keiley, A. M. *In Vinculis; or, The Prisoner of War.* New York, 1866.

McCormick, David I., superintendent, and Mindwell Crampton Wilson, ed. *Indiana Battle Flags.* Indianapolis, 1929.

McPherson, James M. *Battle Cry of Freedom: The Civil War Era.* New York, 1988.

Myers, John C. *A Daily Journal of the 192d Reg't Penn'a Volunteers.* Philadelphia, 1864.

Nichols, Clifton M. *A Summer Campaign in the Shenandoah Valley, in 1864.* Springfield, 1899.

Perkins, George. *A Summer in Maryland and Virginia, or Campaigning with the 149th Ohio Volunteer Infantry.* Chillicothe, 1911.

Reid, Whitelaw. *Ohio in the War: Her Statesmen, Her Generals, and Soldiers.* 2 vols. Cincinnati, 1868.

Roe, Alfred S. *The Fifth Regiment Massachusetts Volunteer Infantry.* Boston, 1911.

Roseboom, Eugene H., and Francis P. Weisenburger. *A History of Ohio.* Columbus, 1988.

Sandburg, Carl. *Abraham Lincoln: The War Years,* vol. 3. New York, 1939.

Sherman, Sylvester M. *History of the 133d Regiment, O.V.I.* Columbus, 1896.

Simonhoff, Harry. *Jewish Participation in the Civil War.* New York, 1963.

Stipp, Joseph A. *The History and Service of the 154th Ohio Volunteer Infantry.* Toledo, 1896.

Vail, Henry H. *What I Saw of the Civil War.* Woodstock, 1915.

Vandiver, Frank E. *Jubal's Raid: General Early's Famous Attack on Washington in 1864.* Lincoln, 1992.

Wallace, Lee A., Jr., and Martin R. Conway. "Military Operations at Petersburg, 1862–1865." U.S. National Park Service's World Wide Web site (http://www.nps.gov), Petersburg National Battlefield pages, 1983, posted 1997.

Wallace, Lew. *Lew Wallace: An Autobiography.* New York, 1906.

———. *Smoke, Sound & Fury: The Civil War Memoirs of Major-General Lew Wallace, U.S. Volunteers.* Portland, 1998.

Welcher, Frank J. *The Union Army, 1861–1865: Organization and Operations.* Volume I: *The Eastern Theater.* Bloomington, 1989.

Williamson, James J. *Mosby's Rangers: A Record of the Operations of the Forty-Third Battalion of Virginia Cavalry from its Organization to the Surrender.* New York, 1909.

Newspapers

Cincinnati *Commercial*
Cincinnati *Enquirer*
Cincinnati *Daily Gazette*
Cincinnati *Times*
Cleveland *Herald*
Cleveland *Plain Dealer*
Dayton *Journal*
Erie County *News,* Sandusky
Gallipolis *Journal*
Guernsey *Times,* Cambridge
Madison County *Union,* London

Mahoning *Register,* Youngstown
Mount Vernon *Republican*
New York *Times*
Ohio State Journal, Columbus
Sandusky *Register*
Scioto Gazette, Chillicothe
Springfield *Republic*
Steubenville *Courier*
Steubenville *Herald*
Summit County *Beacon,* Akron
Toledo *Blade*
Washington (Court House) *Herald*
Zanesville *Courier*

Manuscripts, Diaries, and Papers

"Ohio Volunteer Infantry, 150th Regiment, Reunion Records, Roster & Minutes, vol. 1894–1927." MSS 1204, folders 1 and 2, Western Reserve Historical Society.

"169TH OVI Reunion Scrapbook 1887–1909." Jacob Burgner Collection, LH-6, Box 1, folder 18, Rutherford B. Hayes Presidential Center.

"Program, 61st Annual Reunion, 137th O.V.I." MSS 168, Box 4, folder 4, Ohio Historical Society.

Abbott, Cecil C. "Letters of Cecil C. Abbott, Co. B, 166th O.V.I., to his parents in Wakeman, Ohio." VFM 1476, Ohio Historical Society.

Armstrong, James B. "Copy of a letter, July 19, 1864, from Col. J. B. Armstrong, Cmdr. 134th Regt., O.V.I., to President Lincoln." VFM 101, Ohio Historical Society.

Bailey, George F. "Journal (1864) Kept While Serving with Company G, 132d Regt., Ohio Volunteer Infantry in Norfolk, Va., and Camp Chase, Columbus, Ohio." MSS 30, folder 3, Ohio Historical Society.

Bell, Samuel McCoy, "One Hundred Days' Service: The Civil War Diary of Samuel McCoy Bell." Introduction by Brian A. Williams. PA Box 729, item 18, Ohio Historical Society.

Borton, James Elwood. "Borton Family: Personal Correspondence with Typewritten Transcripts." MS-462, Box 2, folder 1, Center for Archival Collections, Bowling Green State University.

Eames, William Mark. "Papers, 1862–1864." Box 1, folders 4–9 (microfilm No. 1306–1), Tennessee State Library and Archives, Nashville.

Frary, Spencer George. "An Account of the encounter of the 171st Ohio Infantry with Confederate Forces under command of Gen. Morgan and their return to Johnson's Island, 1863–1864." MSS v.f. F, Western Reserve Historical Society.

Green, Thomas. "Letters, to Sarah J. Green, Montezuma, O., from her husband, Sgt. Thomas Green, Co. I, 156th O.V.I." VFM 1451, Ohio Historical Society.

Hambleton, Isaac. "Hambleton Family Papers." MSS 779, Box 1, folder 1, Ohio Historical Society.

Harrod, John, and Sue Harrod. The John Harrod Papers. 1 box, U.S. Army Military History Institute, Carlisle Barracks.

Holtz, Jacob, et al. Jacob Souder Holtz Collection, LH-261, Box 1, folders 2-2, 3-1, 4-1, 5-1, Rutherford B. Hayes Presidential Center.

Hood, Freeland. "Hood Family Papers." 1 folder, Civil War Miscellaneous Collection, U.S. Army Military History Institute, Carlisle Barracks.

Innis, Sarah G. Innis letters. The Charles T. R. Bohannon Collection, 1 box, U.S. Army Military History Institute, Carlisle Barracks.

Kaiser, Peter Henry. "Papers." MSS 1387, folders 1 and 4, Western Reserve Historical Society.

Lincoln, Abraham. "Abraham Lincoln to the 166th Ohio, August 22, 1864." Privately printed by Harry D. Oppenheimer, Chicago, 1943.

Linn, John Brownhill. "Civil War Diaries of Two Brothers, John Brownhill Linn and Thomas Buchanan Linn: Two Volumes in One; Followed by Three More Manuscripts from the 143rd Regiment O.N.G." Typed transcripts, Nancy H. M. Sechrest, ed. State Library of Ohio.

Linville, Benjamin A. "Diary, May–Sep. 1864." VOL 857, Ohio Historical Society.

McClain, Samuel. "Papers, 1864." MS-640, folders 1–19, Center for Archival Collections, Bowling Green State University.

McKee, Edward R. "Papers." MSS 238, Box 1, folder 5 and scrapbook, Ohio Historical Society.

Miller, William, and Silas Miller. "Miller Family Papers." MS-656, Box 2, folders 47–62, Center for Archival Collections, Bowling Green State University.

Morehouse, Charles L. "Diary—1864." VOL 1038, Ohio Historical Society.

Price, Hezekiah. "Papers 1863–1865." Ohio Historical Society.

Rathbone, Thomas W. "Brief Diary of Imprisonment." MIC 17, Roll 16, Ohio Historical Society.

Reeder, William C. "Papers." MSS 647, folder 2, Ohio Historical Society.

Shanks, Tommy. "Weddell Family Papers." MS-484 (microfilm), Center for Archival Collections, Bowling Green State University.

Thompson, Mortimer C. "Two Letters to his Father, Grovenor J. Thompson, Niles, Trumbell County, Ohio from Johnson's Island, June 6 and 9, 1864." VFM 1953, Ohio Historical Society.

Williamson, John C. "Papers." MSS 74, Box 1, folder 12, Ohio Historical Society.

Index of Troops

Page numbers in italics refer to illustrations.

Confederate Army: Army of Northern Virginia, 180, 229*n.14;* Army of the Valley, xvi, 113, 116, 239*n.19;* at Monocacy, 113–115; battle at Cynthiana, 73–76; in Maryland, 112; losses of, 48; near Fort Powhatan, 103–104; near Greenland Gap, 106–109

Delaware troops, xiv; numbers of hundred-days men, 201, 204*n.14*

Illinois troops, xi–xii; Artillery: **1st,** 43; Cavalry: **8th,** 123, 124, 237*n.7;* Infantry: **23rd,** 110, 235*n.10,* 236*n.12;* **134th,** 224*n.1;* **137th,** 104*n.15;* **144th,** 253*n.9;* Light Artillery: **1st,** 108, 146; numbers of hundred-days men, xiii, 201, 204*n.14*

Indiana troops, xi–xii; numbers of hundred-days men, xiii, 201, 204*n.14*

Iowa troops, xi–xii; Infantry: **44th,** 209*n.18;* **46th,** 104*n.15;* numbers of hundred-days men, xiii, 201, 204*n.14*

Kansas troops, xiv; Infantry: **17th,** 253*n.11;* numbers of hundred-days men, 201, 204*n.14*

Kentucky troops: Infantry: **1st,** 73; **2nd,** 73; **30th,** 74; **47th,** 73, 75; **52nd,** 74, 226*n.15;* **168th,** 74

Maine troops: Heavy Artillery: **1st,** 231*n.20;* Infantry: **2nd,** 90; **7th,** 136

Maryland troops, xiv; Infantry: **1st,** 237*n.7;* **2nd,** 43, 66–67, 69, 108, 146, 147, 214*n.14;* **11th,** 120, 204*n.14,* 237*n.7,* 239*n.15;* **12th,** 253; numbers of hundred-days men, 201, 204*n.14*

Massachusetts troops, xiv; Batteries: **16th,** 51; Infantry: **6th,** 104*n.14;* **8th,** 218*n.7;* **10th,**

243*n.23;* **42nd,** 217; Massachusetts Volunteer Militia, 253*n.13;* numbers of hundred-days men, 201–202, 204*n.14*

Michigan troops: Batteries: **13th,** 242*n.8,* 244*n.30*

New Jersey troops, xiv; Infantry: **14th,** 237*n.8;* **37th,** 204*n.14,* 204*n.16,* 249*n.29;* numbers of hundred-days men, 202, 204*n.14*

New York troops, xiv–xv; Artillery, 57; **8th,** 31; **9th,** 237*n.8;* Cavalry: **25th,** 131; Engineers: **1st,** 96; Infantry, 220*n.23;* **8th,** 212*n.12;* **11th,** 208*n.9;* **19th,** 136; **45th,** 136; **77th,** 136; **84th,** 204*n.14;* **106th,** 237*n.8;* **122nd,** 136; **151st,** 237*n.8;* numbering of, 253*n.15;* numbers of hundred-days men, 202, 204*n.14*

Ohio National Guard: Cowen on, 1–2; deaths in, 247*n.4;* duties of, 2–3; formation of, xi; Infantry: **3rd,** 27, 29; **7th,** xv; **8th,** 210*n.28;* **9th,** 208*n.9;* **10th,** xv, 205*n.19;* **23rd,** 32; **27th,** 30; **29th,** 3–4, 208*n.11;* **30th,** 3; **35th,** 35–37; **37th,** 3–4; **39th,** 211*n.6;* **40th,** 208*n.9;* **49th,** 210*n.27;* **54th,** 210*n.27;* **58th,** 29; **60th,** 32–33; **76th,** 29; law creating, 203*n.3,* 205*n.19,* 207*n.5;* naming of, 207*n.4;* numbers of, 201; Oberlin company of (150th, Co. K), 4–5, 51–52, 129–137, 177, 209*n.17,* 214*n.13,* 242*n.20;* performance of, 181; reorganized, xi, xii. *See also* Ohio troops: 130th–172nd Infantry

Ohio troops: Artillery: **135th,** 110; Cavalry: **12th,** 227*n.20;* Infantry, xi, xiii, xiv, xvii, 1–3, 203*n.3,* 207*n.5;* **2nd,** 205*n.19;* **7th,** 226*n.10;* **44th,** 144; **62nd,** 93; **63rd,** 196; **67th,** 87, 196, 250*n.30;* **69th,** 6; **88th,**

261

General Index

Page numbers in italics refer to illustrations.

JIM LEEKE has worked as a reporter in Guam, Michigan, Boston, and San Francisco and is now a freelance writer and editor in Worthington, Ohio. His first book was *Sudden Ice,* a mystery. He is also the editor of *Smoke, Sound & Fury: The Civil War Memoirs of Major-General Lew Wallace, U.S. Volunteers.*